PARENT-TEACHER COLLECTION

Learning

Preschool & Kindergarten

A Christian Parent's Guide

with

Day-By-Day Lesson Plans

Using the Library

As a Resource

By
Ann Ward

Dedicated
to
God, My Teacher
Travis and Kelly, my learners

and special
thanks
to
Craig,
my wonderful,
supportive
husband

Copyright © 1995 by Ann Ward

PUBLISHED BY

Christian Life Workshops
P.O. Box 2250, Gresham, Oregon 97030

ISBN 0-923463-02-X

9 790923 463020

INDEX OF NOTES, MATERIALS & INSTRUCTIONS

A Note From My Husband

As this work neared completion, I asked Ann if she had discussed her qualifications with you. All of us place the quality education of our children at or near the top of our life's priority list. This is doubly true for those who have elected to home school. It is therefore quite understandable, indeed expected, that you would like to know something about the person offering to assist you in teaching your children. However, completely in keeping with her character (and perhaps, therefore, somewhat insightfully) Ann had not done so. Despite the thoroughness which I hope and believe she has brought to this project, genuine modesty (only one of her many virtues) prevented her from talking about her qualifications and accomplishments. Allow me to do so now, briefly.

Ann has a bachelor's degree in Elementary Education from Mount Union College (Ohio), a highly respected private school. After having taught classes in all grades from kindergarten through sixth grade in several school districts, she left the education field and became a trust account management trainee (no, Daddy does not own the bank). She was lured away from the bank by Mary Kay's siren song of flexible hours, workplace and money. Bringing her usual industriousness to the task she became a director with a solid, active unit behind her (yes, the company gave her a pink car to drive around), and a very promising career future.

And then we were blessed with two active, bright and, above all, inquisitive children (just like yours!). It soon became apparent that, "quality time" notwithstanding, the reasonable but full-time demands of our respective careers made little provision for the nurturing of two small, loving human beings who watched their parents' lives from the sidelines. Strangers were raising our children.

When the enormity of this struck, we made some radical adjustments. Figuring it would be easier to come back in a few years and rebuild a business if she wanted to, than it would be to go back and raise our children correctly, Ann gave up her director-ship to devote full time to mothering and homemaking, at which she is also quite adept. It hasn't been easy keeping body and soul together on a police officer's salary, but the love our family shares is beyond riches. By joining you in the investment of value-based home schooling, we believe the benefits will be reaped by our children, our society, and our fragile planet.

Craig Ward

A Note of Introduction

When thinking over the course of the world's history, how natural it has been for parents to teach their children. What a privilege we in America have to be able to pass our values, traditions, and morals on to our children as well as instruct them in a loving atmosphere in subjects that will shape their lives.

This Guide is being written, with God's help, to help those who would love to be able to allow their children to learn at home, but would like help in doing so, either because they are busy now and don't feel like they could plan a curriculum, or because they feel they would have no idea where to begin, etc. I hope to take you step-by-step and lead you through an exciting year with your child.

It will require dedication, a minimum of preparation on your part... and love. But the planning has been done for you. If you feel your child needs more help in a certain area, by all means, allow him/her to practice. Don't feel locked into doing everything in the exact order it is presented. You may switch two days' activities around within a week. Some material, however, is presented in a specific order, building on an earlier concept learned.

This preschool curriculum is designed to interface with the curriculum for the kindergarten year, and hopefully on up, as additional guides are completed. If you are teaching more than one child at a time, you can present some of the same topics to both/all, just more in depth to the older children.

Even though I hold a degree in Education, I believe it has been my training and experience in goal setting and, most of all, in motherhood since my college days, that has helped me most. Thank you for allowing me to help you on your quest. I am excited for you and your children!

With warm friendship extended to you,

Ann Ward
May 1995

Why Teach At Home?

Home teaching is just now beginning to come "of age" again as an option for American parents. Why would you want to consider it as your possible choice? First, I believe, is the quality of education possible. The values learned from some curricula, teachers and peers is far from the ideal character-building situation you would choose for your children. It has been shown in studies that especially up to ages 5-8, a child internalizes activities without being able to resist the wrong. Proverbs 22:6 tells us, "Train up a child in the way he should go, and when he is old he will not turn from it." When you consider the influences outside the family on a young child, and the amount of time he is allowed, it is frightening. I feel a very strong sense of responsibility to guide my children in their values, their spiritual walk, their "education," their ability to make right decisions and their choice of friends. Teaching your child at home allows you to more easily choose the friends your children have.

In teaching at home, the student-teacher ratio is not 30 to 1 or even 20 to 1, but more likely 2 to 1. Therefore, the opportunity is there to provide for us, as teachers, increased caring for each student, that is simply not possible in the traditional classroom setting. You know your children better than anyone else does. Use that to your advantage in providing a setting that will play to your child's strengths and work on his weaknesses. You can easily challenge a gifted child without the boredom, or remediate a weak area without the humiliation, without twenty or more other children in the room demanding your attention at the same time. You will be able to pinpoint and address your child's needs better and sooner, to make his/her learning experience a very positive one. Isn't that exciting?

Next, I believe that teaching at home can strengthen your family. You are in a position as teacher to reinforce your family's values and rules. (By the way, at the beginning, I had my children call me Mrs. Ward, not Mom, when we were in school. I think

it helps add definition to the teacher/learner role.) In our family, although my husband at this point does no formal teaching, he has the title of principal. He makes final decisions, as he is head of our home. As the children get into the more technical aspects of subjects such as science and history, he may become the teacher for those areas.

Home schooling is ideal for you whose husband works a different shift. If our children had attended traditional school, they would not have seen their father from Sunday, at 1:15p.m., when he left for work, until Thursday, at 3:45p.m., when they would have been home from school when he was working swing shift. On Thursdays and Fridays, his days off, they would have been confined to their classrooms. On Saturdays and Sundays, the children's days off, he would have had only about three possible hours of contact with them per day. Yikes! How tragic that would be! Even for a family whose husband works a traditional "8 to 5" job, it makes it so much easier to plan vacations, weekend trips, times to meet dad for lunch, etc. than the locked in schedule of traditional school. I personally want to strengthen the relationships within our family, not weaken them!

A child's self-esteem can be developed more successfully at home school than in the traditional school, I believe. If a child needs extra help in an area, he is not ridiculed or teased, as he may well be in the traditional classroom. There is not the "audience" to act up for, for the child wanting attention. The attention can be given in a much more positive, loving manner. A child at home can learn his value within God's sight and to his family as they work as a team to care for the house, pets, etc.

You have such an opportunity to give your child a beautiful, priceless gift of a top-quality education while strengthening your family. I hope you seize the potential and go with it! Will you? I'll help with some details.

This Curriculum

When we made the decision to teach our children at home, I did not find an acceptable curriculum specifically designed for preschool and kindergarten ages that was easy, inexpensive and from a Christian perspective. This Guide came out of that need. The idea was born on a long piece of paper stretched out on my ironing board as I wrote down all the qualities and content of the curriculum I wanted to present to our children. The more I thought about it, the more I realized that more people would probably teach their children at home if they had a similar resource, being able to teach basics, values, and character building material, without a cash outlay of several hundred dollars.

Besides one cassette ("Sir Oliver's Song" listed in Bibliography) and three books recommended (Phonics for Reading and Spelling [Dettmer], and two children's books used in weeks 34 and 35, Big Thoughts For Little People [Taylor] and Giant Steps For Little People [Taylor]), the only other resource materials you need to complete two or more years of teaching are: this book, the Holy Bible, and your library card! This curriculum uses your public library as a resource for teaching material. (One request I have is that you be real diligent in returning books as soon as you are done with them. That will help other parents be able to use them for their children, too. Be considerate; remember the Golden Rule. I have included a reminder to return them each week in the "Preparation" section. Thank you for your thoughtfulness and consideration!)

I have spent hours upon hours pouring over children's books at the library. Your particular library may not have some of the titles listed, but may have access to them if you request in advance. Also, in the "Bible" and "God's World" areas where card catalog numbers are given, if the specific book(s) listed are not available, you may be able to discover another adequate resource in the same # area. There are, I'm sure, some good books available that I overlooked. I have tried not to include any book that may be offensive to you in any way. Some books I found are not listed because of values not compatible to what I felt were uplifting values, or that referred to "millions of years" of development. There are some science sources that were good and are listed, with a notation showing several specific pages to avoid.

Because of the differing ability levels and age groups served by this guide, personalize and adjust as needed by simplifying and/or enriching various areas to best suit your child. Make it fun for yourself, and your child will "catch" your enthusiasm. Did you know that the word "enthusiasm" comes from two words meaning "God within"? I believe that a love of learning is one of the most precious gifts you can bestow on your child. Teaching your child at home gives you an opportunity to fan the flames of curiosity and interest and love of life and learning, instead of squelching it.

Also, a resource not listed previously is that of a positive, loving attitude toward your child. We need to help instill a "can do" attitude in each child by talking about his "smart head" and catching him succeeding, and praising him right then. If he has done something wrong, how much better it is to say, "Stop. Why, Johnny, that's not like you. You're usually (or "learning to be") so (positive character trait)," rather than "You dummy; I knew you'd have a hard time with this!" (I cringe even to have to write those words.) God tells us to "build others up" and "tell the truth in love." He tells us to correct and discipline our children. We need to do that in a loving, upbuilding way. We need to help our children gain, and maintain, a healthy view of themselves.

Some of the basic concepts I have reinforced over and over again this year (and now I hear our children remind each other) are:
1. Obedience: to God, to parents.
2. Stewardship: being a good steward of their bodies and minds, their toys and books, our home and the earth.

3. Building others up and not tearing them down; guarding their mouths.

4. Thankfulness for what they have; not coveting or comparing.

(Each of these terms is explained in the text.) It's so exciting to hear the material that's been taught (and will apply to their entire lifetime) has been "caught"!

Subject Areas for the Week

The subject areas covered by this lesson plan guide are:

Bible concepts	4 times/week
Reading readiness	4 times/week
Arithmetic readiness	4 times/week
God's World (science, geo-graphy, community)	2 times/week
Character building (habits and values)	1 time/week
Personal Health & Safety, Manners	1 time/week
Art	2 times/week
Music	2 times/week
Physical Education skills	4 times/week
Memory verses	4 times/week
Stories	4 times/week
Field trip	1 time/week

The specific time schedule follows. Don't panic to think of teaching involved lessons for extended periods each day to accomplish all of these subjects. In most cases, the length of each class is 10-15 minutes. It's all mapped out for you. Have fun with it.

In addition to the specific classes mentioned, we begin our school with a routine of the Pledge of Allegiance, prayer for our school time and "calendar time." The calendar time teaches and reinforces different counting and time concepts. I have the child repeat the months of the year after me, the child tells me what month it is, we count from 1-30/31 as I point to each number on the calendar, and the child tells what date it is today. Then we say together, "Today is Monday, September xx,xxxx. Yesterday was Sunday, September xx,xxxx. Tomorrow will

be Tuesday, September xx, xxxx." Then the child colors in the box on the calendar for today's date. I have two children and let them take turns holding our flag for the pledge. The other one says the prayer.

When Do I Teach?

I have found in talking with other parents that most home schoolers are able to complete their schoolwork within 2-3 hours per day. For preschoolers, I believe the structured part should be no more than 1-1/2 - 2 hours per day. Part of that time will be for independent activities and play, part for structured one-on-one activities between teacher and learner and part with any older children you are home teaching on the same topic. For example, my preschooler and kindergartener have Bible class and may work on an art project at the same time. In addition to this class time, allow yourself some time each week as preparation for the coming week's classes.

I have chosen to begin our school at 8:00 a.m. so that we're done before 10:00 a.m., but because that may be unworkable in your situation, I'll list a basic timetable for a school from 9:00-11:00 a.m. Some of the lesson plans have material to fill more than the allotted amount of time; some may take you less. Here's the basic framework:

9:00-9:05	Pledge, Prayer, Calendar Time
9:05-9:15	Bible concepts
9:15-9:25	Independent reading readiness activity
9:25-9:35	Teach reading readiness skill
9:35-9:40	Play
9:40-9:50	Art (Mon. & Wed.)
	Music (Tues. & Thurs.)
9:50-10:00	Arithmetic
10:00-10:10	Character Bldg. (Mon.)
	God's World (Tues. & Thurs.)
	Health and Manners (Wed.)
10:10-10:20	Physical Education
10:20-10:30	Story time

This schedule intersperses play, independent activities, and large muscle activities with the "sitting still" times.

Our school year runs from September through the first week of June, breaking two weeks for Christmas and one for Easter - a total of 36 weeks.

An alternate daily schedule for you who will be teaching a preschooler and a kindergartner is listed in the Kindergarten Curriculum Guide and Lesson Plans. This school day is two hours in length instead of one and a half hours long.

Note that the school week is four days of work in the "classroom," Monday through Thursday, and the fifth day, Friday, is for a Field Trip. These field trips will be incorporated into the classroom activities (followup, etc.) and generally relate to a concept being studied. If there is any work not finished during the first four days for whatever reason (we talked more in depth about a subject or child needed more time to learn a concept), that is completed on Friday, too.

Where Do I Teach?

School can be in any of several places in your home. One family I know uses their dining room table; another, their living room. Another teaches at a desk in the child's bedroom. We use a part of our family room with a child-size table and chairs. Whatever works out as your best option, it will be more convenient for you if you can keep most of your materials nearby. Make it as easy and positive for yourself as you can. If you have to cart many materials to and from a different room daily, it might be a deterrent to you on the days you don't "feel" like having school. You do need some work surface (table or a desk) where a child can comfortably sit and write, glue, color and work. As you teach your children to hold a pencil and position the paper, they will need to be able to sit properly.

I use other "classrooms," too: the grocery store, state park and the library, etc. One real advantage of teaching your children is

to be able to catch and use "teachable" moments. For example, we have "consumer education" in the grocery store, we have counting time each push of swinging, science class as we walk in our woods, and phonics/reading time in the car as the children repeat each phonogram's sounds in alphabetical order after I say them.

Basic/Recommended Equipment

U.S. flag
Paper, pencils, ruler, crayons, scissors, glue
Carton/filing cabinet to store material
Globe
Chalkboard/"blackboard"
Contact paper
U.S. map
Chalk (white & colored)
Chalkboard eraser/washcloth
Dictionary
Clock
Calendar
Magazines - for pictures (tear out any good
    pictures when you find them)
3-ring notebook (one per child)
Notebook paper
Catalogs - seed, Sears (for pictures)
File folders
Gummed hole reinforcements
Thick black marker
Butcher paper/newsprint
Old wallpaper books/samples
Construction paper
Cassette player
Bulletin board & pins/corksquares/card
    board & tape
Piano/recorder/xylophone
Box of art supplies: yarn, fabric scraps, trim,
    TP rolls, cardboard
Balls of different sizes (tennis ball size,
    large 12", soft Nerf, for inside)
Rubber stamps - for art projects, construction of learning materials, motivation charts
Small stickers
Empty food boxes, etc., to use in play store
Opt. - Your Big Backyard magazine
    (National Wildlife Federation)

How Can I Ever Pull This Off?

You may be on "cloud nine" at the prospect of achieving the benefits of teaching at home, but thinking, "Wow! Where do I begin? How will this ever work?" Relax. The first step is to have the desire. If you've read this far, you probably do. Never give that up. Re-inspire yourself if you get discouraged. There will be times when you feel like abandoning your dream. These will pass. Reread the beginning of this guide. Write out why you wanted to teach your child at home, or talk to another home-schooling parent, preferably one that's gone through a few "valleys" and has persevered. It is so worth the commitment.

Now, we'll talk about how you work your school into your life without "losing your marbles!" You will find two weekly plan sheets in this section. Use one as a work sheet (you may do a lot of erasing on the first copy!) and the other to remove from the book and use as your final copy of your weeks as you would want them to look. I use this basic format as an ongoing tool to add specific commitments each week to the "framework" of my commitments. (If you choose to use CLW's Household Organizer you will already have various sheets for this purpose.) You will benefit greatly from taking some time to decide when specifically you will be handling each of your responsibilities on a weekly basis. Remember that each of us has the same 24 hours in a day. It's what we do with them that counts! Here are some guidelines to planning your weekly overview:

1. Write in any committed spiritual activities (church, daily quiet time with God).
2. Write in any other important regular obligations/appointments (weekly date with husband).
3. Block out regular family mealtimes.
4. Considering your and your child's best time of day, fill in your school period(s). If you need to split up the time into two segments, for example, one in morning, and one after nap, do. But remember each time you commit yourself to that schedule, stick with it. Try to schedule doctor appointments, shopping trips, etc., around your school times. Routine is important for children, as well as ourselves.
5. Schedule in a personal renewal interval each day and a short planning session weekly (personal and family goal planning/school preparation).

Here is an example of my current weekly plan. I share it with you not for comparison of any sort, but as a starting point to help you. We all know that the "white spaces" (uncommitted time) do not stay empty for very long!

I have found that it is helpful to use different colored markers/pencils for the various activities. (For example: spiritual = purple, personal = green, cleaning = blue, school = red, meal routines = yellow, etc.) I think it allows you a quicker visual over-

Weekly Plan Sample

Time	Monday	Tuesday	Wednesday	Thursday	Friday	Saturday	Sunday
6:00	Holy Bible and Pray	Holy Bible and Pray	Holy Bible and Pray	Holy Bible and Pray	Holy Bible and Pray	Holy Bible and Pray	Holy Bible and Pray
7:00	breakfast, pack lunches	breakfast, pack lunches	breakfast, pack lunches	breakfast, pack lunches	breakfast, pack lunches	breakfast, clean kitchen	breakfast, clean kitchen
8:00	school	school	school	school	school/ field trip		correspondence
9:00	school	school	school	school	school/ field trip		
10:00	exercise	exercise	exercise	exercise	exercise	exercise	
11:00	lunch	lunch	lunch	lunch	lunch	lunch	church
12:00							church/ lunch
1:00							
2:00							
3:00							
4:00	cleaning	cleaning	cleaning	cleaning	cleaning	cleaning	
5:00	kitchen dinner	kitchen dinner	kitchen dinner	kitchen dinner	kitchen dinner	kitchen dinner	kitchen dinner
6:00	cleanup play w/chil.	cleanup play w/chil.	cleanup play w/chil.	cleanup play w/chil.	cleanup play w/chil.	cleanup play w/chil.	cleanup play w/chil.
7:00	chil. to bed	chil. to bed	chil. to bed	chil. to bed	chil. to bed	chil. to bed	chil. to bed
8:00							
9:00	shower & bed	shower & bed	shower & bed	shower & bed	shower & bed	shower & bed	shower & bed

11

Weekly Plan

Time	Monday	Tuesday	Wednesday	Thursday	Friday	Saturday	Sunday
5:00							
6:00							
7:00							
8:00							
9:00							
10:00							
11:00							
12:00							
1:00							
2:00							
3:00							
4:00							
5:00							
6:00							
7:00							
8:00							
9:00							

view.

I have developed, after trying many "systems," an easy way to keep on top of keeping our home clean and organized. (For those of you who are naturally organized, bear with me.) I drew an outline of a house which is divided to show the relative position of each of the rooms in our home. In each room, I list my weekly "to do" chores. Any once-a-month items I list to the side. I have five "weekly" listings: Week I, II, III, IV, V. Weeks I to IV are done each month during the corresponding weeks. Week V chores are the things that get done in a month with five weeks, obviously not my highest priority items! As I finish a task, I cross it out. When a room is all cleaned, I color it in on my "house." I try to get the entire house colored in by Friday evening. I have a copy of the house for each week.

I also have had the children begin to help me clean. One of my long-term goals is to teach the children to be able to perform all housekeeping skills and beginning cooking skills, etc., by the time they are 12. I believe that those activities are important life-skills and that the children need to have jobs within the family. I have my three- and five-year-olds make their beds, empty wastebaskets, wash the fronts of refrigerator, freezer, dishwasher, oven and washer/dryer, help load and unload the washing machine, feed dogs, unload the dishwasher, pick up their toys, help fold clothes (washcloths, dishcloths, dish towels, socks and their underwear), set and clear the table, and help me cook meals. At this point, it sometimes takes a lot longer to show them how to do something and guide them through it than just to do it myself, but I'm thinking long-term. One other thing that I have learned about cleaning is that "it's easy to clean a clean house." From being on both sides of that fence, I can attest that it is a true statement!

There are several prime activities that help me keep all the balls that I'm juggling up in the air at the same time. I have to say humbly that I "lose it" sometimes, too. I sure don't have it all together, but I have

made progress using a few tools, which I'll pass on to you. Three "biggies" as far as helping us cope with all our roles are:

1. Goal-setting and follow through.
2. Organization - to make our lives flow easier.
3. Time alone for personal refreshment and replenishing. "You can't pour from an empty pitcher."

I believe I am doing what God wants me to do by teaching my children at home. The above three areas assist me in my teaching, and in all other facets of my life. They will help you, too.

Goal-setting: See the lesson plans for weeks 17-19, Bible concepts sections for How-To's. I'd highly recommend you make time (Notice I said make instead of take; I'm a Mom, too!) to write down your Lifetime, One Year (or rest of this year and then reevaluate at the end of this year), and then Monthly Goals. Before you do this, pray that God will direct your choices, and know that He may rearrange and/or change your plans/goals to fit in with His best for you. This technique is a very helpful tool. It helps you keep in mind your most important things to do and helps you to plan for your seasonal projects (canning, vacations, Christmas and birthday gift preparation/shopping, etc.). It is well worth the investment in time! Somehow, some way, you can find/make the time, even if it involves getting a baby-sitter and taking half a day off. Write your goals down, and date them. Keep them in a special place; you'll refer to them later. They help keep you on track. Between them and the weekly plan schedule showing your available/noncommitted times, you'll be able to schedule in "dates" with one child at a time, time for you to read the book you've wanted to, etc. Be careful not to over schedule, though. Then you will be trapped under the pressure of guilt. Ask God for guidance and tell Satan to bug out; don't let him defeat you!

Something very valuable to my life has been an accountability session with a prayer partner. At one point, a friend and I met once weekly for one hour, while our small children played quietly in an adjoining part of the room (so we could supervise them). They knew it was very important to be extra helpful to Mom during this time. We share our short-term and mid-range goals with each other, tell the other what we want to do by the next meeting (and know she'll ask about it!), give each other loving suggestions, and pray for each other. The commitment has been such a blessing to me. We've each benefitted from the structure of the commitment and the power of our Lord (Jesus Christ) working in our lives. I highly recommend this idea to you.

Organization: Basically I am an unor-ganized person, but I can really thank God for the changes He's taken me through over the last few years. I have a long way to go, but I have found some shortcuts and methods that have proven helpful to me. The less disorganization, clutter and chaos you have in your life, the more freedom you'll have to enjoy life because there will be fewer sources of irritation.

I use a master menu plan that has saved me hours in figuring out the grocery list every two weeks. I try to make some items (basics) mentioned on Saturday to tide us through at least one week: granola, yogurt, alfalfa sprouts, biscuits or muffins, and cookies (can be frozen). Here's an example of one week's plan:

Sample Master Menu Plan

Day	Breakfast	Lunch	Snack	Dinner
Sunday	yogurt, granola	grilled cheese sandwich, carrots	fruit	meat, grain, *fish* vegetables *rice*
Monday	eggs, potato pancakes	pizza biscuits with cheese, carrots	yogurt fruit	soup/stew, grain vegetables *fish rice*
Tuesday	7 grain cereal, fruit	egg salad sandwich 2 muffins, carrots	yogurt, cheese (2" squares)	chicken, potato vegetables *chicken potato*
Wednesday	whole-wheat pancakes (plain or w/ honey), fruit	spinich spaghetti carrots, cheese (2" squares)	yogurt, fruit 4T P.B.	meat, grain vegetables *spaghetti dairy*
Thursday	graonola w/milk or yogurt or oatmeal, fruit	lentil burgers, grain, carrots	fruit biscuit	fish, grain, dairy vegetables *potato meatless*
Friday	oatmeal, fruit	leftovers, grain carrots	fruit, 2 eggs yogurt	meatless, grain vegetables *grain chicken*
Saturday	cold cereal w/milk (unsweetened), fruit	P.B. sandwiches cheese (2" squares)	fruit carrots	*meat* chicken/fish grain, vegetables

If I had thought several years ago that I would follow a plan like this, I might have fainted in my tracks! But it has made the task of figuring specific menus and the corresponding grocery lists, a breeze. By the way, I don't spend an extravagant amount of money of food. I recently contacted the Food Stamp Office to see what the maximum amount a family of our size might qualify for and found that we spend less than that maximum amount, and our budget covers non-edible items, too (detergent, etc.). I also have a master grocery list and use a copy of it every two weeks. Because we live 20 minutes from grocery stores, it has been a real blessing to plan well and/or make-do.

To organize information and ideas, I keep a notebook with various sections in it (personal goals, couple, mother's resource, family, thrifting, notes). I change my notebook periodically, weeding out and modifying. It's a storehouse of information in an organized format, instead of a clutter of small notes about different projects that end up getting stashed here and there. I also include a section with phone numbers I frequently call and a master calendar with birthdays and anniversaries on it.

In reading these organizational ideas, you may think there's no room for "fun" things in my life. On the contrary. The small amount of chosen structure provides me freedom to have time to do "fun" things. Everyone goes off his schedule and organization at some time; the important thing is to get back to our priorities!

Time Alone: My morning "alone time" is so missed when I forego it. What a wonderful present thirty minutes or an hour is to yourself at the beginning of a fresh, new day. It is quiet and you are alone with God. It is so much easier to get yourself together, alone, before "the troops" wake up. Ideas that may help you are: shower, dress, pray, quick overview of what you want to do today, read a Proverbs chapter for the day and/or five Psalms (to get you through the book each month), read a chapter in a book you've wanted to read, and spot exercises.

Choose your highest priority items, estimate time to allow for each, juggle them around, sift down, and you'll come up with your present to yourself. Take care to get to sleep early enough in the evening to get your rest. Even if it takes a few mornings of dragging yourself out of bed, it will be worth it in the long run. For those who are really not fond of the morning, try getting up 15 minutes early for a week, then the second week get up the second 15 minutes earlier. Inch by inch...

How To Use This Guide

This Guide is meant to be a timesaver for you by not only providing you with a list of concepts for the preschooler and kindergartner to learn, but also specific day-to-day lesson plans to follow. You will find the lesson plans following page 45. These include all subjects that the preschooler will use. For those teaching a kindergartner, you will be using all the subjects' lesson plans except those for Reading and Arithmetic. Following the lesson plans for Week 36 you will find the Kindergarten/Advanced section, including a School Time Schedule, Helps in Using the Writing Road to Reading reading program, a list of Kindergarten Reading and Arithmetic Concepts, and specific lesson plans for K-Reading and K-Arithmetic.

The subjects' content in the daily lesson plans include wording to use with the child, project information, and resources to use if desired. For the P-Reading plans, it mentions reading a poem to your child each day. You may want to check out some poem books from the library and write out those you want to use during the year. One mom mentioned she had her child illustrate each one as it was read.

There are more books listed for each day than you will ever use. Do not let the number of books throw you. In a few cases you may not be able to find any of the books listed. **Remember: This curriculum can be used without the benefit of a**

library. Simply use the resources available in your home. Be flexible. If a certain book is unavailable, substitute with another. Enjoy the library time with your children. I recommend that when reading the next week's lesson plans you underline or highlight the library books. Then when you go to the library you can more easily spot the resources for which you are looking. If a book is in the picture book section, its title and author are given. If it is in the Juvenile/Junior book section, the Dewey decimal number is also listed. Please make it a priority to be diligent in returning the books quickly so other families can use them.

I would recommend using plastic tabs attached to the outside of the pages or a large clip to mark the Kindergarten section if you are teaching a kindergartner or both a preschooler and a kindergartner.

To assist you in preparing for each week, I have included a section at the end of each week's lesson plans called "Things To Do." These are things to watch for and do while you read through the next week's lesson plans. You can supplement additional activities to reinforce skills taught. I have included the basics.

Making the Materials

Some parents choose to make the materials all at once at the beginning of the year. Others make them as needed in preparation for the coming week. Do whatever suits your situation best.

"The Grid" on the next page is the number one item I've gotten questions about over the past three years. I will try and explain it thoroughly. The grid is meant to be copied. The copies will be used to make matching games to practice various skills throughout the preschool and kindergarten years. The child matches a card (cut from index card weight paper) with an answer you've written on it to the problem you've written on a square of the grid. And then the child matches another

card to its matching grid square, and so on. Some examples of ways this will be used throughout the Guide are: matching a particular small letter to its corresponding capital letter on the grid square; another activity is matching a card with "5¢" written on it to the square with a nickel on it. I hope you get the picture.

Glue the grid to inside of a file folder, in which you also keep the corresponding matching cards. You can use one or two sheets in each folder. The file folders can be labeled and easily stored in a file cabinet or box with matching cards stored in the folder. They are nonconsumable (can be reused), easy to organize, and easy for the child to carry. The matching cards are the same size as the grid sections. Make sure you clip one upper edge of each card, so the child knows which direction is the top (no reversals or upside-down letters/numbers). Purchase from a paper supply store a ream of index weight (#110) stock (8-1/2" x 11" sheets of paper the weight of index cards) that can be cut into whatever size cards you need. You have permission to make copies of the grid.

For picture cards, mentioned in the text, and other projects keep your eyes open for magazine pictures of the following:

Clothing
Shaped objects (circles, squares, etc.)
Animals
Families doing things together
Furniture
Dad as leader
People
Dad working
Objects of each color
Dad protecting
Family members
Dad and Mom teaching
Senses (mouth, nose, fingers, eyes, ears)
Dad and Mom hugging each other
Dad and Mom hugging child
Children obeying
Children helping each other
Children learning
People of different ages

Pictures illustrating:
- (a) temptation
- (b) jealousy
- (c) anger
- (d) selfishness
- (e) pride
- (f) watching TV
- (g) our American freedoms

Some of these pictures are to be used in "classifying" activities, where your child sorts cards (of index size or larger) onto which you've glued pictures (one per card) of various classifications into piles (all furniture cards in one pile, food in another, clothing in a third pile, etc.). The text will tell you when and what kind are needed.

Look in the blue pages of your telephone directory under U.S. Government, Dept. of Agriculture, U.S. Forest Service to locate the posters listed in the Bible Section of weeks 2-4 in the curriculum. Let the people know they are for educational purposes. You can also get the Woodsy Owl song sheet and a Smokey the Bear comic book there. The letter patterns, at the end of the Introduction section, may be copied for your use. These can be used for letter cards (for the child to trace and shape with a finger) and also can be used for headings on a family bulletin board.

How Do I Keep Track of It All?

Keep track of your child's progress in this book. You can circle, date, and make notes in the lesson plans part or inside the covers. If you teach more than one child, note their initials next to a date. Use the section titled "Basic Concepts" as a checklist for skills and accomplishments, with dates. The child's notebook, will also keep track of skills with dated entries.

The Notebook

To record the main points from the lessons of the year, preserve the artwork in an organized manner, and to encourage the love of reading and the importance of the written word, the child will be keeping a 3-ring notebook. Throughout the lesson plans, reference will be made to "Story Pages." These all go into the notebook under the various subject headings. There will be notebook entries for the following subjects: Bible, God's World, Personal Health & Safety and Manners, Character Building, Field Trips, Art, and a section with your child's name. If desired, you could also have a section for Memory Verses, writing each as the child memorizes it.

In addition to the regular pages, the child will be making a number of "books" which can be included in the notebook's main section, put into a pocket of the notebook, put into a large envelope punched with holes, or put into clear vinyl pockets. This notebook will be a summary of the content of your child's work this year. It will be one central place to keep his work in an organized fashion. You, as teacher, will be writing (printing) the summaries and stories. In future years, as your child learns the skills of writing and reading, he will do the written part, first copying sentences from the chalkboard, then working into an independent activity. The skill and method should serve you and your child well. I recommend gummed hole reinforcements for your pages - the notebook will be read many times!

The section of the notebook with your child's name can include height and weight information (several times during the year), full name and address, and a series of 3 blank pages, each to eventually hold 4 photos - one a month for a year. The monthly photo will be to show a positive character trait seen or developing in your child. Underneath each photo write a caption and date. (Example: "Sam is loyal," "Sam is respectful," "Sam is courageous.") You might want to take photos of the child

This page left blank intentionally

actually <u>being</u> helpful (sweeping, working, etc.) instead of just twelve head-and-shoulders views. The listing of traits in the Character Building section should give you a start as to what to notice and/or help your child develop. It will become a self-fulfilling prophecy; our children live up to what they think about themselves. What an opportunity for child development we have!

Motivation For Your Child

I have used stickers and rubber stamps on charts for motivating the children. I usually have two charts going at the same time, one on the refrigerator and one in "school" for school work. In school, I give one rubber stamp time or one small sticker for every "job" or paper completed. I want to reinforce good effort and sticking to the task. If the child disobeys or goofs around, no stamp/sticker is given. They also get to stamp their charts for every memory verse they learn.

I usually divide the "at home" chart into several areas, depending upon which habits/attitudes/jobs are important and currently being worked on. An example of a chart may have these categories: pleasant attitude, picks up toys and clothes, kind to brother/sister, helpful to Dad and Mom, makes wise choices. (I put stick drawings next to the wording so they stamp the right area.) Several times each day we go over the chart categories quickly and I tell them where and how many times to stamp or put stickers. Since I began putting "makes wise choices" on the chart, I've been encouraged to hear the children come to me and say,"Mom, I just made a wise choice. I was going to (bad action), but I told myself, `No, that's not right. I need to do (good action).'" It's working!

I make new construction paper charts each month for each child, usually on regular-sized sheets cut into a different shape. Some suggestions are:

January: snowman, snowflake
February: heart, cloud
March: seashell, shamrock
April: cross, umbrella
May: flower, paper doll chain
June: strawberry, tent
July: flag, shorts/bathing suit
August: sunshine, garden plot
September: open book, teddy bear
October: autumn leaf, pumpkin
November: cornucopia, pumpkin pie
December: Christmas tree, bell

Other Concerns

One question most people who are not familiar with home schooling have is that of "socialization," whatever you interpret that to be. My own view is that the child needs to develop a sense of worth/identity and a sense of obedience and values within the family structure. I also believe it is important for the child to have some time each week developing friendships with a few well-chosen friends. The length of this interaction will need to vary depending on the age and maturity of your child. Each six-month interval of age makes a big difference, developmentally.

I also believe it is good to include Dad, as much as is feasible, in the child's school time. A field trip, not listed, might be to Dad's place of work.

There are so many resources available. Grandparents, neighbors and community workers may each be willing to be a resource for you in specific areas of study.

With rare exceptions, we do not watch television. There are very few excellent programs and it can cause addiction. There are better choices in which we and our children can invest our time, and the values (even on commercials) are inconsistent with those of our family.

When our children were younger, we chose not to allow them to watch one of the most popular children's TV program for the following reasons:
1. It encourages a short attention span;
2. It portrays monsters as being good;
3. It may cause dyslexia (learning disorder)

by the way letters are flashed on the screen (according to Dr. Hilda Mosse);
4. It promotes some values not consistent with those of our family.

Getting the Most out of Your Field Trip

First, ask the contact person what will be covered. Give suggestions, if appropriate. Next, prepare for the visit by telling the child what might be expected (time frame, what to look for, etc.). Review the basic rules:

1. Listen; don't talk.
2. Hold on to my hand (preschoolers).
3. Stay away from all equipment.
4. Be pleasant and polite.
5. Be sure to thank the guide after the tour.
6. Enjoy the trip.

During the field trip, I jot down a few notes of importance, sequence (what we saw first, etc.), and vocabulary (new terms used). I also try to take a photo of the child at the establishment. The following Monday, recap what was seen, telling a story to preserve information and the experience of the trip in a few sentences. Here's an example:

The Airport

I visited the Portland International Airport today.
Thirty-four different airlines fly out from Portland.
Mr. Eldridge showed us an ejection seat and told about airport fire fighters.
I went down the new concourse and saw a plane take off.
Then I saw the baggage area of the airport.
Our airport is a busy place!
Date

Each trip goes on a separate story page, dated and filed in the child's notebook.

Who Am I Teaching?

A Profile Of Your Three-year-old Child:

Loves to play with language and make up new words.
Adores silly rhyming.
Can follow a moving target without losing attention.
Can talk about what he sees in books.
Differentiates between boys and girls.
Shows a growing understanding of time intervals: yesterday, today, tomorrow.
Shows improving memory.
Begins to think problems through in his mind with ideas.
Loves Mom and likes to do things with her.
Is more orderly.
Begins to share toys.
Is more cooperative in putting toys away.
Begins to learn to take turns.
Enjoys play.
Rhythm.
May have difficulty distinguishing between fantasy and reality.
Is eager to help with real family chores.
Will help with housecleaning and keeping things neat.
Shows an interest in babies.
Is learning to cope with anger and fear.
Is developing self-restraint and self-control.

A Profile Of Your Four-year-old Child:

Talks a mile a minute.
Asks more complex questions.
Has boundless energy.
Can be creative or chaotic, depending on environment and materials provided.
Loves to play with words.
Still has difficulty adding correct endings to words.
Asks why, when, how questions and word meanings constantly.
Confuses fact and fiction in children's book.

Enjoys jokes, silly and funny books, silly language.

Has strong feelings for family and home.

Is concerned for young children in distress.

Is aggressive with sibling sometimes.

Understands need to share and taking turns.

Responds to verbal and physical limitations.

Tends to play with children of the same sex.

Is sensitive to praise and blame.

Is noisy.

Shows an interest in the concept of marriage.

Begins an awareness of good and bad.

Is susceptible to colds.

Brain, spinal cord, and nerves reach almost full adult size by 4 to 6 with little growth thereafter.

Responds well to "E" eye test.

A Profile Of Your Five-year-old Child:

Holds pencil and crayon well.

Draws a recognizable human figure with head, arms, legs, and trunk.

Speaks fluently and grammatically correct except for some mispronunciations (s, v, f, th).

Uses plurals, pronouns and tenses correctly in well-constructed sentences.

Loves to be read to; memorizes favorite stories; may act them out.

Likes to practice abilities, shows parents how to print his name, write numbers, and spell words.

Is intent on pleasing parents.

Is acquiring skills of giving, receiving, and sharing.

Likes to impress companions.

Shows more independent behavior.

Has a sense of humor.

Can experience fears.

Is better able to verbally express fears.

Shows a push for autonomy.

Likes to finish what he starts.

Shows greater intent and decisiveness.

Dawdles less.

Can accept fair punishment.

Shows contradictory behavior.

Shows impulsive behavior on occasion.

Is curious about birth, marriage and death.

Is highly imaginative.

Is an expert block builder.

Can play alone or with one to three others fifteen minutes to one hour daily.

Is more interested in "here and now' themes than fantasy.

Uses scissors more skillfully.

Copies what he sees.

Can accompany music with bodily movements, walking like a bear, walking like an old person, moving slowly, etc.

Is interested in science and nature materials.

Has fewer colds.

May have bad dreams/nightmares.

Can use hands and legs competently.

Is cooperative and helpful with tasks.

Thrives on affection.

Seeks adult help and guidance.

Is more involved with dramatic play scenes than one year ago.

Is less restless than a year ago.

Is full of vigor and the joy of life.

Is a delight.

Loves to talk.

Asks questions for information, not for attention.

Is great at telling stories.

What is the Junior Chef and Host/Hostess Program?

This program is one that has been successful short-term, and will be, we hope, very successful in the long run. You will need to adapt this to your particular family, depending on how many children you have. There are two jobs that I delegate, taking turns with each of our two children. One is the Junior Chef for the day, the other is the Host/Hostess for the day. The Junior Chef helps me cook one meal during the day. (S)he helps get the food out of the refrigerator and cupboards, gets the needed supplies, makes the food, puts the supplies and food away as we go along, dishes up the food, and puts it on the table. The Host/Hostess gets the silverware, napkins, and dishes out (ready for the Junior Chef to dish up) and sets the table with the silverware and napkins. They both help unload the dishwasher for the day.

Each child is responsible for clearing his plate, glass, and napkin from the table after each meal.

The children love to be the Junior Chef; they look forward to "their day." I presented the program with a lot of enthusiasm, letting them know how special it would be. They love to be in the kitchen anyway, and they are proud of their skills and accomplishments. It has worked very well for us. Although it takes more of my time now, I feel that it is positive investment in their future.

Using Rubber Stamps as a Teaching Aid

I have been continually amazed at the variety of ways to use rubber stamps, both in personal use and as a teaching aid. Because of the variety of size and content, I'm finding new ways to use them all the time. Following is a list showing some general ways to use rubber stamps:

1. Picture lotto
2. Number lotto
3. Letter lotto
4. Flash cards: letter recognition
5. Flash cards: number recognition
6. Matching capital and small letters
7. Matching numerals with a number of objects
8. Matching folder: numerals
9. Matching folder: number of objects
10. Matching folder: capital letter
11. Matching folder: small letters
12. Matching folder: colors
13. Color lotto
14. Weather charts
15. Picture domino cards
16. Dot domino cards
17. Calendars: small, as gifts
18. Calendars: large, for school
19. Bookmarks: personal and gifts
20. Bookplates: personal and gifts
21. Stationery: personal and gifts
22. Achievement charts
23. Motivation on school papers turned in
24. Tool for following directions (sequence of stamping)
25. Tool for hand-eye coordination practice

And going on, for you as Teacher and Mom:

26. Bookmarks, for you and gifts: regular and embossed
27. Stationery and postcards for you and gifts: regular and embossed
28. Invitations: regular and embossed
29. Gift cards: birthdays, anniversaries, Christmas, Valentine's Day, Easter
30. Gift tags: for all occasions
31. Package wrap decorations
32. Book plates: personal and gifts
33. Canning labels
34. Thank You notes: regular and embossed
35. "To Do" lists/tablets
36. Organization notebook
37. Mark special days on calendar

Besides being fun, I have found them to be a real time and money saver. No mad dashes to the store for cards or even a last minute gift.

With a few simple rules, I have found that my children do very well in using the stamps themselves. This is the sequence I have them follow:

a. They wash their hands.

b. We cover the table with newspaper and then put their stamping paper on top.

c. They choose one stamp at a time.

d. They put the stamp on the inked stamp pad and press once.

e. They put the stamp on the paper and hold it, without wiggling it, for the count of 1,2,3.

f. They put the stamp on a damp washcloth (folded in 1/4's and on plate on the table) to get the ink off it for the count of 1,2,3.

g. They put the stamp back in its proper place.

h. They close the stamp pad box when they are finished with it.

i. They wash their hands after they're done if they did get any ink on them by accident.

They love it. I guess idea #38 for using stamps should be "pure enjoyment and fun!"

His Footprints (26461 Fresno, Mission Viejo, CA 92691), a family business, carries a line of rubber stamps. You may request a catalog from them for $3.00.

I hope you enjoy them as much as I have. And I know your children will love them.

Resources - Books

I. Teaching and Home Schooling:

Blankenbaker, Frances — What the Bible Is All About for Young Explorers

Cangemi, Sam — 50 Tactile and Visual Perception Games for under $10. j790C223f

Coppola, Raymond T. — Successful Children. 371.3C785s.

Flesch, Rudolf — Why Johnny Can't Read.

Harris, Gregg — The Christian Home School. an excellent orientation to the advantages of the Christian home for educating children. from Christian Life Workshops (CLW)

Haycock, Ruth C. — Bible Truth for School Subjects. an excellent resource available by mail through Christian Life Workshops (CLW), P.O. Box 2250, Gresham, Oregon 97030, (See CLW's Mail Order Form on page 32). The set offers everything the Bible has to say about over thirty school subjects. Subjects include: Vol. I: Social Studies; Vol. II: Language Arts/English; Vol. III: Science/Mathematics; Vol. IV: Fine Arts/Health. These books can be used easily to amplify the topics in the Learning at Home: Preschool & Kindergarten curriculum, now and for future levels.

Macaulay, Susan S. — For the Children's Sake.

Nilsson, Leonart — A Child is Born. (photos of baby's growth in womb)

Dettmer, Bonnie — Phonics for Reading and Spelling. (the method I suggest to be used with this curriculum) available from CLW

Toole, Amy L. & Ellen Boehm — Off to a Good Start: 464 Readiness for Reading, Math, Social Studies and Science.

Wade, Theodore Jr. et. al. — The Home School Manual.

II. Child Raising:

Caplan, Theresa & Frank — The Early Childhood Year: The 2 to 6 Year Old. (Although I disagree with some of their views and perspectives, the developmental information is interesting.)

Dobson, Dr. James — Dare to Discipline.
Hide or Seek.
The Strong-willed Child.

III. Spiritual:
Smith, Hannah Whitall — The Christian's Secret of a Happy Life. Great!

IV. Home Management:
Anson, Elva — The Complete Book of Home Management.
Schaeffer, Edith — Hidden Art.
Pride, Mary — The Way Home: Beyond Feminism, Back to Reality.
A life-changing book. Available from CLW
Young, Pam — The Sidetracked Sisters' Happiness File.
& Peggy Jones

V. Goal Setting/Time Management:
Lakein, Alan — How to Get Control of Your Time and Your Life.

Resources - Cassette Tapes

I. For you:
The Challenge of Being a Woman. Alice Painter. Set of 12 cassettes on different facets of a woman's life. Excellent! Available through: Bible Believers Cassettes, 130 N. Spring Street. Springdale, Arkansas 72764.
The Home Schooling Workshop. by Gregg Harris from Christian Life Workshops, 12 cassettes. A must. Learn a great deal and then review periodically for encourage ment and inspiration.

II. For your children:
The Bible: The Amazing Book. The Sparrow Corp.
Charity Churchmouse on the Front Line. Maranatha Music. Application of putting on spiritual armour.
Colby's Missing Memory. Maranatha Music, P.O. Box 1396, Costa Mesa, California 92628.
Lullabies and Nursery Rhymes, Volume I.
Kids' Praise! 5: Psalty's Camping Adventure...Count it all Joy. Maranatha Music. (others in the series must be good, too!)
Sir Oliver's Song. Candle and Agape Force Prep. School. MCA Distributing Corp., 70 Universal City Plaza; Universal City, California 91608. The Ten Commandments in song version.

Resources - Video Tapes

I. Adventure/Classics:

Big Red. (89 minutes)
Charlie, the Lonesome Cougar. (74 minutes)
(The) Legend of Black Thunder Mountain. (90 minutes) Two children get separated from (and reunited with) their father in a covered wagon.
(The) Legend of Lobo. (67 minutes) Wolf.
Mountain Family Robinson. (102 minutes) Family leaves Los Angeles to live in the wilderness.

The Adventures of the Wilderness Family. (100 minutes)

Wilderness Family, II. (104 minutes)

Pollyana. (134 minutes)

Seven Alone. (90 minutes) Based on true story of Sager family on their way to Oregon in covered wagon; parents die; 7 children stick together to finish the journey alone together.

Swiss Family Robinson. (126 minutes)

Treasure Island. (87 minutes)

Westward Ho, the Wagons. (94 minutes) Man leads wagon trains through hardships on Oregon Trail.

(The) Wild Country. (92 minutes) Family moves to Wyoming Territory and meets and triumphs over many problems as a family unit.

II. Animated:

Charlotte's Web. (90 minutes) Stresses friendship, loyalty. It has been a favorite of our children.

(The) Many Adventures of Winnie the Pooh. (74 minutes)

Tales of Peter Rabbit. (43 minutes)

(The) Velveteen Rabbit. (30 minutes)

III. Musical:

Sound of Music. (172 minutes) Presents the joy of music.

IV. Spiritual:

Daniel in the Lions' Den. (39 minutes)

David and Goliath. (37 minutes)

Esther. (50 minutes)

Kings of Kings. (170 minutes)

Moses. (58 minutes)

One Minute Bible Stories, (New Testament). (30 minutes)
   Shari Lewis' Lambchop and Florence Henderson narrate.

One Minute Bible Stories, (Old Testament). (30 minutes)

Basic Concepts Taught

Shari Lewis and Lambchop narrate.

Bible

I. God created the world.

II. God created me.

III. God created families.

IV. God loves us so much that He sent Jesus.

V. Faith: What it is, and how to use it and share it.

VI. God likes order and wants us to plan.

VII. God loves us and wants us to grow.

VIII. God wants us to obey and make the right decisions.

IX. God wants us to be victorious.

X. The Trinity: the three roles of God.

XI. Communication with God: how He talks with us and prayer with Him.

XII. The Final Commandment: Love one another.

Preschool Reading:

I. Name, address, and phone number repetition.

II. Left-to-right eye movement.

III. Visual discrimination.

IV. Auditory discrimination.

V. Classifying.

VI. Rhyming.
VII. Opposites.
VIII. Sequencing.
IX. Following path through a maze.
X. Expressing self in complete sentences.
XI. Hand-eye coordination.
XII. Vocabulary skills.
XIII. Speech skills.
XIV. Listening skills.
XV. Recognition of letters A-Z and a-z.

God's World:

I. Sky
II. Earth.
III . Water.
IV. Animals.
V. Mankind: life cycle, differences, anatomy.
VI. Weather.
VII. Transportation.
VIII. Communication.
IX. Pilgrims.
X. Nature: repetition of night/day, seasons.
XI. Shapes in nature.
XII. Basic food groups and nutrition.
XIII. Directions.
XIV. Maps: USA, State, City
XV. Differences between city and rural areas.
XVI. U.S.A.
XVII. Heat and its effect on matter.
XVIII. Sounds and noises.
XIX. Music & Dance.
XX. Plants.
XXI. Farming.
XXII. Telling time (beginning concepts).
XXIII. Economics.
XXIV. Having your own business.
XXV. Written communication.
XXVI. Gardening.
XXVII. Tools.
XXVIII.Relationships.

Preschool Arithmetic:

I. Top, middle, bottom.
II. Above, below; over, under.
III. Before, after, between.
IV. Color names and recognition: red, orange, yellow, green, blue, purple, brown, black, white.
V. Shape names and recognition: circle, square, triangle.
VI. Parts of a whole.
VII. Time concepts: yesterday, today, tomorrow; days of the week; months of the year.
VIII. Ordinal numbers (first: 1st; second: 2nd; third: 3rd).
IX. Seriation: smallest to largest, lightest to darkest, lightest to heaviest.
X. Counting orally to 30.
XI. Numerals 0-10: recognize amounts and numerals; match numerals with correct number of objects.
XII. Sequence of numerals 0-10: relationship; before/after, more/less.
XIII. Relationships of amounts: many/few, more/less.
XIV. Measurement tools and application: ruler, yardstick, thermometer (oral and outdoor), liquids and solids, speed, loudness.
XV. Maps: directions (north, east, south, west), "reading" maps by legends.
XVI. Money: name, identify and match with cent/dollar value (1 cent, 5 cents, 25 cents, 50 cents, one dollar).
XVII. Shapes and numbers in nature.
XVIII. Review.

Health, Safety & Manners:

I. Personal Health:
   A. Dressing right for the weather.
   B. Personal cleanliness.
   C. Care of teeth and mouth.
   D. Care of eyes.
   E. Importance of rest and sleep.
   F. Importance of exercise.
   G. Good posture.
   H. Germs: coughing and sneezing, washing hands, not sharing food or drinks.

II. Personal Safety:
   A. Fire drills (2).
   B. Eye safety.
   C. Indoor safety.
   D. Outdoor safety.
   E. Safety with medicine, sharp objects, and matches.
   F. Safety in cars and away from home.
   G. "Private zones" and saying "no."
   H. Emergency phone calls.
   I. First aid basics.
III. Manners:
   A. Table manners.
   B. Thank you notes.
   C. Eye contact when speaking and listening.
   D. Being a good guest and host/hostess.
   E. Introductions.
IV. Personal Responsibilities:
   A. Introduction of the Jr. Chef and Host/Hostess program.
   B. Learning new jobs.
   C. Taking care of pets.
   D. Helping elderly people.
   E. Helping with babies.

Physical Education:

I. Ball skills:
   A. Throw ball.
   B. Catch ball.
   C. Kick ball.
   D. Roll ball.
   E. Toss ball into air.
   F. Bounce ball.
II. Body movements:
   A. Walk forward and backward.
   B. Jump forward and backward.
   C. Run regularly and on tiptoe.
   D. Skip.
   E. Hop.
   F. Gallop.
   G. "Animal walks."
   H. Move to music and stop when music stops.
III. Coordination:
   A. Left and right distinction.
   B. Climb on inclined board.
   C. Balance on balance beam/curb/2x4 for 10 feet.
   D. Balance on one foot at a time.

IV. Acrobatics:
   A. Rolls.
   B. Somersaults.
   C. Headstands.
V. Aerobics.
VI. Games:
   A. Bean bag toss.
   B. Indoor bowling.
   C. Simon Says

Art:

I. Painting:
   A. Finger painting.
   B. Tempera painting.
   C. Watercolor painting.
   D. Spatter painting.
   E. Sponge painting.
   F. Stencil painting.
II. Crayon:
   A. Figure drawing.
   B. Object drawing.
   C. Crayon-resist.
III. Other media:
   A. Clay.
   B. Construction paper.
   C. Chalk
   D. Glitter and glue.
   E. Tissue paper.
   F. Materials from nature.
   G. Fabric, yarn, sewing notions.
IV. Construction:
   A. Greeting cards for special occasions.
   B. Gifts for special occasions.
   C. Mobiles.
   D. Chains (popcorn, paper).
   E. Christmas decorations.
   F. Collages.
   G. Field trip scenes.
V. Art Appreciation.

Music:

I. Singing:
   A. American folk songs
   B. Nursery rhyme songs.
   C. Songs with motions.
   D. Religious songs.
   E. Songs that reinforce concepts/ values taught.
   F. Other songs.

II. Rhythm instruments.

Preschool Habits and Values:

I. Stewardship:
    A. Environment.
    B. Our resources.
    C. Our minds and bodies.
II. Humility.
III. Responsibility.
IV. Loyalty:
    A. To God.
    B. To family.
V. Thankfulness:
    A. Abilities, physical things.
    B. Relationship with God, freedom to worship.
VI. Responding to God in the correct way.
VII. Sharing, generosity.
VIII. Hospitality.
IX. Service to others, availability.
X. Orderliness.
XI. Planning and determination.
XII. Endurance, keeping your promises.
XIII. Courage.
XIV. Joyfulness.
XV. Patience.
XVI. Self-control.
XVII. Obedience, decisiveness.
XVIII. Reverence.
XIX. Respect:
    A. For God.
    B. For parents.
    C. For life.
    D. For marriage commitment.
XX. Contentment.
XXI. Faithfulness.
XXII. Overcoming evil, alertness.
XXIII. Praising God.
XXIV. Glorifying God in our lives.
XXV. Being good listeners to God.
XXVI. Power of prayer.
XXVII. Flexibility.
XXVIII. Kindness.
XXIX. Initiative.

Stories:

A variety of stories (4 per week) are to be read for closeness between teacher and child, reinforcement of concepts taught, vocabulary, speech, left-to-right eye movement, art appreciation, and enjoyment.

Also, one or more poems/fingerplays are to be read each class day to reinforce concepts, to celebrate times of the year, for literary style, for memorization (if desired), and for enjoyment.

Mail Order Forms

On the following pages you will find two Mail Order Forms. One is for ordering additional copies of this curriculum or of the companion volumes – <u>First Grade: Learning At Home</u>, <u>Second Grade: Learning At Home</u> – directly from the author through Smiling Heart Press. The other is for ordering various home school materials from my publisher, Christian Life Workshops. Several of the items I have recommended in this curriculum are now available from CLW you cannot find them. Prices from both businesses are subject to change without notice.

AaBb
CcDd
EeFf
GgHh

Notes

This page left intentionally blank

IiJj
KkLl
MmNn
OoPp

Notes

This page left intentionally blank

QqRr

SsTt

UuVv

WwXx

This page left intentionally blank

Notes

This page left intentionally blank

1234
5678
90- +
= # / %

This page left intentionally blank

WEEK 1   MONDAY

1) Go over school rules (see Kindergarten Reading section.)
2) Name your school.
3) Take a picture of child/children.
4) Get notebook.
5) Introduce the Pledge of Allegiance:

> I pledge allegiance to the flag
> of the United States of America,
> and to the Republic for which it stands,
> one nation, under God, indivisible,
> with liberty and justice for all.

WEEK 1   TUESDAY

Bible

Read Gen. 1:1-8, 1:14-18 (Day 1,2, and 4 of Creation).
Explain: the word "Genesis" means "beginning."
What did God make? (light, day and night, sun, sky, moon, stars)
  Begin "God's Creation" poster for notebook. On "sky" part of
    construction paper, glue cut-out moon and sun and gummed star.
  On "God Created the World" story page, write:
    God created the heavens and the earth.
    God made day and night.
    He made Heaven.
    God made the sky.
    God made the light.
    He made the sun, the moon, and the stars.

Reading

Read a poem.
Recognition of own name: What is your name? (Joe Brown) This is how
  your name looks when it is written: <u>Joe Brown</u> (say each letter as it's
  written). (Write name on 1/3 sheet construction paper and tape/pin it to
  the bulletin board; another 1/3 sheet to the refrigerator; the third 1/3
  sheet with name to child's chair or bed.) Your name is very important
  and special.
Take photos of child (to be used in "All About Me" book to be completed
  later this week):

1. child: standing - head to toes view	7. brothers & sisters
2. child: head and shoulders view	8. child and pet(s)
3. child in front of home	9. child in bedroom
4. rest of family (w/out child)	10. child w/favorite toy
5. dad	11. child doing favorite thing
6. mom	12. child helping at home

Have the film developed at a one-day/two-day developing location.

Notes

Music

Heavenly Sunshine, Twinkle, Twinkle Little Star, He's Got the Whole World in His Hands.

Arithmetic

Top, middle, bottom: Have child put blue circle at the TOP of the flannelboard, put the yellow square at the BOTTOM, and the red heart in the MIDDLE. (Repeat with other combinations.)

Look at story book with child. Ask child what's at the TOP of the picture, the BOTTOM of the picture, and in the MIDDLE. Repeat.

God's World

Read a book about the Sun. Talk about it with child.

Show pictures of the moon. Tell child it revolves around the earth. Have child be "moon" and you be "earth." Have child walk in circle around you.

Resources:

j523.3 J42m	The Moon (Michael Jay); talk comparing earth & moon, phases & eclipses of moon, surface, explor. of moon
629.45 W5561	Let's Go to the Moon (Janis Knudsen Wheat); 1977 Books for Young Explorers, National Geographic Society
j523.7	The Sun (Kate Petty); large print, pictures.
j629.45 G799A	A New True Book: Astronauts (Carol Greene); Children's Press, photos and large type
j535 A676S	Sun and Light (Neil Ardly); Action Science Book; the sun, time and direction, mirrors, mag. colors

Physical Education

Throw and catch the ball.

Story

Let's Find Out about the Sun (Martha & Charles Shapp)
It Looked Like Spilt Milk (Charles Green Shaw)

Memory Verse

"In the beginning God created the heavens and the earth." Gen. 1:1
This verse and the rest of the year's verses are taken from The Holy Bible – The New King James Version.

WEEK 1   WEDNESDAY

Bible

Review what "Genesis" means (beginning), who made the world (God), and what God's creations are that we talked about yesterday (light, sun, sky, moon, stars). Read poems: "The Moon" (Child), "I see the moon and the moon sees me, God bless the moon and God bless me." (Anon.) (Have child repeat prayer with you.)

Reading

Read a poem.

(Have child repeat entire name.) Our home address is (123 Oak Street; Town, State). (Child repeats several times. If difficulty, practice with child.) We are going to make a book especially about you, Joe. (On the front of 4 sheets of construction paper folded in 1/2 together, write: ALL ABOUT ME. Have the child draw a picture of himself on a 3x5" unlined card; if there's a goof, child can do another card without having to re-do entire book. Put ALL ABOUT ME on top, picture of child in middle, and name and date on bottom of front cover.)

Art

Make Grandparents' Day cards using rubber stamps/drawings. Send.

Arithmetic

On construction paper folded into 1/3's, have child follow your directions: stamp two bunnies at the BOTTOM of the paper; stamp two hearts at the TOP; stamp one bear in the MIDDLE.

On another piece of construction paper, folded into 1/3's, have child color each part a different color, and then tell you about the picture (TOP, MIDDLE, BOTTOM).

Simon Says: Child touches BOTTOM of his foot, TOP of ear, MIDDLE of his finger, etc.

Health/Manners

Introduce Jr. Chef and Host/Hostess program. Tell how important jobs are; really help family.

> Jr. Chef
> 1. Wash hands
> 2. Put on apron
> 3. Follow directions
>
> Host/hostess
> 1. Wash hands
> 2. Touch only handles on silverware, edges of plates, and bottom part of glasses
> 3. Practice setting table
>   a. Placement of silver
>   b. Placement of plates/glasses
>   c. Placement of napkin

On "Personal Responsibilities" story page write: "Jr. Chef/Hostess washes her hands."

Physical Education

Jump forward and backward over line; run on tiptoes.

Story

The Sun's Asleep Behind the Hill (Mirra Ginsburg)
The Moon Tonight (Gerald Hawkins)
The Moon Jumpers (Janice May Udry)

Memory Verse
"He appointed the moon for seasons; the sun knows its going down."
Ps. 104:19

WEEK 1   THURSDAY

Bible
Read your story page so far. Read poem: "Stars" (Rhoda Backmeister; Poems and Prayers for the Very Young.) Talk about how we are to worship God, the Creator, not the creation (sun, stars, etc.). Who made all the stars, the moon, and the sun? (God did.)

Reading
Read a poem.

Have child repeat name and address. Practice, if difficult.

Help child learn phone number to tune of "Twinkle, Twinkle, Little Star." I taught my children this technique and shortly after I had helped them practice for several days, I was ordering pizza by phone. The man asked for my phone number and the "automatic pilot" kicked in – I almost broke into tune and sang it to him! It goes like this:

(Twinkle, twinkle, little star)	(how I wonder what you are.)
1-2 3-4 5-6 7	"all God's children go to heaven."

Here are suggested endings for phone numbers with each number at the end:

0(oh)	=	"that's the way our phone numbers go."
1	=	"now my rhyme is nearly done."
2	=	"the American flag is red, white and blue."
3	=	"we live in a land of the brave and free."
4	=	"that is all, there is no more."
5	=	"I'm so glad to be alive."
6	=	"our clock in the kitchen tocks and ticks."
7	=	"all God's children go to Heaven."
8	=	"I'm almost (age), I can't wait!"
9	=	"I hope that you are very fine."

(Practice, practice.)

Explain that you do not tell (or sing) just anyone your phone number. If you would ever need help, it's an easy way for you to remember your phone number.

Music
Blow the Man Down
My Bonnie
Michael, Row the Boat Ashore

Arithmetic
Have child make tower of three blocks. Ask which one is on TOP (they point); BOTTOM? in the MIDDLE?

Put your hand, palm down, on the table; have child put one of his/her hands on next; then you put your other hand on top. Have child use free hand to point to hand on TOP, in MIDDLE, on BOTTOM.

Have child make cheese and cracker "sandwich." What comes first? (cracker). It's on the BOTTOM. Next comes the cheese; it's in the MIDDLE. Then comes another cracker; it's on TOP.

God's World

Quick review of sun and moon.
Talk about stars in heaven - some grouped in constellations.
Look at:

j523R45   Find the Constellations (H.A. Rey [of Curious George fame]). Fun book; used to spark interest; great for older children, too.

Resources (Stars):

j523P85w   What is a Star (Daniel Q. Posin, Ph.D.) what are they, kinds (incl. sun), how to study, constellations, galaxies

j523.8 B821s   The Sky is Full of Stars (Franklyn M. Branley)

j523 272   Stars (A Guide to the Constellations, Sun, Moon, Planets, and Other Features of the Heavens) (Herbert S. Zim, Ph.D.); A Golden Nature Guide

j523 z72c   Comets (Herbert S. Zim, Ph.D.)

Physical Education

Rolls on the ground/floor; somersaults.

Story

Mandy's Grandmother (Liesel Moak Skorpen)
A Children's Zoo (Tana Hoban)

Memory Verse

"He counts the number of the stars; He calls them all by name." Ps. 147:4

WEEK 1   FRIDAY

Visit the zoo.

Preparation for next week:

General:
_____Read over lesson plans
_____List materials needed
_____Collect materials needed
_____Story pages etc., to notebook

Library:
_____Return books used this week
_____Check out books for week after next

Field Trips:

_____Reconfirm next Friday's trip

_____Thank you note for last trip

_____Set up trip for week after next

WEEK 2   MONDAY

Bible

Read Gen. 1:9-10 (part of day 3 of Creation: Creation of land and seas).
What did God make on the first part of Day 3 of Creation? (dry land/
earth and water/seas/oceans)

Have child draw and color a lake/ocean and some mountains on the "God's
Creation" poster.

Read poem: "At the Seaside".

Write on story page: God made the land and the seas.

Talk about the differences between ground (soils of different kinds) and
sand.

Who made the land and the oceans/seas? (God did.)

Reading

Read a poem.

Put developed photos into book as follows:

> Ask child's name. Have him answer in complete sentence: "My name is_____."

Page #	Picture	Write:
1	Standing view of child	My name is_____,
2	House	My address is_____,
3	Family	This is my family.
4	Dad	Here is Dad.
5	Mom	Here is Mom.
6	Brothers & Sisters	Here are my brothers and sisters.
7	Pets	I have 2 dogs.
8	Bedroom	This is my bedroom.
9	Helping	I help my parents at home.
10	Toys	My favorite toy is_____.
11	(Have child color index card favorite color)	My favorite color is_____.
12	Doing favorite thing	I like to (swing, etc.)_____.
13	(Mag./drawn pic. of phone)	My phone number is_____.
14	Head & shoulders of child	Good-bye!

Number the pages; put clear Contact paper on the cover; punch two or
three holes in book; tie with string/yarn, leaving about one finger's width
extra space to be able to turn pages. Opt.: cover punched holes with
gummed hole reinforcements before using string/yarn.

(Alone) Hand-eye coordination: Child colors page in coloring book; hang on
bulletin board when done.

Art

Fingerpaint oceans and glue construction paper fish onto it when it's dried.

Arithmetic

Read: <u>Over, Under, Through</u>. (Tana Hoban)

Ask child: What's ABOVE you? What's BELOW you?

Using the table as "middle," give child directions to "put a box ABOVE the table, put a toy UNDER the table," etc. Repeat with several instructions.

Character Building

Stewardship of the earth's resources (Part I of III): Being thankful and not greedy.

Who created the world? (God did.) What does stewardship mean? (to take the very best care of the blessings God has given us.) We need to be good stewards of all God has given us in our world - our land, air, water, and resources. To be good stewards of all we have, we first need to be thankful. God created this beautiful world for us to enjoy. We need to be thoughtful of God by taking good care of all He made, and not being greedy. Many people in the world do not have a nice home like you do, or toys to play with, or books to look at. We need to watch what we ask for, to enjoy all that God has given us (our home, our family, our clothes, etc.) and to be thoughtful of others: in using our money and the things that God's given us. We need to enjoy the trees, the sweet-smelling flowers, the red sunsets, the warm feel of sun on our arms and grass tickling our feet. We need to be thankful and good stewards.

On Character Building story page, write: Stewardship means taking good care of what God has given me. I need to be thankful to be a good steward.

Resources:

<u>Living More With Less</u> (Doris Jantzen Longacre)

j301.3E61i   <u>It's Your Environment - Things to Think About - Things to Do</u> (Environmental Action Coalition)

Physical Education

Skipping; kicking ball.

Story

<u>Noah's Ark</u> (Peter Spier)

<u>My Big Book of the Outdoors</u> (Jane Werner Watson)

Memory Verse

"...worship Him who made heaven and earth, the sea and springs of water." Rev. 14:7b

WEEK 2   TUESDAY

Bible

Review yesterday's lesson of God creating land and oceans/seas.

Read poem: "Poem of a Breton Fisherman." "Dear God, Be good to me, The sea is so wide, And my boat is so small."

Read Gen. 1:11-13 (rest of Day 3 of Creation).

What did God make on the rest of the third day of Creation? (vegetation/plants, herbs, fruit-bearing trees)

Cut out pictures of plants, herbs and fruit trees from seed catalogs and glue to "God's Creation" poster.

Reading

Read a poem.

Read child's "All About Me" book.

Review name, address and phone number (in complete sentences).

Listening: Tell the child you are going to say a word and then he is to repeat it back to you.

God	stars	host	trees
world	sky	hostess	landform
creation	constellation	land	continents
sun	zoo	oceans	globe
moon	Junior Chef	plants	earth

(Alone): Visual discrimination: Sort cards (wallpaper samples cut into shapes) by shapes; "circles in one pile, squares in another, etc."

Music

The Ballad of Woodsy Owl (U.S. Dept. of Ag., Forest Service)

Arithmetic

Using flannelboard with string/yarn dividing the board into halves, have child put a circle ABOVE the line, put a heart BELOW, etc.

Talk about what animals live ABOVE ground and which ones live BELOW the ground.

God's World

Geography: Landforms: Globe (land and oceans); seven continents

Show child globe. On it point out: North Pole (top), South Pole (bottom), seven continents (name and count out), oceans, U.S.A., your state, your city (approx. location).

Resource:

j551F3411 The Land We Live On (Carroll Lane Fenton and Mildred Adams Fenton) Good Amer. Geog.-landforms; full page b&wh photos.

Physical Education

Running broad jump; hopping.

Story

McElligot's Pool (Dr. Seuss)

The First Seven Days (Bible)

Memory Verse

"Surely the world is established; so that it cannot be moved." Psa. 93:1d

WEEK 2   WEDNESDAY

Bible

Review Day 3 of Creation (God created the land and seas, vegetation of all kinds).

On story page, write: God created plants and trees.

Talk about different kinds of plants (wildflowers, flowers in the garden, herbs, vegetables, bushes). (Have the child name as many as he can.)

Look at poster of Wildflowers (U.S.Dept. of Ag. - Forest Service poster 84CFFP20).

Who made all these plants? (God did.)

Resources:

j581P74t   The True Book of Weeds and Wild Flowers (Illa Podendorf); water color drawings of most; wildflowers divided into Spring and Summer/Fall

j581V464w   Wildflowers of North America (Frank D. Venning); Golden Press; full color drawing

j581S46d   The Doubleday First Guide to Wild Flowers (Millicent Selsam); color drawings

j581Z72f   Flowers, A Guide to Familiar American Wildflowers (Herbert S. Zim); color

j581.6S29d   Dandelion, Pokeweed and Goosefoot, How the early settlers used plants for food, medicine, and in the home (Elizabeth Schaeffer); also has info on making own garden, collecting and drying plants, making teas and salads, dyeing cloth

j581A73   Field Book of Western Wild Flowers (Margaret Armstrong); b&w, some water color drawings

j581D791   Look at a Flower (Anne Ophelia); technical; good ref. bk.

j581H35   1967 Wild Flowers of the Pacific Coast (Leslie L. Haskin); photos; some colored

j581H71w   Weeds (Dorothy Childs Hogner); b&w drawings

j582L654f   Flowering Plants (Action Science Book) (Alfred Leutscher); good color drawings & some experiments; reference book for this age

j586S56n   Non-Flowering Plants (Ferns, Mosses, Lichens, Mushrooms, and Other Fungi) (Floyd S. Shuttleworth & Herbert S. Zim); Golden Nature Guide

j588.2J69m   Mosses (Sylvia A. Johnson); good photos, text advanced

j588.2J69m   Mushrooms (Sylvia A. Johnson); good photos, text advanced

Reading

Read a poem.

Read book: "All About Me."

Review name, address and phone number (complete sentences).

Auditory discrimination: Introduce activity of their listening and repeating your clapping patterns. (Make patterns increasingly more difficult.)

(Alone) Hand-eye coordination: Have child do sewing card (purchased one or one made from center part of bleach bottle cut into an animal or shape, and holes punched with paper punch). Lace shoelace through holes.

Art
Seed art collage: Glue beans and seeds onto paper plate. Outside of plate forms "frame."

Arithmetic
Read: Here a Chick, There a Chick (Bruce McMillan).
Jump rope: Tie jump rope so it's about one foot above ground. Have child jump/climb OVER and then crawl UNDER the rope. Repeat.

Health/Manners
Table Manners:
1. Napkin on lap; use it instead of clothes, tablecloth to wipe mouth, fingers.
2. Don't speak with food in your mouth.
3. Chew with your mouth closed.
4. Say, "Please, may I have _____," when you'd like something.
5. Use silverware, not fingers.
6. Don't touch others' plates, etc.
7. Be pleasant!
Act out situation of someone with poor manners and have child tell you what's wrong.
On "Manners" story page, write:
> **Table Manners**
> 1. I use my napkin.
> 2. I chew with my mouth closed.
> 3. I don't talk with food in my mouth.
> 4. I say "Please" and "Thank you."
> 5. I use my silverware.
> 6. I am pleasant.

j170M13e   Etti-Cat, The Courtesy Cat (Jo Mary McCormick); etiquette and manners.

Physical Education
Left/Right; Simon Says.

Story
The Circus Baby (Maud and Miska Petersham)
What is a Flower (Jennifer W. Day) Golden Science Book

Memory Verse
"The earth is the Lord's and all its fullness." Ps. 24:1a

WEEK 2   THURSDAY

Bible
Read story page so far.
Talk about different kinds of trees (fruit trees, evergreens, deciduous trees). Have the child name as many as possible.

Talk about the parts of trees (trunk, roots, branches, leaves) and how each
   tree differs.
Look at the posters: Leaves (84CFFP17); and Trees and their Leaves
   (84CFFP23) from the Forest Service.
Who made all these trees? (God did.)
Resources:

j582A42e	The Everyday Trees (Gertrude D. Allen); pencil drawings
j582S46m	Maple Tree (Millicent E. Selsam); photos; some color; good
j582Z72	Trees, A Guide to Familiar American Trees (Herbert S. Zim); Golden Nature Guide
j585.2A752B	The Biggest Living Thing (Caroline Arnold); Sequoia trees

Reading

Read a poem.
Read book: "All About Me."
Review name, address and phone number (complete sentences).
Classifying: Show child one picture card at a time, setting it to the right of
   the previous one (beginning left-to-right eye movement). Have child
   name each of the 10 cards after you have them all set out, beginning
   with the left card and going right, pointing to each card as it's being
   named. Then ask the child to please hand you all the clothing cards
   (put in one pile); all the people cards (second pile); and the furniture
   cards (third pile). Then have the child hand you the first pile (one on
   left), second pile (middle) and the third pile.
(Alone) Hand-eye coordination: have child string beads onto shoelace.

Music

Ash Grove
Mulberry Bush

Arithmetic

Using flannelboard, review with child concepts of TOP, MIDDLE,
   BOTTOM, ABOVE (BELOW, OVER, UNDER).
Look at story book pictures and have child show you these concepts as you
   ask questions to him.

God's World

Geography: Canyons and gorges; islands; deserts; swamps; mountains.
Using the resource books, show child examples of these landforms.
Resources:

j575.3 G7381	Let's Discover the Floor of the Forest (Ada & Frank Graham, Jr.); color photos
j574.526 C828e	Explore a Spooky Swamp (Wendy W. Cortesi); National Geographic Book
j570 K59d	Desert Life (Ruth Kirk); fairly easy text, photos
j549 272r	Rocks and Minerals (Herbert S. Zim); A Golden Nature Guide

Physical Education

Climb on inclined board; somersaults.

Story
   The Little Island (Margaret Wise Brown)
   The Dead Tree (Alvin Tresselt)

Memory Verse
   "For every creature of God is good." I Tim. 4:4a

WEEK 2   FRIDAY

Visit a recycling center/drop off place.

Preparation for next week:

General:
_____Read over lesson plans
_____List materials needed
_____Collect materials needed
_____Story pages etc., to notebook

Library:
_____Return books used this week
_____Check out books for week after next

Field Trips:
_____Reconfirm next Friday's trip
_____Thank you note for last trip
_____Set up trip for week after next

WEEK 3   MONDAY

Bible
   Read Gen. 1:20-23 (Day 5 of Creation).
   Talk about what God created (all kinds of water creatures, fish, etc. and
      birds).
   Have child draw and color several small fish/water creatures (starfish,
      octopus, etc.), cut out, and glue to poster.
   Write on story page: God created all kinds of fish and water creatures.
   Have child name as many water creatures as he can name: fish (all kinds),
      sharks, whales, porpoise, dolphins, starfish, octopus, stingray, clam,
      lobster, shrimp, crabs, etc.).
   Resources:
   j595.3R67c   The Crusty Ones: A First Look at Crustaceans (Solveign
                    Paulson Russell); b&wh drawings, ref.
   j599H316s   Swimming Mammals (Susan Harris); large color
                    illustrations, fairly easy text
   j599.745C953w   The Wonderful World of Seals and Whales (Sandra Lee
                    Crow); National Geographic
   j599.5G879b   The Blue Whale (Donna Grosvenor); National Geographic
   j599.5S468f   A First Look at Whales (Millicent E. Selsam and Joyce
                    Hunt); b&wh drawings; ref.
   j599.5W542   Whales (Henry Pluckrose, ed.); easy text, color illus.

j599.51M146L	<u>Little Whale</u> (Ann McGovern); story of young whale; drawings
j599.53B851p	<u>The Playful Dolphins</u> (Linda McCarter Bridge); National Geographic
j599.53F535n	<u>Namu: Making Friends with a Killer Whale</u> (Ronald M. Fisher); National Geographic
j597H58s	<u>SeaHorses</u> (Lilo Hess); b&wh photos; ref.
j591.92C62t	<u>Tide Pools and Beaches</u> (Elizabeth Clemons); b&wh drawings; ref.
j591.92S462	<u>See Along the Shore</u> (Millicent E. Selsam); drawings; sections on the world is round, tides
j591.92S896a	<u>Animals that Live in the Sea</u> (Joan Ann Straker); National Geographic
j591.92Z72	<u>Seashores, A Guide to Animals and Plants Along the Beaches</u> (Herbert S. Zim and Lester Ingle); Golden Nature Guide
j593.9S58s	<u>A Star in the Sea</u> (Alvin and Virginia Silverstein); life of starfish
j594D84	<u>Seashells</u> (Ruth H. Dudley); b&wh drawings
j595.3J69c	<u>Crabs</u> (Sylvia A. Johnson); color photos; ref.
j591.526A525L	<u>Life in Ponds & Streams</u> (William H. Amos); National Geographic

Reading

Read a poem.
Read book: "All About Me."
Review name, address and phone number.
Sequence and complete sentence: Have child dictate "story" of several
  sentences about last Friday's visit to the recycling center. Guide him
  through, if necessary:

You say:	They answer and you write:
Where did we go?	We went to the recycling center.
What did we take?	We took glass bottles and aluminum cans.
What did we do with them?	We put them in bins.
What else is recycled?	Cardboard, paper and tin are also recycled.
What happens to these things?	These items are sold to be recycled.
What is the money used for?	The money is used to help hungry people have food to eat.

(Alone) Hand-eye coordination: Have child do puzzle(s).

Art
Make fish out of playdough/clay. Let dry.

Arithmetic
Read: <u>Becca Backward, Becca Frontward: A Book of Concept Pairs</u> (Bruce
  McMillan)
Retell story of Peter Rabbit (or other familiar story). What happened
  BEFORE (event)? AFTER? BETWEEN_____and_____?

Character Building

Stewardship of the earth's resources (Part II of III):

Review last week's concepts of being thankful and content in order to be a good steward. Today, we will be talking about practical ways of how we can save resources:

1. Saving earth/soil: Plant flowers, vegetables, trees.
2. Saving oxygen: Plant trees, plants, bushes.
3. Saving resources (gasoline, electricity, trees, water):
   Ride bicycle, walk, stay at home, or take mass transportation (gasoline).
   Play games instead of TV (electricity).
   Turn off lights (electricity).
   Dress warmer in winter; turn heat down (electricity).
   Put draft-stoppers by windows, doors (electricity).
   Reuse paper cup - put your name on it (trees).
   Recycle paper and cardboard (trees).
   Turn water off all the way (water).
   Recycle aluminum, glass (resources).
4. Saving beauty:
   Don't litter; pick up litter.
   Don't pick wildflowers in parks.
   Plant flowers and trees.
5. Saving wildlife:
   Put out seed and bread for birds in the winter.

On Character Building story page write: I need to be a good steward of the earth and its resources. I can save the earth's resources and recycle products by being thoughtful and using my smart head.

Physical Education

"Animal" walks (elephant, bear, kangaroo, snake, etc.).

Story

The Beach Before Breakfast (Maxine W. Kumin)
Houses from the Sea (Alice E. Goudey); seashells

Memory Verse

"I know that whatever God does, it shall be forever; Nothing can be added to it, and nothing taken from it…" Ecc. 3:14

WEEK 3   TUESDAY

Bible

Review of God creating fish and water creatures.
Talk about different parts of fish (gills, tail, fins, etc.), and differences among fish (color, size, habitat, etc.).
Look at poster: Fish (8CFFP24, U.S. Forest Service); and other pictures of fish.
Who made all these sea creatures? (God did).
Resources:
j598.1I47r   The Reptiles (Robert Inger); color drawings
j598.1S84t   Turtles (Bertie Ann Stewart and Gordon E. Burks); A Golden Science Reader; color drawings

j597Z71f   <u>Fishes, a Guide to Fresh- and Salt-Water Species</u> (Herbert S. Zim and Hurst H. Shoemaker); (Note: skip "origin and development" p. 14-15); Golden Nature Guide

j597.55C689f   <u>A Fish Hatches</u> (Joanna Cole and Jerome Wexler); b&wh photos, easy

j590.7Z71   <u>Goldfish</u> (Herbert S. Zim)

j590.7B65   <u>An Aquarium</u> (Glenn O. Blough)

j590.7B86t   <u>The True Book of Tropical Fishes</u> (Ray Broekel); includes how to make aquarium

j590.7S819h   <u>How to Raise Goldfish and Guppies, a Child's Book of Pet Care</u> (Sara Bonnett Stein); color photo; ref.

j590.7C777a   <u>All About Goldfish As Pets</u> (Kay Cooper); b&wh photos; ref.

Reading

Read a poem.

Read book: "All About Me."

Review name, address and phone number.

Listening: child repeats each word back to you:

fish	swimming	river	stewardship
oceans	birds	lake	resources
beaches	flying	waterfall	respect
tides	air	conservation	privacy
currents	water	world	property

(Alone) Hand-eye coordination: Have child trace over lines and figures (on index cards you've prepared) with crayon. Have him do one, then go to the next one, etc. Figures to draw: | - \ / (2 of each).

Music

Woodsy Owl (ballad); (U.S. Dept. of Ag., Forest Service)

Eency, Weensy Spider

Alouette

Arithmetic

Sequence of three things: Make up 5 sets of sequence cards (3 cards each). Using one set at a time, have child tell you what each is a picture of and then ask questions about it. (Ex: sock, sock on foot, sock and shoe on foot) Where was the sock BEFORE is was put on the foot? (plain sock card) Then what happened AFTER the sock was put on? (shoe on) Which happened in BETWEEN the other two? (sock on foot) Have the child put the other sets in sequential order. Tell child (going left to right) which card is the first, second, third. Which is BEFORE the second? AFTER? BETWEEN the first and third?

Line up dolls or Lego/action figures. Which one is BEFORE the doll with the pink dress? AFTER? Which figure is BETWEEN the policeman and the mailman? Repeat with other questions. Then have the child ask BEFORE, AFTER, BETWEEN questions to you.

God's World

Seas: Lakes; oceans; beaches; tides, currents.

Talk about differences between oceans (salt water) and lakes (fresh water); tides - two times a day due to the pull of the moon.

Resources:
j551.4 H14w	What is Water? (Adaline Hagaman, M.S.)
j551.46271w	Waves (Herbert S. Zim); more detailed text; good ex. of power of waves (p. 40-42+)
j574.92 A525+	Exploring the Seashore (William H. Amos) National Geographic

Physical Education
Run on tiptoe and then stand on tiptoe 10 seconds.

Story
The Seashore Noisy Book (Margaret Wise Brown)
At Last to the Ocean: The Story of the Endless Cycle of Water (Joel Rothman)

Memory Verse
Choral reading Psalm 136:1-9, 25, 26
(Child says, "for his steadfast love endures forever")

WEEK 3   WEDNESDAY

Bible
Read Gen. 1:20-23 again and ask what else God created then besides water creatures. (birds)
Have child punch out gummed bird stickers; lick and stick to sky in poster.
Write on story page: God created all kinds of birds.
Talk about different parts of birds (beaks, wings, feathers, etc.).
Look at posters: Birds (#84CFFP18), Butterflies (#84CFFP21) from U.S. Forest Service.
Show pictures of differences in birds (color, size, habitat, etc.).
Who made all these birds? (God did.)
Resources:

j598.2G22w	What Makes a Bird a BIRD? (May Garelick); color illus.
j598.2C75i	If I Were A Bird (Gladys Conklin)
j598.2F92	The True Book of Birds We Know (Margaret Friskey); easy, good drawings
j598.2M364f	Familiar Birds of Northwest Forests, Fields and Gardens (David B. Marshall); color paintings
j598.2P23b	Birds in Your Backyard (Bertha Morris Parker); large color paintings
j598.2P48f	A Field Guide to Western Birds (Roger Tory Peterson); b&wh/color drawings
j598.2A75f	Five Nests (Caroline Arnold); includes robins, redwing blackbirds, cowbirds; drawings; role of father and mother birds; easy text
j598.2Z71	Birds, A Guide to the Most Familiar American Birds (Herbert S. Zim & Ira N. Gabrielson); (Note: skip "Family Tree of Birds," p. 12-13)
j598.44J71p	Penguins (Sylvia Johnson) color photos; ref.
j598.44S541p	The Penguin (Angela Sheehan); full page color pictures; fairly easy story
j595.7S64w	Western Butterflies (Arthur C. Smith); b&wh/color pictures

j595.78W613c	<u>A Closer Look at Butterflies and Moths</u> (Ralph Whitlock); large color drawings; ref.
j595.7M128m	<u>Moths and Butterflies and How They Live</u> (Robert M. McClung); ref.
j595.7C59g	<u>A Golden Book of Butterflies</u> (J. F. Gates Clarke); color drawings
j595.7M68b	<u>Butterflies and Moths</u> (Robert T. Mitchell & Herbert S. Zim); Golden Nature Guide
j595.7G 59c	<u>A Child's Book of Butterflies</u> (Elizabeth Godwin); b&wh/ color drawings

Reading

Read a poems.

Read book: "All About Me."

Review name, address and phone number.

Opposites: Smile and say, "Do I look happy or sad? (Happy) Show me a sad face. (Child frowns.) Stand up as tall as you can. Now make yourself as short as you can. Sad is the opposite of happy, short is the opposite of tall. Here are some more:

> When you're awake it's (day); asleep, it's (night).
> The light in the sky in the day is the (sun); in the night is the moon).
> A turtle walks very (slowly); a rabbit hops (fast).
> The top cupboard is very (high); the bottom shelf is very (low).
> An elephant is very (big); a mouse is very (small).

Day and night, sun and moon, slow and fast, high and low, big and small - these are opposites. Can you think of any others?"

(Alone) Classifying: Have child sort picture cards into three stacks: clothes, people, and furniture.

Art

Use fir/pine cones, construction paper, and pipe cleaners to make "birds."

Arithmetic

Talk about another familiar story; review events quickly. Then ask, what happened BEFORE (event)? AFTER? BETWEEN_____and_____?

Line plastic animals up like they are going onto Noah's Ark. Ask child: Which animal is BEFORE the hippo? AFTER? BETWEEN the giraffe and the monkey? Etc.

Health/Manners

Respect for others' property and privacy.

How would you feel if someone got into your special treasures and broke them or lost them?

We need to treat others' property with respect (Mom and Dad's, house guests', at others' homes, in stores).

Privacy (Moms and Dads need quiet time to study Bible/think/plan).

Have them think of ideas of what they could do instead of interrupting.

On "Manners" story page, write: I respect other people's property and privacy.

Physical Education

"Animal" walks.

Story
If Everybody Did (JoAnn Stover)
Hide and Seek Fog (Alvin Tresselt)

Memory Verse.
"Let all the earth fear the Lord...for He spoke, and it was done; He commanded, and it stood fast." Ps. 33:8,9

WEEK3   THURSDAY

Bible
Continue talking about different kinds of birds: North American (incl. migration; owls); pets (parakeets, pigeons); ducks & geese.
Tell each child that God made each kind different.
Resource:
j598.81K22r   Robins Fly North, Robins Fly South (John Kaufman); color drawings; story of migration

Reading
Read a poem.
Read book: "All About Me."
Review name, address and phone number.
Talk about communication. "The way we exchange ideas with other people is by talking and listening, by reading and writing. In school we will practice all four - being a good listener, speaking well, reading and writing. What do we use to talk? (mouth) What do we use to listen? (ears) To read and write we use our eyes and our hands (hold pages, finger under each letter or word) and some symbols called letters. When letters are put together, they can make words, which can make sentences (a complete thought). The sentences put together can make a story, just like the story you wrote about the recycling center, and from books we read. Next week, we will begin learning one letter at a time so you will get to recognize them and the sounds they stand for. There are 26 letters in the alphabet."
(Alone) Visual discrimination: Have child sort silverware into sectioned divider or into piles on table (knives, dinner forks, salad forks, tablespoons, teaspoons, iced tea spoons).

Music
Looby Lou
Little White Duck

Arithmetic
(Note: For the next two weeks, the child will be making a MY COLORS book. Use one sheet of construction paper of corresponding color to the color studied each day. On the front, print MY COLORS on the top, and the child's name and date centered near the middle/bottom.)
RED: On red construction paper page, write the word red on the top of the page. From magazines find red objects; cut and glue to the front of the red sheet.

For the back of the red sheet, have the child stamp image with rubber
    stamp and red ink onto white unlined index card; mount on to back of
    red sheet. Label that side red, too.
Read: <u>Seeing Red</u> (Robert Jay Wolff).

God's World
Other water forms: using rivers, lakes, and waterfalls.
Using these and previous resources, show these water forms.
Talk about likenesses and differences.
j575.3 W87p   <u>Pond Life: Watching Animals Find Food</u> (Herbert H. Wong
                     and Matthew F. Vessel)
j575.3 W87p   <u>Pond Life: Watching Animals Grow Up</u> (Herbert H. Wong
                     and Matthew F. Vessel)

Physical Education
Introduce headstand.

Story
<u>Make Way for Ducklings</u> (Robert McCloskey)
<u>The Brook</u> (Carol and Donald Carrick)
<u>The Robin Family</u> (Miss Frances) Golden Book
<u>My Goldfish</u> (Miss Frances) Golden Book

Memory Verse
"But be glad and rejoice forever in that which I create." Is. 65:18a

WEEK 3   FRIDAY

Take a walk in the autumn woods.
Resource:
j570P95d   <u>Discovering the Outdoors: A Nature and Science Guide to</u>
                <u>Investigating Life in Fields, Forests and Ponds</u> (Laurence P.
                Pringle, ed.); ref.; good info and some good pictures
Preparation for next week.

General:
_____Read over lesson plans
_____List materials needed
_____Collect materials needed
_____Story pages etc., to notebook

Library:
_____Return books used this week
_____Check out books for week after next

Field Trips:
_____Reconfirm next Friday's trip
_____Thank you note for last trip
_____Set up trip for week after next

WEEK 4   MONDAY

Bible

Read Gen. 1:24-25 (part of Day 6 of Creation).

What did God make next after water creatures and birds? (livestock, reptiles, wild beasts)

Stick farm animal stickers on land poster.

On story page, write: God made every kind of animal - livestock, reptiles, and wild beasts.

Begin talking about farm animals. What are some animals you can think of that people raise on a farm (cows, horses, pigs, sheep, goats, dogs, rabbits)?

Who made all these animals? (God did)

Use resources listed for Week 27 & 28, God's World sections on farm animals.

Reading

Read a poem.

Introduce "A a" letter shape and three sounds (a like in apple; ay, aahhh). Have child trace letter shapes (cut from patterns onto sandpaper or indoor/outdoor carpet), while he repeats sounds.

Sequence and complete sentences: Have the child dictate story about Friday's walk in the woods (four or more sentences).

(Alone) Classifying: sort capital and small letter cards (A and a) into two piles; then match each card with corresponding match in file folder.

Art

"Feely board": glue pinecones, etc., from Friday's walk in the woods to board. Close eyes; feel; try to tell what each item is.

Arithmetic

ORANGE: On orange construction paper page, write the word orange on the top of each side of the sheet. From magazines find orange objects; cut and glue to the front of the orange sheet.

For the back, stamp images(s) with rubber stamp using orange ink on to white unlined index card; mount on to back of orange sheet.

Read: Colors (John J. Reiss).

Character Building

Stewardship of the earth's resources (Part III of III):

Review ideas discussed so far about being a good steward of the earth:

1. To be thankful and content.

2. We can save electricity, water, trees, beauty, and wildlife by being thoughtful.

(As a personal note, I feel we have a responsibility in this age of "throwaways" of everything from unborn babies to newspapers, to educate our children in the value of our resources, the items we buy/use, and human life. Most all we bring into our homes in the way of consumable products can be recycled somehow. As a family of four, we have less than one garbage can-full of waste per month and I

continue to look for ways of reducing that).
Today we will talk about practical ways we can recycle the things we have instead of wasting them. How could we recycle (reuse):

paper? (recycle, burn in woodstove for heat, use as scratch paper)
clothes? (give to others, use material for another project)
food waste? (not waste as much, give to pet dog, compost pile)
plastic containers? (milk jugs: to recycling center; other containers: hold toys, food leftovers)
magazines? (give to others)
wrapping paper? (art project, decoration, other wrapping)
paper bags? (reuse, book covers, wrapping for mailing packages)
toys? (give to others)
newspapers? (recycle at center)
glass bottles? (recycle at center)
aluminum cans? (recycle at center)

Physical Education
Hopping on one foot at a time; "animal" walks.

Story
Mousekin's ABC (Edna Miller)
What is a Mammal? (Jennifer W. Day) Golden Science Book

Memory Verse
"For every beast of the forest is Mine, and the cattle on a thousand hills. I know all the birds of the mountains, and the wild beasts of the field are Mine." Ps. 50:10-11

WEEK 4   TUESDAY

Bible
Have child draw and color turtle, reptiles; cut and glue to poster (or use stickers, if you can find them).
Talk about reptiles, creeping things.
Who made all these reptiles and creeping things? (God did)
Resources:

j595.4D94s	Spiders (Ramona Stewart Dupre); color drawings
j595.4P74t	The True Book of Spiders (Illa Podendorf)
j595.44P512s	Spiders (Kate Petty); easy text; large color drawings
j595.7B65d	Discovering Insects (Glenn O. Blough); ref.
j595.7B78m	Moths (Jeanne S. Brouilette); color drawings
j598.1Z72rl	Reptiles and Amphibians (Herbert S. Zim and Hobert M. Smith); Golden Nature Guide; (Note: skip "history" p. 4-7)
j598.1M49s	Snakes (Esther K. Meeks); color drawings
j597.8H71f	Frogs and Polliwogs (Dorothy Childs Hogner); b&wh illus.; ref.
j597.8L266f	The Frog (Margaret Lane); full page large color picture; fairly easy text
j597.96C689s	A Snake's Body (Joanna Cole)

Learning At Home

j598.1B87w	The Western Diamondback Rattlesnake (Evelyn Brown & M. Vere De Vault); drawings/some color; ref.
j595.79L459h	Honeybees (Jane Lecht); National Geographic
j595.7Z72	Insects, A Guide to Familiar American Insects (Herbert S. Zim & Clarence Cottam)
j595.76J69L	Ladybugs (Sylvia A. Johnson); good color photos; ref.
j595.77C752i	I Watch Flies (Gladys Conklin); large color drawings
j595.7N33w	What Is An Insect? (Charles D. Neal); large color photos
j595.7N33wb	What Is A Bee? (Charles D. Neal); large color photos
j595.7P52g	Grasshoppers (Robert E. Pfadt); color photos
j595.7P74i	Insects (A New True Book) (Illa Podendorf)
j595.7S46w	Where Do They Go? Insects in Winter (Millicent E. Selsam)
j595.7P825i	Insects (Action Science) (Joyce Pape); large color pictures & experiments; ref.
j595.7D274w	What is an Insect? (Jennifer W. Day); large color drawings
j595.7E64b	The Beginning Knowledge Book of Ants (Anne Orth Epple); large color pictures; ref.
j595.7H71g	Grasshoppers and Crickets (Dorothy Childs Hogner); b&wh drawings
j592B42w	What We Find When We Look Under Rocks (Frances L. Behnke); b&wh drawings
j594.3J69s	Snails (Sylvia A. Johnson); color photos; ref.
j595.1	Earthworms (Dorothy Childs Hogner); b&wh drawings
j595.1S59d	Discovering What Earthworms Do (Seymour Simon); ref.; b&wh drawings

Reading
Read a poem.
Left-to-right eye movement: put 5 colored picture cards in a row in front of your child. Say, "Point to each card, starting at your left. Tell me what you see on each." Then put 5 different cards down and repeat.
(Alone) Visual discrimination: Give child two boxes of crayons. Have him match crayons by color (start with set of 8; may try box of 16).
Speech: Have child "read" familiar book to you by looking at the pictures.

Music
One More River (Noah's Ark)

Arithmetic
YELLOW: On yellow construction paper page, write the word yellow on the top of each side of the sheet. On the front, glue yellow pictures from magazines. On the back, mount white card with yellow image rubber stamped on to it.
Read: Hello, Yellow (Robert Jay Wolff)

God's World
Animals - Growing Up - Life Cycle
Talk about life cycle of animals. Read about animals being born (see also Week 2, Tue.-Thur. resource books).
j591.391366w   What's Hatching Out of That Egg? (Patricia Lauber); see ways 11 animals are born; photos of eggs

j591.5 C582h   How Animals Live (Anne Civardi & Cathy Kilpatrick); color pictures

Physical Education
Running broad jump.

Story
ABC Book (C. B. Falls); woodcuts; color
Gobble, Growl, Grunt (Peter Spier)

Memory Verse
"The earth is full of Your possessions..." Ps. 104:24c

WEEK 4   WEDNESDAY

Bible
Have child punch out, lick and stick wild animal stickers on to poster.
    Begin talking about North American wild animals. See how many child
    can name (bears: polar, grizzly, brown, black; deer family: muledeer,
    whitetail, blacktail; coyote; fox; wolf; raccoon; elk; caribou; moose; etc.).
Look at posters from U.S. Forest Service: Animals & their young
    (#84CFFP22); and Animal tracks (#84CFFP26).

Resources:

j599H87a	Animal Friends of the Northwest (Fran Hubbard); b&wh drawings
j590.4M15	Wildlife of the Pacific Northwest (Margaret McKenny); b&wh photos
599.32G845	Grey Squirrel (Oxford Scientific Films); color photos
j599.74N778L	Little Raccoon (Susanne Noguere); water color illus
j599.74R59f	Foxes and Wolves (Charles L. Ripper); b&wh drawings; medium text
j599.74C285b	The Black Bear Book (Joe Van Wormer); lots of b&wh photos
j599.744S881b	Bears (Bernard Stonehouse); color photos; ref.
j599.7 B86c	Coyotes (Wilfrid S. Bronson); b&wh drawings; large type
j599.7E16b	Bears Live Here (Irmengarde Eberle); b&wh photos; ref.
j599.7H58m	The Misunderstood Skunk (Lilo Hess); b&wh photos; ref.
j599.7W87d	The Deer Family (F. Dorothy Wood); drawings; ref.
j599.74E16f	Foxes Live Here (Irmengarde Eberle); b&wh photos; ref.
j599.74M466c	Cascade Cougar (Julian May); illus. story of small cougar growing up
j599.32H842	House Mouse (Oxford Scientific Films); color photos
j599.32L266s	The Squirrel (Margaret Lane); full page color illus; fairly easy text
j599.32Z71	Rabbits (Herbert S. Zim)
j599.3E16b	Beavers Live Here (Irmengarde Eberle); b&wh photos; ref.
j599.3W87b	Beavers (Dorothy Wood) color illus.; fairly easy text
j599.32B99n	Nature's Pincushion: The Porcupine (Ralph Buxton); drawings; fairly easy
j599W73f	The First Book of Mammals (Margaret Williamson); drawings; ref.

j599Z71m	<u>Mammals, A Guide to Familiar American Species</u> (Herbert S. Zim & Donald Hoffmeister); Golden Nature Guide; (Note: skip p. 7, 12-16 [evolution])
j599L33m	<u>Mammals of the Northwest</u> (Wash., Or., Idaho, & Br. Col.) (Earl J. Larrison); some color photos; animal tracks; b&wh drawings
j599B150	<u>Our Wild Animals</u> (John Bailey; photos by Leonard Lee Rue III); photos; tracks
j599D862	<u>Album of North American Animals</u> (Clark Bronson); large color illus. of 26 animals
j590B96z	<u>Zoology, An Introduction to the Animal Kingdom</u> (R. Will Burnett) (Note: skip 2 pages on "prehistorical mammals")
j590Z72	<u>What's Inside of Animals?</u> (Herbert S. Zim); clam, starfish, earth worm, grasshopper, fish, frog, dog
j590.4B92i	<u>In Yards and Gardens</u> (Margaret Waring Buck); b&wh drawings; ref.
j590.4B92	<u>In Woods and Fields</u> (Margaret Waring Buck); b&wh drawings; ref.

Reading

Read a poem.

Auditory discrimination: Have child repeat your clapping patterns.

(Alone) Missing parts: Have child match missing part from each of 5-10 pictures.

Sequencing: Have child put set of 5 cards in size order from small on left to largest on right (circles, 3 different sets).

Listening: Have child repeat after you series of words you say:

grizzly	wolf	giraffe	snake	
coyote	orangutan	turtle	musk ox	
fox	elephant	lion	tiger	wildebeest
antelope	baboon	rabbit	bear	raccoon

Art

Glue raisins to paper in shape of animals.

Arithmetic

GREEN: On green construction paper page, write the word green on the top of each side of the sheet. On the front, glue green pictures from magazines. On the back, mount white card with green images stamped on to it.

Read: <u>A Color of His Own</u> (Leo Lionni)

Health/Manners

Read book: <u>When There's a Fire, Go Outside</u>.

Talk about and practice fire drill "escape routes" for various areas of your house.

Talk about importance of:
1. Not hiding.
2. Firemen being there to help you/rescue you.
3. Not going back into house to get toys, etc.

On "Personal Health and Safety" story page, write: If there's a fire, I go outside.

Physical Education
Gallop to music and stop when music stops.

Story
Animal Babies (Ylla)
Fox and the Fire (Miska Miles)

Memory Verse
"These all wait for you, that You may give them their food in due season."
Psalm 104:27

WEEK 4　　THURSDAY

Bible
Continue talking about wild animals - this time those from the rest of the
world (elephant, giraffe, lion, tiger, panda bear, gazelle, wildebeest,
rhino, hippo, donkey, lla ma, etc.).
Who made all these different kinds of animals? (God did.)
Resources:

j220B582L	Animals of the Bible (Dorothy P. Lathrop)
j599.7B851	Lion Island (William Bridges); b&wh photos; story of NY Zoo lions
j599.2N7781	Little Koala (Suzanne Noguere); illus.; story of little animal
j599.725G879w	The Wild Ponies of Assateagne Island (Donna K. Grosvenor); National Geographic
j599.6E16e	Elephants Live Here (Irmengarde Eberle); b&wh photos; ref.
j599.6V285e	Elephants (Joe Van Wormer); b&wh photos; medium text but interesting
j599.6Z71	Elephants (Herbert S. Zim); b&wh drawings; fairly easy text
j599.61096e	Elephants (Cynthia Overbeck); color photos; ref.
j590.744G879z	Zoo Babies (Donna Grosvenor); National Geographic
j590.744J72a	Andy Bear, A Polar Cub Grows Up At the Zoo (Ginny Johnston & Judy Cutchins); photos (some color)
j591B315h	Hosie's Zoo (Leonard Baskin); watercolors of animals
j591.96P34w	Wild Animals of Africa (Klaus Paysan); color photos

Reading
Read a poem.
Rhyming: Say the word "at"; have child think of as many words that rhyme
as he can. Then rhyming words for: "an," "as," "aid."
(Alone) Hand-eye coordination: Sewing card.
Kinesthetic: Have child use two fingers (pointer and big finger) and repeat
sounds of "A a" as he traces shapes on letter cards, in air, and on your
back.

Music
Where Has My Little Dog Gone
For the Beauty of the Earth

Arithmetic

BLUE: On blue construction paper page, write the word blue on the top of each side of the sheet. On the front glue blue pictures from magazines. On the back mount white card with blue images rubber-stamped on to it.

God's World

Animals: Food, homes, defenses.

Talk about animals' food (differences, and how they get their food), homes (different types), and their defenses.

Resources:

j591.57 M128h	How Animals Hide (Robert M. McClung); National Geographic
j591.5 C613t	Tricks Animals Play (Jan Nagel Clarkson); National Geographic; defenses
j591.5 H58a	Animals That Hide, Imitate & Bluff (Lilo Hess); b&wh photos; defenses
j591 A316c	Creatures That Look Alike (Susan Harris); color drawings
j591 S596a	Animal Fact/Animal Fable (Seymour Simon)
j591.042 N277a	Animals in Danger: Trying to Save Our Wildlife (National Geographic)
j591.3 S46	Egg to Chick (Millicent E. Selsam)

Physical Education

Somersaults; rolls.

Story

Autumn Story (Jill Barklem); Brambly Hedge story.

I Am Eyes - Ni Macho (Leila Ward, illus. Nonny Hogrogian); Africa; animals.

Memory Verse

"All the earth shall worship You and sing praises to You; They shall sing praises to Your name." Ps. 66:4

WEEK 4   FRIDAY

Visit point of interest in your area.

Preparation for next week:

General:

_____Read over lesson plans

_____List materials needed

_____Collect materials needed

_____Story pages etc., to notebook

Library:

_____Return books used this week

_____Check out books for week after next

Field Trips:

_____Reconfirm next Friday's trip

_____Thank you note for last trip

_____Set up trip for week after next

WEEK 5   MONDAY

Bible

Read Gen. 1:26-31 (rest of Day 6 of Creation).

What did God make? (man and woman)

What did God ask the man and woman to do? (have children; fill the earth; rule over the fish, birds and creatures)

Have child cut out pictures of man and woman; glue them to poster.

Write on story page: God created man and woman.

Reading

Read a poem.

Introduce "B b" letter shape and sound. Have child trace letter shapes, starting at x and repeat the sound.

(Alone) Classifying: Have child sort the capital and small b's from A's & a's and match with corresponding B's and b's on file folder.

Sequence and complete sentences: Have child dictate story about the visit to a point of interest.

Art

Trace outline of child as he lays on white butcher paper; cut out and tape to door. If desired, add features and "clothes."

Arithmetic

PURPLE: On purple construction paper page, write the word purple on the top of each side of the sheet. On the front glue purple pictures from magazines. On the back mount white card with purple images rubber-stamped on to it.

Character Building

Stewardship of our minds and bodies - we are the temple of God.

God tells us that our bodies are the temple of God. He says we need to care about what we think about and how we treat our bodies. We need to guard what goes into our bodies to meet our physical needs: thoughts, food, rest, exercise and fresh air.

What would happen to you if you thought about bad things all the time? Ate bad food? Didn't sleep enough? Didn't get enough fresh air and exercise?

Humility is understanding who God is and knowing who I am in relationship to God. Remember that God is the Creator of the entire world. He is the Creator of all people, including you.

We need to remember that although God has given us gifts and abilities that:

1) they don't even begin to compare with Him and His abilities.

2) we need to make sure HE gets credit for them - not us.

3) we need to take good care (be good stewards) of all the parts of our bodies and minds for God.

We need to remember never to be proud and boastful.

On Character Building story page, write: God wants me to be a good steward of my mind and my body.

Physical Education
Toss ball in air; walk backward.

Story
Becky's Birthday (Tasha Tudor); read first half; continue Tuesday.
Smokey the Bear (Jane Werner); Golden Book.

Memory Verse
"Therefore, humble yourselves under the mighty hand of God."
  I Peter 5:6a
"I will not set nothing wicked before my eyes."
  Psalm 101:3a

WEEK 5   TUESDAY

Bible
(Background: Gen 2:15-20 - Adam naming animals; God wanting helper for him.)

Read Gen. 2:21-25. A woman was made to be a helper for her husband. Talk about the differences between man and woman (physical characteristics and abilities; for example, man is stronger because of shoulder and chest muscles, etc.).

Then read Gen. 2:1-3 (7th Day of Creation - Rest!).

God had created heavens and earth and all in it; He ended His work; He rested from His work; He blessed the seventh day and consecrated it.

Talk about the importance of our resting the seventh day (Sabbath).

God saw all that He had created and saw that it was good.

On Story Page, write: God saw that all He made was good. Then He rested.

Reading
Read a poem.

(Alone) Left-to-right eye movement: Make a line of 5 shape cards on the table in front of the child. Have the child "read" the pattern to you and then have him duplicate the pattern of another set of shape cards. (Make sure he begins at the left; repeat with several sequences, if time..

Visual discrimination: Put two blue and one red crayon on the table. Have child find the one that is different (not the same). Do this several times with different colors and combinations.

Speech: Have child "read" familiar book to you using the pictures as a guide, if necessary.

Music
Jesus Loves Me
Oh, Be Careful Little Mind

Arithmetic

BROWN: On brown construction paper page, write the word brown on the top of each side of the sheet. On the front glue brown pictures from magazines. On the back mount white card with brown images rubber-stamped on to it.

God's World

Life Cycle of Person - Stages of Growth & Ability (Part I)
Talk about the usual life cycle of a person:
1. Conceived, growing inside mother.
2. Born; baby stages.
3. Toddler - beginning to walk.
4. Preschooler - learning more things.
5. Age 5-12 - bigger and more responsible each year.
6. Adolescent 12-13 - body changing more.
7. Teenager 13-19 - learn to drive a car, more responsibility each year.

Look at baby pictures of child.

Physical Education

Jump from 1-2' height; walk on inclined board.

Story

<u>Becky's Birthday</u> (Tasha Tudor); finish from yesterday
<u>Faces</u> (Barbara Brenner); photos

Memory Verse

"So God created man in His own image; in the image of God He created him; male and female He created them. Then God blessed them..."
Gen. 1:27-28a

WEEK 5   WEDNESDAY

Bible

Talk about differences among people (have children think of examples for each of them):

Characteristics:	Differences due to:
Physical	1. Boy/girl
Emotional	2. Size
Intellectual	3. Age
Social	4. Where you live (geography; climate; food available)
	5. God's special design for you

Reading

Read a poem.
Auditory discrimination: Say a set of two words and have the child tell you if the words are the same or different:

bat, bat	ball, baby	basket, basket
bark, bottle	ben, bin	bottle, bottle
bit, bat	bit, bit	bell, bill
bell, ball	ball, balk	belt, bell

Notes

(Alone) Maze: Have the child use matchbox car and go through maze you've made on a large piece of cardboard. Explain that where there is an obstacle, they must go around it, not through it.

Listening: Have the child repeat sequences of words:

create, God, joy	baby, toddler, child
young, family, baby	people, different, me
special, unique, each	happy, gift, day
man, woman, family	wife, children, husband
father, mother, children	steward, mind, body

Art

(Newspaper on table first.) Write/print child's name on construction paper, then write over it with glue. Sprinkle cornmeal/glitter/sand over it; shake excess off onto newspaper.

Arithmetic

BLACK AND WHITE: On black construction paper page, write the word black (with white crayon) on the top of each side of the sheet. On the front glue black pictures from magazines. On the back mount white card with black images rubber-stamped on to it.

On the white construction paper page, write the word white on the top of the front side of the sheet. On the front glue white pictures from magazines. On the back have child color in the stripes of the rainbow that you've outlined and put a dot of color in each stripe, so the child will know what color to put where.

(Note: To finish book, use gummed hole reinforcements after punching 3 holes through each sheet. Tie with yarn/string, allowing a small amount of excess so the pages can be easily turned).

Health/Manners

Dressing Right for the Weather

Why wear clothes?

1. Cover private zones.
2. Keep us warm in cool, windy, cold, rainy weather, and cool in warm weather.
3. Protect our skin (insects, thorns, rain).

Have child tell you what he thinks he should wear for various situations: berry-picking (arms and legs covered); hiking in snow-covered mountains (wood); camping at coast (rain/wind protection, short and long pants, sweater, hat); and other situations.

On "Personal Health and Safety" story page, write: I dress right for the weather and to protect myself.

Physical Education

Jump to music and stop when music stops.

Story

Bread and Jam for Frances (Russell Hoban)
The Important Book (Margaret Wise Brown)

Memory Verse

"Then, God saw everything that He had made, and indeed it was very good…" Gen. 1:31a

WEEK 5　　THURSDAY

Bible

Introduction to: God created me!

Tell child that God knows all about us. He made us. "He made you, (child)."

Read Psalm 139:13-16. "God created you inside your mother. He made each part of you special. There is no one else in the entire world like you. You are unique. God loves you. Even your fingerprints are different from everyone else in the whole world."

Take picture of the child. Show pictures of him/her as an infant, baby, toddler, on up to the present time, recalling one or two special and unique things about him.

Begin "God Created Me!" story page. On it, write: God created me. I am special to Him. He made me different from everyone else; I am unique. God made every part of me (for each body part to be listed following these sentences, glue a cut out picture/drawing of each body part after the corresponding sentence).

Who created me? (God did)

Reading

Read a poem.

Rhyming: Say "ball" and have child think of as many words as he can that rhyme. Then rhymes for "bind," "bear," and "beam."

(Alone) Hand-eye coordination: have child do puzzle(s).

Kinesthetic: Using two fingers (pointer and big finger) and repeating sounds, trace B and b on letter cards, in the air, and on your back.

Music

Paw Paw Patch

God Made Me

Arithmetic

Smallest to largest; youngest to oldest.

Child arranges wallpaper samples of different sizes in same pattern in sequential order, beginning with the smallest on the left. After he completes one set and you check it, have him do several more.

Using picture cards you make of people af all ages (baby, child, teenager, parent, grandparent), have child arrange them in sequence from the youngest (at the left) to the oldest (at the right). Repeat with another set.

God's World

Stages of Growth & Ability (Part II)

Review Stages 1-7. Continue:

    8. Adult - responsible for own living

    9. Married - husband/wife

    10. Parent - father/mother

    11. Grandparent

    12. Elderly person

Notes

Cut out pictures from magazines of each step. Glue on to timeline. On bottom write: God makes each stage of our life special.

Physical Education
Somersaults; headstands

Story
The Ugly Duckling (Hans Christian Anderson)

Memory Verse
"Your hands have made and fashioned me;" Psalm 119:73a

WEEK 5   FRIDAY

Visit Natural History Museum (see "Invisible Man/Woman" if available).

Preparation for next week:

General:
_____Read over lesson plans
_____List materials needed
_____Collect materials needed
_____Story pages etc., to notebook

Library:
_____Return books used this week
_____Check out books for week after next

Field Trips:
_____Reconfirm next Friday's trip
_____Thank you note for last trip
_____Set up trip for week after next

WEEK 6   MONDAY

Bible
On story page, write: God made my bones, muscles, blood system, and my skin. (Add pictures.)
Talk about the function and examples of:
1. bones (framework for body; grow as body grows) Look at your arm bones and ankles. (See an X-ray, too, if possible.)
2. muscles (increase with use) Look at your tongue, bicep, thigh muscles.
3. blood system (highway to provide blood for your body) Look at the veins in your arm.
4. skin (protective organ; largest organ in body; differences in skin on body due to function and use; it is elastic; it grows a new layer; it can heal). Look and feel difference between skin on face and on bottom of foot.

Who made my bones, muscles, blood and skin? (God did.)

Reading

Read a poem.

Introduce "C, c" letter shapes and sounds (cuh, sss). Have child trace letter shapes, starting at x as they repeat the two sounds.

(Alone) Classifying: Sort capital and small C's from A's, a's, B's, and b's. Match with the C's and c's on the file folder.

Sequence and complete sentences: Have child dictate story about trip to science museum last Friday. (4 or more sentences; guide through it, if necessary.)

Art

Autumn leaves pressed (with iron, by you) between two pieces of waxed paper. Tape to windows to let sun shine through.

Arithmetic

Using stacking/nesting cups (Discovery Toys/Fisher-Price), have the child (after you've mixed them up) arrange them sequentially with the smallest on the left and the largest on the right. (Note: if there are quite a few in the set, start with four. Then add more cups as the child's skill increases.)

Using picture cards of people of varying ages (or photos of people in your family!), have child arrange from youngest to oldest.

Character Building

Review humility. Talk about reverencing God: treating God so special in our thoughts about Him, in our words about God to others, and in our words and actions (the things we do and say each day) to make sure they would make God happy.

We need to remember that NO ONE or NOTHING can ever compare to our God. Last week we talked about humility. What is it? (Knowing who God is and who we are in relationship to Him.)

What is our relationship to God? Who are we to Him? (We are His people; we are His creation; we are to be His helpers, to build Him up to others, not to break Him down by our thoughts, words, and actions.)

Physical Education

Throw and catch the ball.

Story

<u>Ola</u> (Ingri and Edgar Parin d'Aulaire)
<u>The Me I See</u> (Barbara Shook Hazen)

Memory

"For My thoughts are not your thoughts, nor are your ways My ways, says the Lord. For as the heavens are higher than the earth, So are my ways higher than your ways, And my thoughts than your thoughts." Is. 55:8-9

WEEK 6   TUESDAY

Bible

On story page, write: God made my arms, hands and fingers. (Add pictures)

Have child look at arms, hands and fingers. Talk about joints that connect arm and allow it to move (shoulder, elbow, wrist and knuckles).

What do we use our arms and hands for? (hugging, holding, writing, eating, getting dressed, throwing ball, etc.)

What covers our arms? (skin and tiny arm hair)

What's underneath? (bones, muscles, blood)

Who made your arms, hands and fingers? (God did.)

How many arms do you have? How many fingers on each hand? If you couldn't use your arms/hands, what other body part could you use? (mouth to hold pencil; feet for feeding yourself) How should we care for our arms? (protect them, keep them clean, eat right foods to nourish them)

Reading

Read a poem.

Left-to-right eye movement: Have child take different types of steps (giant, baby, etc.) to the right/left as you direct him.

(Alone) Visual discrimination: Have child sort AaBbCc cards into piles of all like letters (5-10 of each card).

Speech: Have child "read" familiar story to you, turning pages as you go.

Music

Where is Thumbkin?

Arithmetic

Give child four to six boxes - ones that will fit on top of each other - in varying sizes. Have him make a line with the smallest box at the left up to the largest box on the right.

Have child arrange wallpaper shapes from smallest to largest. (Use several sets; different shapes.)

God's World

My Specialness

Take fingerpaints. Write down specifics about child: height, weight, hair color, photo, moles, distinguishing marks, etc., birthdate. Put in section of notebook titled with the child's name.

Physical Education

Balance on curbstone/2 x 4 - 10 ft. long; jump forward and backward over line.

Story

Quick as a Cricket (Audrey Wood)

Farm Alphabet Book (Jane Miller) color photos

Memory Verse

"Since you were precious in My sight, you have been honored, And I have loved you…" Is. 43:4

WEEK 6   WEDNESDAY

Bible

On story page, write: God made my mind. (Add picture)

Talk about brain - how complex it is and how different parts control different areas of your body. There are two different sides to your brain: two "helpers." (Simplify the following)

Left side	Right side
Verbal skills, language skills	Emotions, feelings
Communication	Artistic ability; visual and sensory ability
Ability to analyze and think things through and reason; to put things in order; to remember facts, figures and dates.	
Organization	Physical ability, motor skills
Reading & Arithmetic skills	Creativity, dance, music
Intellectual" ability	Looks at whole picture/situation
Goal oriented	Good reaction in emergency situations.

God gave you both parts of your brain and you use both parts for different tasks, skills and situations. Here are some examples of how each "helper" helps you:

Your "left friend" helps you:	Your "right friend" helps you:
1. learn to talk and express yourself.	1. feel happy, excited, sad.
2. learn your arithmetic and learn to read.	2. draw, paint, tell stories, dance.
3. get dressed-what to put on first, etc.	3. jump, hop, move
4. to be organized.	4. react well in emergency situation.

Who made your mind? (God did.)

Read poem: "God Be in My Head" (from a children's prayer book, 1558):

God be in my head, and in my understanding;
God be in my eyes, and in my looking;
God be in my mouth, and in my speaking;
God be in my heart, and in my thinking;
God be at mine end, and at my departing.

Reading

Read a poem.

Auditory discrimination: Say sequence of two words and have child tell you whether they start with the same or different sounds:

apple, cat	caboose, comb	call, ball
cabbage, car	circus, century	come, break
cauliflower, cotton	celebrate, cent	cow, act
basket, candle	call, bat	clip, clop

(Alone) Missing parts: Show child picture of face with all of the parts on it. Name the parts together. Then give child paper on which you've drawn six face shapes, each with one to three parts missing. Have child draw in missing parts.

Listening: Have the child repeat the sequence of words you say:

skeleton, tongue, bones	create, muscles, hands
finger, liver, lungs	legs, ankles, toes
fingers, knuckles, wrists	skin, blood, veins
toenails, hair, fingernails	heart, intestines, stomach
foot, knee, hip	shoulder, elbow, neck

Art

Crayon resist - use bright color crayons (press rather hard) to draw picture/ design. Paint over it with blue/black water colors.

Arithmetic

Have child arrange 4-6 pencils according to size, smallest on the left to the longest on the right. (Make sure that they can distinguish size differences among them.)

Have child arrange family photos and then set of magazine pictures in sequential order from youngest to oldest.

Health/Manners

Personal Cleanliness

Talk about being good stewards of our bodies and protecting them against germs, and dirt.

1. I wash my hands before eating.
2. I wash my hands after going to the bathroom.
3. I wash my face each day.
4. I scrub with soap and a washcloth each bathtime.

On "Personal Health and Safety" story page, write: I keep myself clean.

Physical Education

Walk to music and stop when the music stops.

Story

The Story of Dumbo (Walt Disney) Golden Book

The Pantheon Story of Art for Young People (Ariane Ruskin); j709R95p; look at some of the paintings (art appreciation)

Memory Verse

"A glad heart makes a cheerful countenance." Prov. 15:13a

WEEK 6   THURSDAY

Bible
On story page, write: God created my inside organs: my heart, lungs, liver, stomach, intestines, and all the rest. (Add pictures)

Talk about the functions and locations of:
1. Heart: pumps blood throughout your body (feel your heartbeat)
2. Lungs: chambers to hold air (take a deep breath and let air go)
3. Liver: filters and cleans blood
4. Stomach: (pull in and push out) digestive system
5. Intestines: process food; digestive system

How should we care for our inside organs? (eat right foods, exercise, rest)

Reading
Read a poem.

Rhyming: Have child name as many words as he can with "cake," "cent," "cape," and "car."

(Alone) Hand-eye coordination: Have child string beads onto shoelace.

Kinesthetic: Using two fingers and repeating sounds, trace C c letter cards in the air and on your back.

Music
Songs of your choice.

God's World
Anatomy

Read:

j611 H66t   The True Book of Your Body & You (Alice Hinshaw); drawings. Talks re: individuality; skeleton; muscles; brain; nerves; skin; eyes; ears; nose; blood; heart; limbs; spirit.

Physical Education
Somersaults; skipping.

Story
Poems for Weather Watching (Laurie Israel)

Busy Feet (Elizabeth Elaine Watson); A Happy Day Book

Memory Verse
"For You have formed my inward parts; You have covered me in my mother's womb." Ps. 139:13

WEEK 6   FRIDAY

Visit a special place of your family's.

Preparation for next week:

Notes

General:
____Read over lesson plans
____List materials needed
____Collect materials needed
____Story pages etc., to notebook

Library:
____Return books used this week
____Check out books for week after next

Field Trips:
____Reconfirm next Friday's trip
____Thank you note for last trip
____Set up trip for week after next

WEEK 7   MONDAY

Bible
On story page, write: God made me a special size. He made me a (boy/
    girl). He made my hair (color) and my eyes (color). He loves me.
Talk about individuality of your child, any special characteristics that are
    dear to you and/or evident to others (physical: moles, birthmarks;
    positive temperament qualities; abilities shown thus far).
Talk about how important it is for us NOT TO COMPARE with others. God
    gives each of us special gifts, characteristics. We are to be thankful, to
    find and best develop our God-given abilities, always giving <u>God</u> the
    glory.

On construction paper, draw a pentagon of 5 dots, as shown: o   o   o. Save
    page.

Reading
Read a poem.
Introduce "D d" letter shapes and sound. Have child trace letter shapes
    while repeating letter sound. (Make sure he starts at the right spot.)
(Alone) Classifying: Have the child sort capital and small letters D d from
    other letters; match with the D's and d's on the file folder.
Sequence and complete sentences: Have the child dictate story about last
    Friday's trip.

Art
Make picture with blue construction paper, brown "tree" (you cut, they
    paste), and bits of torn construction paper (red, orange, yellow, green,
    brown) for leaves glued to tree and falling to ground.

Arithmetic
Read: <u>Circles, Triangles, and Squares</u> (Tana Hoban)
Show child circle cut out of sandpaper/indoor-outdoor carpeting. Name it
    as a CIRCLE. Have the child say (complete sentence), "This is a circle,"
    as he traces around the edge with his finger.

Have child color worksheet you've made of eight circles (color one each of the colors he did pages for in the past weeks: red, orange, yellow, green, blue, purple, brown, black). Save this page as it will be page one of his Circle book.

Character Building

On Character Building story page, write: Humility means knowing who God is and who I am in relationship with Him.

Talk about responsibility (answering for your own obligations and actions).

Talk about God's chain of authority - the umbrella of protection. When it is raining, we use an umbrella to protect us from the rain. On the hot beaches sometimes people use a beach umbrella to protect themselves from sun and wind. God has an "umbrella" of protection for us.

> The husband is responsible for his wife.
>
> The wife has the delegated responsibility from the husband for the children.

God
|
husband
|
wife
|
children

The children's job (responsibility) is to:
1) Respect, honor and obey God and your parents.
2) Do your best to make God and your parents happy and pleased.

We need to do our jobs cheerfully - without grumbling. How would you feel if you were a storekeeper and there was a person who worked for you who was always grumbling and whining whenever you asked him to do anything? Would you say he was being responsible? Was he doing his best?

On the Character Building story page, write: God has given me a chain of authority. I need to be responsible and do my jobs quickly and cheerfully, without grumbling.

Physical Education

Kicking ball.

Story

Rachel (Elizabeth Fanshawe); wheelchair

The New Baby (Ruth and Harold Shane); Golden Book

Memory Verse

"...the head of every man is Christ, the head of a woman is her husband, and the head of Christ is God." I Cor. 11:3

"So a man's heart reveals the man." Prov. 27:19a

WEEK 7   TUESDAY

Bible

On story page, write: God made my legs, feet and toes. (Add pictures)

Have child look at his/her legs, feet and toes.

Talk about joints that connect leg and allow it to move (hip, knee, ankle, toe joints/knuckles).

What do we use our legs and feet for? (holding up our body, walking, skipping, hopping, climbing, running, etc. toes gripping, getting around)

What covers your leg? (skin, tiny leg hairs)

What's inside your leg? (bones, muscle, blood) How many legs do you have? How many toes on each foot? If you couldn't use your legs, what other body parts could you use? (arms to crawl and push wheelchair/crutches) How should we care for our legs and feet? (protect them, keep them clean, eat the right foods to nourish them) Who made your legs? (<u>God</u> did.)

Resource: Rachel (Elizabeth Fanshawe); girl in wheelchair has busy life with help of family and friends.

Reading

Read a poem.

(Alone) Left-to-right eye movement: Have the child copy the patterns of beads you've strung (and laid down on the table, knot end at the left).

(Alone) Visual discrimination: Have child match crayons from 2-3 boxes of crayons by color.

Speech: Have child "read" book to you.

Music

The Lord is My Shepherd

Arithmetic

Draw a circle on the chalkboard. Ask the child what the shape is. Have him answer in a complete sentence: This is a circle. Tell him that we always start drawing a circle at the spot where 2:00 is on the clock (show him the spot on the circle you made).

Classifying: Sort circle wallpaper shapes on cards from cards with triangles and squares. Then match the circle wallpaper shapes to the matching patterns on the file folder.

Have child paint with watercolors another set of eight circles on another worksheet page. This will be page two of his circle book.

God's World

Weather: Rain, Snow

Talk about rain (drizzle, sprinkle, rain, downpour), snow (drops of water from clouds that freeze around a bit of ash, sand and dust).

Begin keeping weather chart each day.

Read:

j551.5 S99w   <u>What is Weather</u>? (B. John Syrocki, EdD.)

Resource:

j551.5 LS2w   <u>Weather: Air Masses - Clouds - Rainfall - Storms - Weather Maps -Climate</u> (Paul E. Lehr, R. Will Burnett, Herbert S. Zim); Golden Nature Guide; ref.; good info.

Physical Education

Galloping; standing on tiptoes.

Story
One Morning in Maine (Robert McCloskey)
The Snowy Day (Ezra Jack Keats)

Memory Verse
"Set a guard, O Lord, over my mouth; Keep watch over the door of my lips."
Ps. 141:3

WEEK 7   WEDNESDAY

Bible
On story page, write: God created my mouth. (Add pictures)
Ask child what we use mouth for. (speaking, eating) We need to be good
stewards of our mouth in three ways:
1) Swallowing: We need to make sure that we eat good food.
2) Teeth: we need to take good care of our teeth.
3) Speech: we need to make sure that what comes out of our mouth builds
others up ("speaking the truth in love").
Who made your mouth? (God did.)

Reading
Read a poem.
Auditory discrimination: Have child repeat your clapping pattern.
Memory: Have three objects on tray; child looks and then closes eyes; you
take one object away; he names missing object. (Increase number of
items as skill increases.)
Listening: Have child repeat sequences of words after you:

mind, head, steward	thoughts, me, memory	mouth, tongue, gums
teeth, brush, floss	hair, fingerprint, me	name, unique, special
taste, mouth, tongue	sweet, salty, bitter	taste buds, ridges, senses
wind, rain, weather	clouds, dew, dust	snow, hail, precipitation
fog, frost, chart		

Art
Draw picture of himself with crayons.

Arithmetic
Have child look around the room for circles he can see.
Classifying: Sort circle shapes from others; match with correct patterns on
file folder.
Stamp rubber stamps along penciled outline of circle. (Page 3 of book)

Health/Manners
Care of Teeth, Mouth
1) Show correct way of brushing teeth.
2) Use disclosing tablet, if possible, to show areas they are missing in brushing.
3) Talk about foods that are good for strong, clean teeth. (apples, carrots,
celery)
4) Show how to floss teeth and why we floss. (clean between teeth, get
particles you can't reach with toothbrush; help strengthen gums)
On "Personal Health and Safety" story page, write: I brush and floss my teeth
well each day to keep them clean.

Physical Education
Dance to music and stop when music stops.

Story
The Five Chinese Brothers (Claire Huchet Bishop and Kurt Wiese)
Rain Drop Splash (Alvin Tresselt)

Memory Verse
"But the very hairs of your head are all numbered." Matt. 10:30

WEEK 7   THURSDAY

Bible
Today and the following four classes, the child will be gluing a picture on each of the dots to represent one of the five senses God has given us. On the upper left-hand corner of the paper, write: God has given me 5 senses.

Taste: Talk about what part of his body tastes food. (mouth) What kinds of foods do you like? Your tongue helps you taste your food. It has "taste buds" on it.

Have child look in the mirror at his/her tongue. Show him which areas of the tongue taste the various tastes: sweet, sour, salty.

Find, cut out, and glue pictures of mouth to top dot on the "5 Senses" poster.

Blindfold child and tell him you are going to have him do a taste test. Have him open mouth and guess what each of the following samples is:
1) honey (sweet)
2) potato or corn chip (salty)
3) dill pickle (sour)
4) peanut butter sandwich bite (combination)

Who gave me the ability to taste? (God did.)
Resource:
j612.8M382m   Messengers to the Brain-Our Fantastic Five Senses (Paul Martin); National Geographic

Some things are not safe to taste; they are poison.

Reading
Read a poem.
Rhyming: Have child name rhyming words for: "dad," "day," "dip."
(Alone) Hand-eye coordination: Have child cut out parts of a face (eyes, nose, mouth, hair, ears) and glue them to a construction paper oval to make a clown.
Kinesthetic: Using two fingers while repeating the "d" sound, have child trace letter shape of "D d" on the letter card, in the air, and on your back.

Music
Song of your choice.

Arithmetic
Have child count out circular objects from magazine pictures; glue to page 4. Put book pages together; punch holes; reinforce holes; tie with yarn/string. Label front of book: CIRCLES

God's World

Weather: Wind Dust, Dew, Frost, Fog, Air

Talk about differences between these terms: wind; dust (fine, dry pulverized particles of earth or other matter); dew (moist, condensed on cool bodies [air warmer than ground] at night); frost (covering of minute ice crystals on a cold surface); fog (vapor condensed to fine particles of water suspended near the ground [lower atmosphere]); air (invisible, odorless, tasteless gases that surround the earth).

Explain what these terms/conditions mean.

Physical Education

Walk in a circle without losing balance; jump forward and backward over line.

Story

The Berenstein Bears Visit the Dentist (Stan and Jan Berenstein)
Snow is Falling (Franklyn Branley)

Memory Verse

"For we are His workmanship…" Eph. 2:10a

WEEK 7   FRIDAY

Visit the dentist's office; tour.

Preparation for next week:

General:
_____Read over lesson plans
_____List materials needed
_____Collect materials needed
_____Story pages etc., to notebook

Library:
_____Return books used this week
_____Check out books for week after next

Field Trips:
_____Reconfirm next Friday's trip
_____Thank you note for last trip
_____Set up trip for week after next

WEEK 8   MONDAY

Bible

Sense of Touch: What part of the body feels things? (all over, especially hands) Look at your hands and fingertips. What are different things we can feel? (breeze on face, sharp, stickery weed when walking barefoot, tickling on tummy, baby's smooth skin, Daddy's scratchy beard and big bear hug, Mommy's face and hair as we lay our head on her shoulder as she holds us) Ask child to name as many words as he can to describe how things feel. (soft/hard, smooth/rough, sticky, sharp, velvety, crumbly, wet/dry, scratchy)

Tell child that some things are not safe to touch.

Blindfold child and have him describe characteristics of several items and try to decide what they are. (Ex.: uncooked elbow macaroni, cooked elbow macaroni, Scotch tape, different fabrics [velvet, satin, silk, corduroy, plastic], wet washcloth, dry washcloth, crumbly cheese, tip of nail, his own vocal cords while talking/singing)

Find, cut out, and glue picture of hand/fingers to the dot at 10:00 position (left of the "taste" picture).

Who gave me the ability to touch and feel? (<u>God</u> did.)

Resource:

<u>Red Thread Riddles</u> (Virginia Allen Jensen and Polly Edman); (parents' shelf) riddles with Braille markings and thread (raised markings) to follow with fingers through book.

Reading

Read a poem.

Introduce letter shape "E e" and the two sounds (eh, ee). Have child trace letter cards while repeating the sounds.

(Alone) Classifying: Have child sort the letter cards E and e from A-D and a-d cards. Then match with the E's and e's on the file folder.

Sequence and complete sentences: Have child dictate story about trip to the dentist's office.

Art

Glue eyes, nose and mouth on to orange pumpkins (construction paper).

Arithmetic

Squares: Read Listen to a Shape (Marcia Brown).

Show child square cut out of sandpaper/indoor-outdoor carpeting. Name it as a SQUARE. Have the child say (complete sentence), "This is a square," as he traces around the edge with his finger. Note with him that a square has (count them) four straight lines as its edge.

Have child color worksheet you've made of eight squares (one of each color), beginning from the left to the right, top row to bottom.

Character Building

Review humility and responsibility to God and your parents.

Our responsibility to God and to our parents:

  1) Be thankful - for protection and provisions and love.

  2) Be cheerful - not grumbling.

  3) Be obedient - first time asked!

  4) Be respectful of authority.

On Character Building story page, write: My job is to be thankful, be cheerful, be obedient, and be respectful to God and to my parents.

Physical Education

Throwing and catching the ball.

Story
    <u>Face Talk, Hand Talk, Body Talk</u> (Sue Castle)
    <u>The Dead Bird</u> (Margaret Wise Brown)

Memory Verse
    "Deliver those who are drawn toward death..." Prov. 24:11a

WEEK 8   TUESDAY

Bible
Sense of Smell: What part of your body do you smell things with? (nose)
Look at your nose in the mirror. What kinds of things can we smell?
    (fragrant flowers, bread baking, talcum powder, soap, gas stations,
    garbage, wonderful forest scent of rich soil and wildflowers, cologne,
    pizza, Vicks vap-o-rub, fresh oranges, cinnamon) Blindfold child and
    have him sniff several samples (from above list or your ideas). Have
    child name as many samples as he can.
Some things are not good or safe to smell.
Find, cut out, and glue picture of nose to the poster at the 2:00 position dot.
Who gave you the ability to smell? (God did.)

Reading
Read a poem.
Left-to-right eye movement: Have child copy pegboard patterns that you've
    made (different colors in a horizontal line). Make sure that he starts at
    the left side. When one pattern is completed, repeat with another.
Speech: Have child "read" story to you.

Music
Head, Shoulders, Knees and Toes

Arithmetic
Draw a square on the chalkboard. Ask the child what the shape is. Have
    him answer in a complete sentence: This is a square. Ask him what
    kind of lines makes a square. (straight, 4)
Classifying: Sort square wallpaper shapes on cards from cards with triangles
    and circles. Then match the square wallpaper shapes to the
    corresponding matching patterns on the file folder.
Have child paint with watercolors another set of eight squares on another
    worksheet page. This will be page two of his square book

God's World
Things That Happen To Me
Explain the following concepts/terms. Why do I:
    1) Tear (from tiny sacs/glands in corner of eye. Wash eyes to keep clean
       and healthy)
    2) Sleep (body and brain needs rest; brain needs rest more than any other
       part of body)
    3) Sneeze (when something gets in nose that doesn't belong there)
    4) Shiver (muscles moving to warm me up)
    5) Hiccup (muscle [diaphragm] jerks suddenly - air pulled in and out of
       lungs sounds HIC instead of breath)

6) Yawn (when body is tired or not getting enough fresh air)

7) Sweat (tiny tubes [sweat glands] just under skin push sweat [mostly water   mixed with salt] through tiny holes [pores] in my skin)

Physical Education

Balance on one foot and then the other.

Story

The Storm Book (Charlotte Zolotow)

The Truck Book (H. McNaught); Golden Book

Memory Verse

"But by the grace of God I am what I am." I Cor. 15:10a

WEEK8   WEDNESDAY

Bible

Sense of Hearing: What part of the body do we hear with? (ears) How many ears do we have? What kind of sounds can we hear? (Nature: birdsong, coyote howling, rippling brook, ocean waves, wind in the trees, thunder, rain hitting the roof, cat purring, owl hooting; man-made: walking through dried leaves, refrigerator hum, piano music, singing, car horn and traffic, hammer pounding)

Some sounds are harmful to our ears (too loud, too shrill). Sometimes people need ear protectors to do their jobs (lawn mowing a lot, heavy machinery, hunters shooting practice).

Blindfold child and have him listen to several sounds and name as many as possible (Ex.: water dripping, refrigerator humming, piano note, stomping boots, whisper, scream, two pan lids hitting, can opening with can opener).

Find, cut out, and glue picture of ear to dot at 7:00 position on the poster.

Who gave me the ability to hear? (God did.)

Resources:

j362.4W853a   Anna's Silent World (Bernard Wolf); photos

j362.7L665L   Lisa and her Soundless World (Edna S. Levine)

Reading

Read a poem.

Auditory discrimination: Say sets of two words; child tells you if his beginning sounds are the same or different.

duck, doll	egg, elephant
dim, dog	enter, if
dress, best	eggplant, rooster
desk, teacher	Edith, Easter
dream, nest	eat, aim
date, doctor	elm, old

(Alone) Missing parts: Have child draw the missing parts on the 6-8 faces you have drawn on the chalkboard (with one to four parts missing on each).

Listening: Have child repeat sequences after you.

senses, five, God	touch, hear, taste
senses, smell, see	nose, ears, mouth
eyes, mind, blessing	tears, sleep, sneeze
yawn, hiccup, shiver	goosebumps, itch, fever
chapped, itchy, dry	eyelash, eyebrow, eyelid
humility, God, love	blister, responsibility, me
feelings, mind, glorify	safety, eyes, glasses
earache, toothache, nosebleed	

Art

"Spatter" paint: autumn leaves, toothbrush, tempera paint, construction paper. Hold leaf down; tape underside and then use finger/screen to spatter paint from toothbrush onto paper.

Arithmetic

Cut out pictures in the shapes of squares from magazines. Glue to page 4. Put book pages together; punch holes; reinforce holes; tie with yarn/string. Label front of book: SQUARES.

Health/Manners

Care of Eyes and Eye Safety
1) Don't put anything in or near your eyes.
2) Don't get sharp things near your (or others') eyes.
3) Some liquids would burn your eyes.
4) Don't rub eyes.
5) Tears wash eyes if you get something in them.
6) If you get something in eyes and it won't come out with tears, wash out with cool water.

Have child act out what he would do if he got eyelash in eye.
On "Personal Health and Safety" story page, write: I am very careful of my eyes and others' eyes, too.

Physical Education

Move to music and stop when it stops.

Story

The Noisy Book (Margaret Wise Brown)
Deer at the Brook (Jim Ainosky)

Memory Verse

"The hearing ear and the seeing eye, The Lord has made them both." Prov. 20:12

WEEK 8 THURSDAY

Bible

Sense of Sight: What part of the body do we see with? (eyes) How many do we have? Look at your eyes in the mirror. Just as we need to be careful of what we taste, touch, smell, and hear, we also need to be careful of what we look at. There are some bad things and scary things we should not see. God wants us to be careful of what our eyes see. We also need to be careful to keep things away from our eyes - and other people's eyes. Eyes can get scratched, burned, and hurt just like other parts of our body.

Blindfold child. Have him try to walk from one place in the house to another place without bumping into anything.

If you didn't have the ability to see, what other senses could you develop to help you? (touch, hearing especially)

Find, cut out, and glue picture of eye to dot at 5:00 position on poster.

Who gave you the ability to see? (<u>God</u> did.)

Read: "A Great Grey Elephant" (National Society for the Prevention of Blindness; <u>Poems and Prayers for the Very Young</u>)

Review the five senses as you label each picture on the poster: taste, touch, smell, hearing, sight.

Resources:

j362.4W853c	<u>Connie's New Eyes</u> (Bernard Wolf); girl with guide dog
j636.7R22b	<u>"Banner, Forward!": The Pictoral Biography of a Guide Dog</u> (Eva Rappaport) b&wh photos; detailed text

Reading

Read a poem.

Rhyming words: Child thinks of as many rhyming words as he can for "egg," "ear," "eat," and "ease."

(Alone) Hand-eye coordination: Child traces over lines and figures you've drawn on worksheet (| -\ /) - several of each.

Kinesthetic: Using two fingers and repeating sounds for E e, trace letter shape on the letter card, in the air, and on your back.

Music

Bridge of Avignon

Arithmetic

Have child look around the room for the squares he can see.

Classifying: Sort square shapes from others; match with correct patterns on file folder.

Stamp rubber stamps along penciled outline of square. (Page 3 of book)

God's World

Things That Happen to Me

Explain these concepts/terms:

1) Goosebumps (tiny muscles under hair or skin tighten up and make hair stand on end)

2) Fever (temperature of 103 degrees or more; means you have infection or disease)

3) Itch (message brain gets from skin nerves about irritation)

4) Chapped skin (red, rough and cracked skin from natural skin oil being dried up/licked off/washed off)

5) Blister (bump of watery stuff [tissue fluid] that pops up when you get a burn rub from shoe, sunburn]; tissue fluid protects burned skin and helps burn stop hurting)

Physical Education
Somersaults; jump forward and backward over the line.

Story
Mousekin's Golden House (Edna Miller)
Spectacles (Ellen Raskin)

Memory Verse
"My eyes are ever toward the Lord…" Psa. 25:15a

WEEK 8   FRIDAY

Visit blind/deaf school - or - make popcorn balls.

Preparation for next week:

General:
_____Read over lesson plans
_____List materials needed
_____Collect materials needed
_____Story pages etc., to notebook

Library:
_____Return books used this week
_____Check out books for week after next

Field Trips:
_____Reconfirm next Friday's trip
_____Thank you note for last trip
_____Set up trip for week after next

WEEK 9   MONDAY

Bible
Label top of new sheet of construction paper: God Created Families.
Tell child that God created families as units to care for each other. Talk
    about what families do. (have children, take care of each other,
    celebrate each others' good times, help each other through sad times,
    way for children to learn, provide basic necessities-food, clothing,
    shelter)
Each family is special and has its own rules. Also, God gives us guidelines
    and rules to help our family:
        1) We are to love one another.
        2) The husband and wife are to be faithful to each other.
        3) Parents are to train their children.
        4) Children are to honor and obey their parents.
        5) We are to speak kindly to each other.
        6) We are to be loyal to our family and take care of each other.
Find, cut out, and glue on poster pictures of families doing things together.
Who gave us our families? (God did.)

Reading

Read a poem.

Introduce "F f" letter shape and sound. Have child trace letter while saying sound.

(Alone) Classifying: Child sorts F f cards from A a-E e cards and matches them with the F's and f's on the file folder.

Sequence and complete sentences: Have child dictate story to you about making popcorn balls last Friday.

Art

Draw and color pictures of each family member. Save for Wednesday.

Arithmetic

Triangles: Read Shapes, Shapes, Shapes (Tana Hoban)

Show child triangle cut out of sandpaper/indoor-outdoor carpeting. Name it as a TRIANGLE. Have the child say (complete sentence), "This is a triangle." Have him trace around edges. Note with him that a triangle has three straight sides and that the first few letters of the word "tri" mean "three" (Ex.: tricycle, tripod, tricornered hat).

Have child color eight triangles on worksheet you've made (one of each color). This will be page one of his book on triangles.

Character Building

Loyalty to God: I need to learn all that God wants me to do and say, and to follow His suggestions/plan. I need to stick to God, and not let anyone or anything tempt me into saying or doing something that would make God sad. We need to build God up, not break Him down in our words about Him and about other things. No matter what others say about God, we need to defend Him and His honor.

A dog is a good example of loyalty. When he sees his master coming home, he's so glad to see him that he wags his tail and gets all excited. He follows the master and wants to be near him. He always depends on him. That's how we need to be with God - loyal!

On Character Building story page, write: God wants me to be loyal to Him.

Physical Education

Throwing and catching ball.

Story

The Little Family (Lois Lenski)

Rainy Day Together (Ellen Parsons)

Memory Verse

"What is desired in a man is kindness." Prov. 19:22a

WEEK 9   TUESDAY

Bible

When a man and a woman get married, they are partners in a new "company" - their family. They each give the other ideas to solve many problems and situations. What happens if they each have a different idea to solve a problem? God has said that the man, the husband, is the head of the household. He makes the final decision. Dad is the leader of our family. He makes his decisions, with love for our family, the best he can. God says this is how a family is to run. The mom and children are to respect his authority and be supportive of him.

Divide piece of construction paper into three areas. On top 1/3 write: Dad; on middle 1/3 write: Mom; on bottom 1/3 write: Children.

For top area, cut out picture (magazine/drawing) of father as leader; glue.

Who said Dad is our family's leader? (<u>God</u> did.)

Reading

Read a poem.

(Alone) Left to right eye movement: On worksheet you make up, have child color objects, shapes in horizontal rows, starting from left and going to the right.

Visual discrimination: (Equip.: bread tags [6 of each of 4 colors], 2 sets of crayons) Hold up different "sets" of objects and have the child find the exact objects to make a matching set. (Ex.: 2 blue bread tags, 2 white bread tags, and a green crayon) Do several times.

Speech: Have child "read" book to you.

Music

I've Been Working on the Railroad

Down By the Station

Arithmetic

Draw a triangle on the chalkboard. Ask the child what the shape is. Have him answer in a complete sentence, "This is a triangle." Ask how many straight lines make a triangle. (3)

Classifying: Sort triangle wallpaper shapes on cards from cards with circles and squares. Match the triangle cards with corresponding matching patterns on the file folder.

Have the child paint with watercolors each of another set of eight triangles on another worksheet page. This will be page two in his triangle book.

God's World

Transportation: Individual

Talk about ways of a person or family traveling: walking, bicycle, horse, motorcycle, car, truck, taxi. Talk about differences in 1) cost of method (purchase, upkeep), 2) time it takes, 3) upkeep, 4) how weather would affect method used, and 5) benefits of each.

Poem: "Stop/Go" (Dorothy Baruch)

Resources:

j629.1 S538w	<u>What Happens at a Gas Station</u> (Arthur Shay); photos
j629.224 R517t	<u>Trucks & Super Trucks</u> (Norman & Pat Richards); '80 photos (Truck: tractor-trailer, dump truck, delivery truck, emergency, recreational)

Physical Education

Balance on one foot and then the other; running.

Notes

Story

I Read Symbols (Tana Hoban)

William's Doll (Charlotte Zolotow)

Memory Verse

"Every kingdom divided against itself is brought to desolation, and a house divided against a house falls." Luke 11:17b

WEEK 9   WEDNESDAY

Bible

Dad also provides for our family. He gives us lots of love and he works to provide for us a home, food, clothes, and other nice things. Three "basic necessities" for every person are food, home/shelter, and clothing. These are different in type depending on where you live in the world, what the culture is, personal taste, and income. It is important for us to be thankful to Dad for the food, home, and clothes we have. God tells us we must not compare.

Draw/cut out from magazines/take instant photographs of Dad working to earn a living to provide for our family. Glue in the top 1/3 of poster.

Besides being a leader of our family, what else does Dad do? (provides us with food, clothing, and shelter)

Reading

Read a poem.

Auditory discrimination: Have child sort wallpaper shapes on cards into three piles of circles, triangles, and squares (10 of each shape).

Listening: Have child repeat your sequences of words.

family, rules, loyalty	partner, head, Dad
provider, protector, caregiver	transportation, walk, drive
bicycle, motorcycle, scooter	bus, train, airplane
individual, group, airport	depot, caboose, chugging
freight car, engine, passenger	jetway, baggage, captain
engineer, co-pilot, attendant	gasoline, horsepower, oil
fuel, cost, exercise	rest, relaxation, sleep

Art

Cut out Monday's pictures of family members. Glue each on to tongue depressor/popsicle stick to make puppets.

Arithmetic

Have child look around the room for the triangles he can see.

Classifying: Sort triangle wallpaper shapes from others; match with correct patterns on file folder.

Stamp rubber stamps along penciled outline of triangle. (Page 3 of book)

Health/Manners

Importance of Rest/Sleep

1) God tells us to rest.
2) Sleep allows body to grow.
3) Sleep allows many organs to slow down, rest.

4) Sleep helps you be alert and learn well.
5) It is essential for maintenance of general health.
6) Sleep helps protect you against colds, germs, diseases.
7) Sleep helps you have a pleasant attitude (grumpy when tired).
8) Sleep helps you be able to do your best.
On "Personal Health and Safety" story page, write: I get plenty of sleep
    each night to take good care of my body.

Physical Education
Up and down from squatting position to music.

Story
Cars (Anne Rockwell)
A Special Birthday (Symeon Shimm)

Memory Verse
"Wives, submit to your own husbands, as is fitting in the Lord. Husbands,
    love your wives and do not be bitter toward them. Children, obey your
    parents in all things, for this is well pleasing to the Lord." Col. 3:18-20.

WEEK 9   THURSDAY

Bible
Dad is our family's protector. He does his best to keep our family safe and
    to make sure we don't see or read bad things. He may say "no" when
    you ask him to do something or go somewhere because he loves you
    so much he wants to protect you. Can you think of some way Dad has
    protected you? (Held child when afraid, held hand in crossing street,
    said child could not watch a TV program) God has given you your Dad
    to help you stay safe.
Draw/cut out from magazine/take instant photograph of Dad protecting
    you; glue to top 1/3 of poster.

Reading
Read a poem.
Rhyming: Child names as many rhyming words as possible with "fish,"
    "food," "frog," and "five."
(Alone) Hand-eye coordination: Child colors picture from coloring book.
Kinesthetic: Using two fingers and repeating "f" sound, child traces "F f" on
    letter card, in air, and on your back.

Music
Old Brass Wagon
Home Sweet Home

Arithmetic
Cut out pictures in the shapes of triangles from magazines. Glue to page 4.
Put book pages together; punch holes, reinforce holes; tie with yarn/string.
    Label front of book: TRIANGLES.

Learning At Home

Notes

God's World

Explain "mass transportation" - a form of transportation that runs on a schedule and carries a large number of people. Talk about these ways of mass transportation: bus (city, cross country); train (commuter, cross-country); airplane (commercial).

Talk about differences between these and individual: pay each trip; not responsible for maintenance; must go at scheduled time; less privacy.

Read:

j656 S253t	Train Whistles, A Language in Code (Helen Roney Sattler); whole page color illus.; easy text

Resources:

j656 B96h	How Engines Talk (David Robert Burleigh); trains; easy text; color illus. Talks re: train whistler
j656 E51a	All Aboard! The Railroad Trains That Built America (Mary Elting); some good pictures; ref., history
j629.344 R978s	See Inside An Airport (Jonathan Rutland); some photos, some color drawings, quite a bit of words
j385 L766p	Peter Lippman's Busy Trains
j385 R643g	The Great Book of Railways; great color pictures and photos

Physical Education

Walk in circle without losing balance.

Story

My Little Island (Frane Lesac); bright color paintings of older boy and friend who visit island that boy grew up on

We're Taking an Airplane Trip (Dinal Moche); Golden Book

The Bunny Book (Patricia and Richard Scarry); Golden Book

Memory Verse

"But as for me and my house, we will serve the Lord." Joshua 24:15

WEEK 9   FRIDAY

Visit an airport.

Preparation for next week:

General:

_____Read over lesson plans

_____List materials needed

_____Collect materials needed

_____Story pages etc., to notebook

Library:

_____Return books used this week

_____Check out books for week after next

94

Field Trips:
_____Reconfirm next Friday's trip
_____Thank you note for last trip
_____Set up trip for week after next

WEEK 10   MONDAY

Bible
God tells parents to train their children (Prov. 22:6). Dad and Mom are teachers. They teach roles, skills and school subjects. What roles do Dad and Mom teach? (boy will be father/husband - leader, provider, protector, loving family; girl will be mother/wife - teacher, loving family, homemaker, caregiver) What skills do you learn from Dad and Mom? (homemaking, housekeeping, maintenance on things, carpentry, sewing/crafts, etc.) What school subjects do Mom and Dad teach you? (reading, arithmetic, writing/communication, history, science [learning about the world that God has made], physical education, art, music, etc.)

The fourth thing that Dad and Mom teach you are values, spiritual guidelines, and service to others. The Holy Bible is the "textbook" on how to live successfully and be happy and obedient.

Take photo/draw and cut out pictures/cut out from magazines and glue pictures of Dad and Mom teaching in some way. Glue to the top 1/3 and middle 1/3 of poster.

Who told parents to teach and train their children? (God did.)

Reading
Read a poem.

Introduce letters "G g" and its two sounds (guh, juh). Child repeats the two sounds as he traces letter cards.

(Alone) Classifying: Child sorts G and g cards from A a - F f cards; matches with the G's and g's on the file folder.

Sequence and complete sentences: Child dictates story about trip to the airport.

Art
Draw and color airport on butcher paper. Label.

Arithmetic
Today we are going to look at a whole object and the parts to make a whole. (Fold construction paper circle in half. Cut in half. Show child how to fit the pieces together and then have him do it. Tell him that each half is a semi-circle.

Have child use file folder matching game (drawing of two circles in file folder: one with marking to divide in halves, other with markings to divide in quarters). Have child choose the correct pieces to match on to the patterns to fill in the circle. Repeat with another size/pattern.

Show child how we write this fraction (part) of the whole: 1/2 (one part of two) and 1/4 (one part of four).

Have child match fraction symbols with pieces of the whole.

Character Building

Loyalty to your family: Each family has different rules. We need to respect our parents' decisions by obeying our family's rules, no matter if we are at home or not, no matter if our parents are there or not. We still need to obey what we know is right.

Loyalty to our family means that we show love and that we care for our family always, no matter what happens to them.

We need to stick up for our family, to build it up, never saying anything against our parents or brothers/sisters or our family as a unit, no matter what anyone else says to disagree or make fun of anything about our family.

On the Character Building story page, write: God wants me to be loyal to my family.

Physical Education

Kicking ball; running

Story

Blueberries for Sal (Robert McCloskey)

But Not Billy (Charlotte Zolotow)

Memory Verse

"…hear the instruction of your father, and do not forsake the law of your mother;" Prov. 1:8

WEEK 10   TUESDAY

Bible

God wants Dads and Moms to love each other and their children. Let's talk about how we do this. Mom and Dad are faithful and loyal to each other. (They don't like any other man/woman more than each other.) Dad and Mom treat each other special. Dad brings flowers for Mom and builds her up; he treats Mom with respect/manners, gives Mom ideas/guidelines to help her; is thoughtful; listens to Mom. Mom tries to fit in with Dad's plans and be flexible and thoughtful of Dad; she tries to help Dad face job prepared - have clothes ready and lunch packed; listens to Dad. Dad and Mom care for and play with children; listen and talk with children to show love for them. They try to help children see God's love. Because they love their children, they discipline them for their good, to train them. Also, hugs and kisses for all!

Take photo/draw/cut out from magazine pictures of Dad and Mom showing love to each other or to children.

Reading

Read a poem.

(Alone) Visual discrimination: Child sorts beans and seeds (about 5 each of 6-12 different kinds) into segments in egg carton.

Speech: Have child "read" book to you.

Music

Row, Row, Row Your Boat

Arithmetic

Have child use file folder with circles marked in 1/3's and 1/6's. Talk about the whole being divided into 3 parts. One of those parts is one of three, so it is called one third. Talk about how we write 1/6.

Cut piece of bologna (or other circle of food) in thirds and then in sixths. It began as one whole slice of bologna. Now we have six smaller pieces. They all fit back together to make one whole piece.

Have child match fraction symbols with pieces of the whole. Work with file folders to match the correct pieces to fill up the circles divided in 1/2, 1/4, 1/3, 1/6.

God's World

Transportation: "Olden day" - Horse and wagon, stagecoach, covered wagon.

Look at pictures of "olden day" transportation and talk with child about what changes have been made in all forms of transportation. (walking, bicycle, motorcycle, car/truck, horse, bus, train, airplane)

Resources:

j380 K791   The Look-It-Up Book of Transportation (Bernice Kohn); good photos, detailed text

j380 T92   Wheels: A Pictoral History (Edwin Tunis); detailed text; but wonderful line drawings

Physical Education

Walk backwards; tiptoe.

Story

Little Toot (Hardie Gramatky)
The Runaway Bunny (Margaret Wise Brown)

Memory Verse

"Train up a child in the way he should go, And when he is old he will not depart from it." Prov. 22:6

WEEK 10   WEDNESDAY

Bible

Mom helps Dad and cares for the children.

I. Mom is helper to Dad (Ex.: holds tools/flashlight when Dad is working on project; gets lunch and clothes cleaned and ready for work; takes care of paying household bills). Explain that a bill is an amount of money to be paid for a thing (water, electricity) or a service (doctor, taxes).

II. Mom cares for the children. Have child give examples of what Mom did to care for him as a baby, and then now. Include physical needs: food, clothing, shelter, medical care, keeping them clean; emotional needs: hugs and kisses, holding them, disciplining them; intellectual areas: reading to them, helping them use their mind; spiritual areas: answering questions about God, nature, etc.; social: helping children develop good manners and learn how to be a good friend.

These jobs are very important.
Find/draw and cut out/take photo of Mom helping Dad and caring for the children; glue to the middle 1/3 of poster.

Reading

Read a poem.
Auditory discrimination: Child listens to sets of two words and tells you if beginning sounds are same/different.

fog, fan	goat, go
frog, vine	goat, boat
valley, follow	goal, glory
farm, friend	home, gate
fantastic, feet	gentle, generous

(Alone) Closure: On worksheet, draw 12 shapes (circles, triangles, and squares) with parts of their lines missing. Child fills in the gap with crayon/pencil.
Listening: Child repeats sequence of words after you.

Dad, teacher, Mom	
training, Proverbs, obedience	roles, skills, school
caregiver, Dad, children	loyalty, love, partners
ferryboat, bridge, road	transportation, stagecoach, horse
Mom, caring, helping	ship, sailboat, waterway
exercise, muscle, heart	homemaker, organizer, attitude
children, responsibility, fun	husband, wife, partners
jump, backwards, aerobic	kicking, running, tiptoe

Art

Make Thanksgiving cards for family and friends using rubber stamps/ stickers/drawings.

Arithmetic

Using 3 graham crackers, show child how one whole graham cracker looks; break second one in half; break a third one into fourths. Show how each different fractional part is a different size and they all fit together to make whole crackers.
Have child use file folder matching squares into halves and fourths with the pieces of the whole.
Have child match fraction symbols with pieces of the whole.

Health/Manners

Importance of Exercise
1) Stewardship of our body.
2) Helps strengthen muscles.
3) Helps us relax and get rid of tension.
4) Helps strengthen our lungs.
5) Gives our whole body oxygen needed for building body.
6) It is fun.
7) Makes us feel good.
8) Helps us learn to control parts of our bodies.
9) Strengthens our heart.
Have child name different kinds of exercise he can think of.
Optional: Tell child about aerobic exercise.
On "Personal Health and Safety" story page, write: I exercise daily to keep my body healthy and fit.

Physical Education
Walk on a straight line; jump forward and backward over line. (I use masking tape on carpet and take it up as soon as we are done so it comes up easily.)

Story
Freight Trains (Donald Crews)
Goodnight, Aunt Lilly (M. Madigan); Golden Books

Memory Verse
"Marriage is honorable among all..." Heb. 13:4a

WEEK 10   THURSDAY

Bible
Mom is a homemaker. She makes sure the house is cared for. She cleans and teaches children skills so they can clean, too. Part of Mom's role are:
1) Cleaning home (sweeping, dusting, cleaning, vacuuming, changing sheets, etc.) and delegating this and other jobs
2) Planning menus, making grocery list, shopping for food
3) Cooking meals
4) Doing laundry and ironing
5) Being best steward of dollars/income to provide clothing, food and other purchases
6) Coordinating gift-making/purchasing for birthdays, Christmas
7) Setting tone for home - cheerful, pleasant, relaxing, thankful
8) Hostessing to guests
9) Making sure home runs as smoothly as possible

Take photo/draw/find picture of Mom doing one of her jobs in the homemaking role.

Explain about step-parents: one parent had been married before. Then he/she married another woman/man. That woman/man is the child's step-parent.

Reading
Read a poem.
Rhyming: Child names words to rhyme with "go," "gate," and "gem."
(Alone) Hand-eye coordination: Child completes sewing card(s).
Kinesthetic: Using two fingers and repeating two sounds, child traces "G g" on letter cards, in the air, on your back.

Music
She'll Be Coming Round the Mount
London Bridge

Arithmetic
Cut sandwich in half. Ask child how many parts there are. Then cut each half again in half. How many parts are there now? (4) Then again cut each part in half. How many parts are there now? (8) As we divide the whole into more parts, each piece gets smaller, doesn't it?

Have child complete the file folder matching 1/8's into the whole circle marked with 1/8's.

Have child do worksheet you make: Draw circles/squares marked in fractional parts with a fraction next to it (Ex.: 1/3 next to circle divided into thirds). Child colors part shown by fraction. (one part in three) Have child do several on the page.

Read: <u>What's Inside</u> (Duane Daughtry)

God's World

Transportation: Roads, Bridges, Tunnels, Waterways

Talk about what "paths" are needed to get from one place to another: roads, bridges, tunnels, railroad tracks, waterways.

Look at book(s) about ships/boats or read Boat Book (Gail Gibbons).

Resources:

j387 B274s	<u>Picture Library - Ships</u> (N. S. Barrett)
j387 Z17	<u>The Big Book of Real Boats & Ships</u> (George Zaffo)
j387.1 M186B	<u>Big City Port</u> (Betsy Maestro & Ellen Del Vecchio)
j387.2 G441B	<u>Boat Book</u> (Gail Gibbons)

Physical Education

Balance on balance beam/curbstone for 10 feet.

Story

<u>The Quilt Story</u> (Tony Johnston and Tomie dePaola)
<u>Dig, Drill, Dump, Fill</u> (Tana Hoban)
<u>We Help Mommy</u> (Jean Cushman) Golden Book
<u>We Help Daddy</u> (Mimi Stein) Golden Book
<u>My Little Book of Boats</u> (M. Hanrahan) First Golden Book

Memory Verse

"Children, obey your parents in the Lord, for this is right." Eph. 6:1

WEEK 10   FRIDAY

Scavenger hunt in woods/park.

Preparation for next week

General:
_____Read over lesson plans
_____List materials needed
_____Collect materials needed
_____Story pages etc., to notebook

Library:
_____Return books used this week
_____Check out books for week after next

Field Trips:
_____Reconfirm next Friday's trip
_____Thank you note for last trip
_____Set up trip for week after next

WEEK 11   MONDAY

Bible

Children's jobs within the family

I.   Love family - do thoughtful, kind things (flowers to Mom, pretty rocks to Dad, putting others' toys and clothes away without grumbling, hug, build others up - not break them down). Have child give as many examples as he can think of.

II. Help and encourage each other (come tell Mom/Dad if other one hurt, help with a skill or pouring a cup of milk; encourage each other to meet a goal or learn a skill-encourage sister not to be afraid of climbing to top of slide; encourage brother to throw a ball well).

Take photo/find or draw picture of children loving, helping, and encouraging one another. Glue to bottom 1/3 of poster.

Reading

Read a poem.

Introduce "H h" letter shape and sound. Child repeats sound while tracing letter card.

(Alone) Classifying: Child sorts H and h cards from A a-G g cards; matches them with the H's and h's on the file folder.

Sequence and complete sentences: Child dictates story about scavenger hunt in the woods/park from last Friday.

Art

Make collage from magazine cutouts of what child is thankful for.

Arithmetic

Introduce concept of first, second, third. The FIRST is the thing/person at the beginning. The SECOND is the thing after the first. The THIRD is just after the second thing.

Say three words. Ask your child which word you said first? second? third? (Repeat concept with other words.)

Read: What Happens Next? (Bill Gillham)

For first page of FIRST, SECOND, THIRD book child will be making, on middle of worksheet page with three items in a row across, have child color the first (house/heart, etc.). On top of the page write first 1st.

Character Building

Talk about thankfulness. Ask child to name all the things he is thankful for - his physical things and abilities.

On the Character Building story page, write: I am thankful for _____.

Physical Education

Hop on one foot at a time.

Story

Peter's Chair (Ezra Jack Keats) sibling rivalry

Talking Without Words (Marie Hall Ets)

Memory Verse
"Let your father and mother be glad…" Prov. 23:25a
"God shall bless us…" Ps. 67:7a

WEEK 11   TUESDAY

Bible
Children's jobs within the family (continued)
Review yesterday's lesson.
- III. Respect parents.
  - A. Respect their authority and position and their care for you.
  - B. Work with willing hands.
  - C. Speak without grumbling; with cheerful, pleasant voice.
  - D. Speak nicely to others about their parents.
  - E. Listen carefully to what their parents say.
  - F. Have attitude of thankfulness and gratitude.
- IV. Obey parents. So important to God. Obey the first time you are asked to form the habit of obedience (important in relationship with God, too), to stay safe when parents are trying to protect you, to show them you love them and trust them, as an example to other children as to how you should treat parents (be a leader), and to learn discipline so when you get older self discipline will be easier and more of a habit.

Take photo/find or draw picture of children obeying and respecting parents. Glue on to bottom 1/3 of poster.

Reading
Read a poem.
(Alone) Left-to-right eye movement: Make worksheet with X on left side and dots across page from it to right side (6-10 lines on a page). Child starts at the X and connects the dots to the other side of the page.
Visual discrimination: Child sorts cards with two letters on each into sets of like cards (2 each of aa, ab, cd, ce, df, dg, ea, ee, fi, fe).
Speech: Child "reads" book to you.

Music
Prayer of Thanksgiving
We Gather Together

Arithmetic
Ask child to do three things (Ex.: hop, nod, wave). Which did you do first? Second? Third? (Repeat concept with other movements.)
For second page of FIRST, SECOND, THIRD book, on top of another worksheet write: second 2nd and have child color second item in a row of three things.

God's World
Communication with those we love
Post Office - how a letter gets delivered
Read:
j383.4 G441p   The Post Office Book - Mail and How it Moves (Gail Gibbons)

Physical Education
Bounce ball and catch.

Story
A Letter Goes to Sea (Lore Leger)
Bright Fawn and Me (Jay Leech and Zane Spencer)

Memory Verse
"Let no corrupt communication proceed out of your mouth..." Eph. 4:29a

WEEK 11   WEDNESDAY

Bible
Children's jobs within the family (continued)
Review jobs so far: 1) love family; 2) help and encourage each other; 3) respect parents; 4) obey parents
V. Be good learners. Accept parents' wisdom, instruction (Prov. 19:20). Learn well future roles and skills, good values and habits, and school subjects. How can you best be learners?
  A. Respect parents.
  B. Want to learn.
  C. Want to do your best.
  D. Get enough rest, so brain can think well.
  E. Eat right, so body not thinking of food during school; "machine" running well.
Take photo/find or draw and cut out pictures of child learning. Glue to bottom 1/3 of poster.

Reading
Read a poem.
Auditory discrimination: Child repeats clapping patterns after you.
(Alone) Missing part: Child matches missing part cards with picture cards (animals, people, buildings).
Listening: Child repeats sequence of words after you say them:

posture, back, spine	neck, aligned, tummy
shoulders, straight, tall	children, responsibility,
jobs, qualities, attitude	helpers love, sister, brother
encourage, build up, loyalty	thankfulness, family, God
respect, obey, honor	learner, skills, roles
school, attention, progress	provider, protector, caregiver
teacher, homemaker, children	communication, letter, post office
mail, postage, delivered	telephone, dial, lines

Art
Make Pilgrim hats (butcher paper and construction paper).

Arithmetic
Show child three pictures that tell a story. What happened first? second? third? Mix pictures up and have child put into sequential order.

For third page in FIRST, SECOND, THIRD book, on top of the third worksheet, write third 3rd. Have child color the third item in the row of three items.

Health/Manners
Good Posture
Show correct ways to sit and stand.
Checklist: head back, shoulders back and down, tummy in, bottom tucked in.
Good posture lines up backbone. It helps all inside organs stay in place. Practice showing poor posture and good posture.
Review "Personal Health and Safety" story page so far.
On "Personal Health and Safety" story page write: I stand straight and tall.

Physical Education
Jump to music and stop when music stops.

Story
The Everyday Train (Amy Ehrlich)
Emily (Domitille De Presence)

Memory Verse
"Apply your heart to instruction And your ears to words of knowledge."
Prov. 23:12

WEEK 11   THURSDAY

Bible
Review each family member's role over/next to picture with medium tip marker. (Dad: leader, provider, protector, teacher, loves family; Mom: teacher, loves family, Dad's helper, cares for children, homemaker; Children: love family and help each other, respect and obey parents, good learner.)

Reading
Read a poem.
Rhyming: Child names as many words as possible to rhyme with "hot," "huff," "huge," "hid."
(Alone) Hand-eye coordination: Child does puzzle(s).
Kinesthetic: Using two fingers and repeating sound, child traces H h on letter card, in air, on your back.

Music
Over the River and Through the Woods
Come Ye Thankful People Come

Arithmetic
Line up four shapes (three same and one different). Ask child which one is different (first, second, or third)?
For fourth page in book, write at top:

The 1st house is red.
The 2nd house is yellow.
The 3rd house is blue.

Then have the child color the houses correspondingly.
On cover of book write: FIRST, SECOND, THIRD
by Name
Date
Punch holes, reinforce with gummed reinforcements, and tie together.

God's World

Communication - Phones
Talk about telephones. How are they used? (emergencies: fire, police,
    medical help; talk with friends and relatives; call stores; get information)
Make string and paper cup/tin can telephones.
Optional - Read:
j001.56 G659s   Signs (Ron and Nancy Goor); photos of signs

Physical Education

Balance on balance beam/curbstone for 10 feet.

Story

Angus Lost (Marjorie Flack)

Memory Verse

"The Lord has done great things for us; whereof we are glad." Ps. 126:3
"...be thankful." Col. 3:15c

WEEK 11   FRIDAY

Visit the post office, or make Thanksgiving cookies.

Preparation for next week

General:
_____Read over lesson plans
_____List materials needed
_____Collect materials needed
_____Story pages etc., to notebook

Library:
_____Return books used this week
_____Check out books for week after next

Field Trips:
_____Reconfirm next Friday's trip
_____Thank you note for last trip
_____Set up trip for week after next

WEEK 12   MONDAY

Bible

Begin family tree. Tell child that it shows names of each family member for several generations. What is a generation? (Note: this will be going back three generations from child; can be referred back to whenever you read passage of Scripture "to the third and fourth generations.")

Put parents' names and birthdates on family tree. Then put child's name and birthdate (and those of brothers and sisters, too) on the family tree.

Ask child to name grandparents on father's side. Add their full names and birthdates. Tell a little about each of the people: where they grew up; how they met; where they lived; what they did. Select one or two positive character traits about each. You can write a short "story" using a few sentences about each of the child's ancestors - to follow the family tree in the child's notebook.

Child can draw a picture of each grandparent.

Reading

Read a poem.

Introduce letter shape "I i" and its two sounds (ih, eye). While repeating sounds, child traces letter card.
(Alone) Classifying: Child sorts I and i cards from A a - H h cards and then matches to the I's and i's on the file folder.

Sequence and complete sentences: Child dictates story about making Thanksgiving cookies last Friday.

Art

Make different textures collage (macaroni, string, fabric, yarn, etc.)

Look at book: A Family (Carl Larsson, painter); j759.85L334f.

Arithmetic

Using three items of differing weights, have your child feel each one and arrange the items in sequential order from lightest to heaviest.

(Construction note: Make 4 gradations of each of the 8 colors in a box of watercolors - paint onto index card squares. Let dry. These will be used for today and the next two days and will be mounted by child on to empty squares of the same size on a LIGHTEST TO DARKEST page for his notebook - 8 rows of 4 spaces each.)

Using the red and then the orange color gradations, have child arrange in order from lightest to darkest. You check for accuracy. Then have the child glue the red gradations onto the top row; orange on the second.

Character Building

Talk about thankfulness for the freedom to worship God freely and for God's love to us. Explain that in many countries in the world it would not be as easy for us to worship and learn about God.

On Character Building story page, write: I am thankful God loves me. I am thankful I can learn about God and sing songs to Him.

Physical Education

Stand on one foot and then the other (balance); hop.

Story

Little Bear's Thanksgiving (Janice Brustlein)
The Patchwork Quilt (Valerie Flournoy)

Memory Verse

"You are my God, and I will praise You;" Ps. 118:28a

WEEK 12   TUESDAY

Bible

Review family tree thus far. Today, follow yesterday's format, only talking about child's maternal grandparents. Tell "story" about each one; put names and birthdates on family tree; draw picture of each one.

Reading

Read a poem.
Left-to-right eye movement: Put 5 colored picture cards in a horizontal row on the table. Child "reads" the sequence by naming each card in the row, beginning at the left.
(Alone) Visual discrimination: Dominos - child matches like ends together, seeing how long a line he can make.
Speech: Child "reads" book to you.

Music

Over the River and Through the Woods
Prayer of Thanksgiving

Arithmetic

Have child arrange three or four items in order from lightest to heaviest by feeling their weight.
Using the yellow and then the green gradations (4 each), have child arrange each set in order from lightest to darkest. You check for accuracy. Then have child glue yellow cards to third row; green to fourth.

God's World

Talk about pilgrims' courage to follow beliefs in God and wanting freedom for their families.

Physical Education

Balance on balance beam/curbstone for 10 feet.

Story

The Coming of the Seasons (E. Brooks Smith)
Dandelion Hill (Clyde Robert Bulle)

Memory Verse
"I will praise You, O Lord with my whole heart." Ps. 9:1

WEEK 12   WEDNESDAY

Bible
Brief review of family tree. Add names and birthdates for children's great-grandparents. Follow Monday's format. ("Story"; names and birthdates on "tree"; photo, if possible, of each one.)
Resource:
j575.1S559m   Me and My Family Tree (Paul Showers)

Reading
Read a poem.
Rhyming: Child names as many rhyming words as possible for "it," "is," "ill," "if."
(Alone) Maze: Child uses matchbox car to go through maze drawn with marker on large poster/cardboard.
Listening: Child repeats sequence after you say it.

ancestors, grandma, family	grandpa, heritage, thankful
pilgrims, New England, brave	Holland, Mayflower, Bradford
England, freedom, religion	God, worship, voyage
manners, politely, please	table, thank you, napkin
chewing, turkey, quiet	November, winter, corn
Indians, harvest, courage	houses, crops, hats
shelter, food, clothing	preserving, wise, prepare
hospitality, thank, God	

Art
Make red and green construction paper chain for counting the days until Christmas.

Arithmetic
Have child arrange color gradations from lightest to darkest for blue, purple, brown, and then black. They do one set; you check; they glue to next row. Then they go on to next color (you hand them next set of four cards). Repeat until entire page is done. Put page into notebook.
Read: Big, World, Small Word (Jeanne Titherington)

Health/Manners
Review table manners (see Week 2, Wednesday).

Physical Education
Skip to music and stop when music stops.

Story
My Grandpa Died Today (Joan Fassler)
Over the River and Through the Wood (Lydia Marie Child)
Mailman Mike (Mabel Watts) Golden Book

Memory Verse
"It is good to give thanks to the Lord." Ps. 92:1a

WEEK 12   THURSDAY

H A P P Y   T H A N K S G I V I N G !

WEEK 12   FRIDAY

Visit flour mill if possible

Preparation for next week

General:
_____Read over lesson plans
_____List materials needed
_____Collect materials needed
_____Story pages etc., to notebook

Library:
_____Return books used this week
_____Check out books for week after next

Field Trips:
_____Reconfirm next Friday's trip
_____Thank you note for last trip
_____Set up trip for week after next

WEEK 13   MONDAY

Bible
Read Gen. 2:15-17, 3:1-24 (or tell story using flannel board/drawn pictures). Talk about Adam and Eve's disobedience that led to sin, which led to death.
Review: What did God ask Adam not to do? (eat from the tree of knowledge of good and evil.) What did He say the consequence would be if Adam disobeyed? (He would surely die) Who tempted Eve to question authority, rule? (serpent - Satan) Then Satan/serpent lied to Eve and said, "You will not surely die." What did Eve do next? (She looked at the fruit and thought of how good it looked. She took some and ate it. She gave some to her husband, Adam.) Did Adam eat it? (yes) Did he know it was wrong? (yes) What happened next? (They realized they didn't have any clothes on, so they sewed fig leaves together and made coverings for themselves.) What did Adam and Eve do when they heard God walking in the garden? (they hid) Then God called Adam. Adam answered. God asked Adam how he knew they were without clothes. How did Adam answer? (He blamed God and

Learning At Home

Eve. "The woman you put here with me, she gave me some fruit." Gen. 3:12) God then asked Eve what she had done. How did she answer? (She blamed the serpent.) Did Adam or Eve apologize to God for what they had done that was disobedient? (No, not that we know of.) Did Adam and Eve have consequences because of their disobedience? (yes) What were the consequences to the serpent? (God made it crawl on the ground and made the woman and serpent hate each other.) What was the consequence of disobedience to Eve? (When she gave birth to babies, she would have more pain.) What were the consequences of disobedience to Adam? (He would have to work to eat and live; he would not live forever; he was banished from the Garden of Eden.) Was God happy or disappointed that Adam and Eve had sinned? (disappointed) What can we learn from this story? (Because of their sin, all people must die; obedience is very important to God; there are consequences for our wrong choices.)

Reading

Read apoem.

Introduce letter shapes J j and sound (juh). Child traces letter while repeating sound.

(Alone) Classifying: Child sorts J and j cards from A a - I i cards; matches them to the J's and j's on the file folder.

Sequence and complete sentences: Child dictates story about last Friday's trip to the flour mill.

Art

Draw a picture of flour mill and send it with thank you note to the flour mill.

Arithmetic

Today we are going to learn the symbol to show nothing - that there are no objects at all somewhere. This is the symbol: 0. It is called ZERO. You say it: "Zero." We are going to make a counting book of 0.

On front cover write:　　My Counting Book of 0
                                            by Name
                                            Date

Character Building

Talk about how we respond to God and His love is very important; thankfulness; obedience; sharing with others/generosity; hospitality; service.

On Character Building story page, write: How I respond to God and His love is important.

Physical Education

Indoor bowling.

Story

Linda and Her Little Sister (Golden Book)
A Farmer's Alphabet (Mary Azarian) woodcuts

Memory Verse
"For as in Adam all die, even so in Christ all shall be made alive."
   I Cor. 15:22
"...having heard the word with a noble and good heart, keep it and bear
   fruit with patience." Luke 8:15b

WEEK 13   TUESDAY

Bible
God loves us so much he sent Jesus. Read/tell story of Luke 1:26-56.
   (God, through angel, tells Mary she'll be the mother of Jesus; her
   response.) Use flannel board, if desired, to dramatize the story.
Review: What did the angel say to Mary? ("Greetings, you who are highly
   favored! The Lord is with you.") How did Mary respond? (She was
   afraid.) What did the angel tell Mary? (Not to be afraid; that she, Mary,
   had found favor with God; that she would be pregnant and give birth to
   a son whom she was to name Jesus; and that He, Jesus, would rule over
   a kingdom that would never end.) Mary didn't see how this could be
   since she was a virgin ("was not married" - you choose wording with
   your child). What did the angel say? (That the Holy Spirit of God would
   come upon Mary and that Jesus would be called the Son of God. That
   "nothing is impossible with God." Luke 1:37) How did Mary respond to
   this? (She said, "I am the Lord's servant. May it be to me as you have
   said." Luke 1:38. She was willing to be used by God.)
How we respond to God is so important. We need to be obedient and
   willing, like Mary.
Make puppets (popsicle stick/construction paper on sticks/paper bags) of
   angel and Mary. (These and puppets to be made on following days will
   be used at the end of Week 15 to act out the Christmas story.)

Reading
Read a poem.
Left-to-right eye movement: Put five colored shape cards in a horizontal
   row in front of the child. Child "reads" sequence by naming card ("red
   triangle," etc.) beginning at the left side.
(Alone) Visual discrimination: Child matches two half-pictures that you've
   mounted and then cut in two (faces, etc.). (Make 8-12 sets.)
Speech: Child "reads" familiar book to you.

Music
All Day, All Night
Jingle Bells

Arithmetic
Because zero represents no objects, this counting book will be shorter than
   the rest of the books that you will make.
Have child glue numeral shape 0 to first page.
If there is extra time, have child begin review of folders of shapes/colors/
   seriation work.

God's World

"Again and Again": Night and Day (Sunrise, Sunset, Moon)

Read Gen. 1:14-18. Talk about difference in night and day. What causes it? What does the sun do in the morning? (rise) What does the sun do in the evening? (set) What do we do in the day? In the night? Watch the sun rise and/or set with your child.

Physical Education

Beanbag toss

Story

Christmas Tree on the Mountain (Carol Fenner)

My Big Book of the Seasons (also known as The Wonders of the Seasons) (Bertha Morris Parker)

Memory Verse

"For God so loved the world that He gave his only begotten Son, that whoever believes in Him should not perish but have everlasting life." John 3:16

"This is the day which the Lord has made; we will rejoice and be glad in it." Ps. 118:24

WEEK 13   WEDNESDAY

Bible

Read/tell story of Matt. 1:18-25. (Angel of Lord appears to Joseph to tell him about Mary and Jesus to be born; to take Mary as his wife. He did marry Mary and name the baby Jesus.)

Review: Was Joseph a good man? (yes) Who appeared to Joseph? (angel) What did the angel tell Joseph? (That the baby Mary was going to have was to be named Jesus and that He was special to God.) When Joseph woke up, what did he do? (He obeyed the angel of the Lord and took Mary as his wife. He named the baby Jesus.)

This shows another person who was so obedient to the Lord, even though it probably didn't make sense to him. He didn't question or grumble or procrastinate (put off 'til later); he obeyed right away.

Make Joseph puppet.

Reading

Read a poem.

Auditory discrimination: Child repeats clapping patterns after you.

(Alone) Closure: Child fills in missing parts of 6-8 faces you've drawn on a worksheet.

Listening: Child repeats sequence of words after you.

Adam, disobedient, sin	Eve, consequences, sadness
Satan, tricky, tempting	questioning, rebelling, death
respect, obey, thankfulness	obedience, trust, wisdom
Jesus, love, Christmas	Mary, angel, obedient
donkey, Joseph, journey	Elizabeth, John, cousin

sunrise, moon, revolution	axis, sun, sunset
earth, seasons, again	summer, autumn, spring
winter, night, day	germs, cough, health
virus, sneeze, tissue	balance, bowling, toss

Art

Make bookmarks with magazine picture cutouts and rubber stamps, on index cards cut into strips; cover with Contact paper. Use as Christmas gifts.

Arithmetic

Review what the number name is for No things? ZERO. What does it look like? (0) Where is it on a number line? (at the beginning; it is the point from which we start counting)

For a second page in ZERO book, have child look with you at number line you have made on a sheet of construction paper. Point to the 0. Because it represents no items, we do not color any part of the number line.

Put pages one and two with the cover of the ZERO book, punch and reinforce holes, and tie book together.

Health/Manners

Germs - Coughing and Sneezing
Talk about how colds are passed.
  1) Cover your mouth and nose when coughing or sneezing.
  2) Don't sneeze or cough toward another person.
  3) Don't cough or sneeze over plates of food.
On "Personal Health and Safety" story page, write: I fight germs: I cover my mouth and nose when I cough or sneeze.

Physical Education

Balance on one foot while music is playing and change feet when music stops.

Story

Mousekin's Fables (Edna Miller)
Silent Night (Susan Jeffers)

Memory Verse

"For this purpose the Son of God was manifested, that He might destroy the works of the devil." I John 3:8c

WEEK 13   THURSDAY

Bible

Read/tell story of Luke 2:1-5 (Mary and Joseph's trip to Bethlehem).
Review: The government issued a rule that all the people in the Roman world were to be counted; a census was to take place. All were to go to their town. How did Joseph respond to the government's decree/

rule? (he obeyed) Did he go alone? (No, he took Mary, his pregnant wife.) People back then did not have cars or paved roads. How do you think Mary would have felt traveling on bumpy, dusty roads? (tired, dirty/dusty, uncomfortable)

Reading

Read a poem.

Rhyming: Child names rhyming words for "jet," "job," "jam," "jig."

(Alone) Hand-eye coordination: Child strings beads onto shoelace.

Kinesthetic: Using two fingers and repeating letter sound, child traces J j on letter card, in the air, and on your back.

Music

Go Tell It On the Mountain

Silent Night

The First Noel

Bring a Torch, Jeannette, Isabella

Arithmetic

Review concept of 0.

Have child review folders and activities dealing with previous topics. How many rainbows do you have in your hair? How many koala bears are there in the refrigerator?

God's World

"Again & Again": The Four Seasons

Talk about the four seasons. Read one or more of these books:

j570 B415w	<u>What Happens in the Spring</u>? (Kathleen Costella Beer) National Geographic
j574.543 S237s	<u>Summer, Discovering the Seasons</u> (Louis Santrey)
j574.543 S237sp	<u>Spring, Discovering the Seasons</u> (Louis Santrey)
j574.543 S237a	<u>Autumn, Discovering the Seasons</u> (Louis Santrey)
j574.543 S237w	<u>Winter, Discovering the Seasons</u> (Louis Santrey)
j570 A439r	<u>The Reasons for Seasons: The Great Cosmic Megagalactic Trip Without Moving Your Chair</u> (Linda Allison). Some good ideas for experiments and well-presented information if you overlook references to "millions" of years and some anti-Christ attitudes; good as ref.; present good bits and pieces to children

Physical Education

Balance on balance beam/curbstone for 10 feet.

Story

<u>Around the Year</u> (Tasha Tudor)

<u>Green Eyes</u> (A. Birnbaum)

Memory Verse

"To everything there is a season, A time for every purpose under heaven."
Ecc. 3:1

WEEK 13   FRIDAY

Visit whole wheat bakery

Preparation for next week

General
_____Read over lesson plans
_____List materials needed
_____Collect materials needed
_____Story pages etc., to notebook

Library:
_____Return books used this week
_____Check out books for week after next

Field Trips:
_____Reconfirm next Friday's trip
_____Thank you note for last trip
_____Set up trip for week after next

WEEK 14   MONDAY

Bible
Review Christmas story so far (angel with Mary; Mary pregnant with Jesus; angel with Joseph; Joseph and Mary get married; they travel to Bethlehem to register for census).
Read/tell story of Luke 2:6-7.
Review: What was it time for while Mary and Joseph were in Bethlehem? (Jesus to be born) Did they stay at the inn? (no) Why not? (There was no room for them.) Where did Mary and Joseph and Jesus stay? (in a stable) Do you think the innkeeper knew how important the baby to be born was and would be? (no) How should we treat Jesus in our lives? (very important; as the most important priority; we should always have room in our heart and life for him)

Reading
Read a poem.
Introduce letter shape and sound for K k; child repeats sound as he traces letter card.
(Alone) Classifying: Child sorts K and k cards from A-J and a-j cards; matches them with the K's and k's on the file folder.
Sequence and complete sentences: Child dictates story of last Friday's trip to whole wheat bakery.

Art

Make gingerbread boys/girls for tree decorations: construction paper or cardboard with yarn, pieces of construction paper cut for features, ribbon for bow; punch hole at top to attach ribbon/yarn for hanging.

Arithmetic

Introduce number one and symbol 1. We are going to make a counting book of 1. (Note: Use 3 pieces of construction paper folded in half.) On outside cover, write:

My
Counting Book
of
1
Name   Date

On paper plate with numeral 1 written on middle, have child clip the correct number of spring clothespins to its edge.

For page 1 of "1" book, have child color one shape on worksheet you've made. Cut out picture and mount on page 1.

Have child glue numeral 1 and one object shape to page 2.

Character Building

Sharing/Generosity

Read Hebrews 13:5 "Keep your lives free from the love of money and be content with what you have..."

God doesn't want us to KEEP all we have. He wants us to share some of it with others. What do we have? How can we share? What do others need? (money, friendship, clothes, toys, good example, our friend Jesus)

On Character Building story page write: To share what I have I need to be content and to care about others.

Physical Education

Indoor bowling; hopping.

Story

Christmas in the Barn (Margaret Wise Brown)

Memory Verse

"But do not forget to do good and to share..." Heb. 13:16a

WEEK 14   TUESDAY

Bible

Read poem: "The Friendly Beasts" (anon.)
    Jesus our brother, kind and good,
    Was humbly born in a stable rude,
    And the friendly beasts around Him stood,
    Jesus our Brother, kind and good.

"I," said the donkey, shaggy and brown,
"I carried His Mother up hill and down;
I carried His Mother to Bethlehem town,
I," said the donkey, shaggy and brown.

"I," said the cow, all white and red,
"I gave Him my manger for His bed,
I gave Him my hay to pillow His head,
I," said the cow, all white and red.

"I," said the sheep with curly horn,
"I gave Him my wool for a blanket warm,
He wore my coat on Christmas morn,
I," said the sheep with curly horn.

"I," said the dove from rafters high,
"Cooed Him to sleep so He would not cry,
We cooed Him to sleep, my mate and I,
I," said the dove from rafters high.

Thus, every beast who loved Him well;
In the stable rude was glad to tell
Of the gift he gave Emmanuel,
Of the gift he gave Emmanuel.

Was Jesus born in a fancy place? (no) Did He come into the world in a
    royal way since God said He would be a king? (No, it was a very
    humble beginning.)
Make puppets of a few animals and a manger.

Reading
Read a poem.
Left-to-right eye movement: Child takes different steps (giant, medium,
    baby) left and right as you direct them to.
(Alone) Visual discrimination: Child sorts and matches wallpaper pattern
    cards (3 each of 10 patterns).
Speech: Child "reads" you a book.

Music
The Friendly Beasts
Away In A Manger
O Christmas Tree

Arithmetic
Show child a card with one dot on it. "How many dots are there?" Write 1
    on chalkboard and have child hold up this many fingers. Write
    previous numerals on chalkboard; child holds up correct number of
    fingers.

For page 3 of "1" book have child use 1 strip of paper (1/2" x3")to make loop for chain. Glue ends together. Glue to page 3.

For page 4 of "1" book have child put one sticker on page.

God's World

Shapes in Nature

Talk about the different shapes of mountains, lakes, landforms, islands, earth.

Begin to look through:

j500 S29s   <u>The Seeing Eye</u> (Victor B. Scheffer) An nspired naturalist shows you how to see the marvelous forms, textures and colors of nature, color photos classified by FORM (the outline structure), TEXTURE (the inner parts of the pattern), COLOR

Physical Education

Beanbag toss

Story

<u>Mousekin's Christmas Eve</u> (Edna A. Miller)
<u>Christmas in the Stable</u> (Astrid Lindgren)

Memory Verse

"God loves a cheerful giver." II Cor. 9:7c

WEEK 14   WEDNESDAY

Bible

Read/tell story of Luke 2:8-16 (shepherds and angels)

Review: Who were in the nearby fields? (shepherds) What did the shepherds see? (An angel of the Lord appeared to them.) The Holy Bible says that "the glory of the Lord shone around them" Luke 2:9b. How did they react? (They were terrified. Luke 2:9c) Why do you think they felt this way? (It was probably very bright and they'd probably never experienced/seen anything like this before.) What did the angel say? (Not to be afraid; that he was bringing "good tidings of great joy which will be to all people. For there is born to you this day in the city of David, a Savior, who is Christ the Lord. And this will be the sign to you: You will find the Babe wrapped in swaddling clothes, lying in a manger." Luke 2:10-12) After the angel said that, what happened? (A great company of the heavenly host appeared, "praising God and saying, 'Glory to God in the highest, and on earth peace, good will toward men!'" Luke 2:13b, 14) When the angels left and went to heaven, what did the shepherds do? (They decided to go and hurried off "to see this thing that has come to pass which the Lord has made known unto us." Luke 2:15b, c) Did they find Mary and Joseph and Jesus, the baby? (yes)

Make puppets of more angels and several shepherds.

Reading

Read a poem.

Auditory discrimination: After you read a series of two words, child tells
   whether the beginning sounds are the same or different.

kite, kitten	individual, ask
kept, swept	injury, immediate
pencil, kingdom	elephant, illness
key, kin	Indian, insure
hammock, helpful	jam, jungle
heritage, inherit	valley, joyful
ink, hammer	jubilant, jacks
hopeful, happy	jump, pump

Memory: Have your child look at tray with four items on it; child closes
   eyes; you remove one item; child names missing item. (Increase number
   of items as child's skill increases.)

Listening: Child repeats sequence of words after you.

innkeeper, stable, crowds	manger, animals, birthday
hay, Jesus, humble	sharing, generosity, love
shepherds, sharing, angel	afraid, walking, joyous
gift, meaningful, remember	germs, washing, hygiene
hands, food, health	earth, round, sphere
mountains, lakes, landforms	icicles, snowflakes, crystals
miracles, special, thanks	

Art

Make angels for the table (Using construction paper, glitter, crayons and/or
   paint). Make tabs on either side of "robe" to connect for standing up.

Arithmetic

Have child (with your assistance if needed) match card with numeral 1 on it
   with card that has one object on it. (Have 4 of each and use 4 of 0 cards
   and cards showing no objects, too.)

For page 5 have child use one popsicle stick to make design. Glue to
   page 5.

Stamp one rubber stamp image on page 6.

Review pages done so far. Write numeral 1 on each page as you review
   with child and ask how many items on each page.

Health/Manners

Germs - Washing Hands and Not Sharing Food/Drink

Talk about how germs need to be washed off hands.

   1) Wash hands before eating.

   2) Wash hands after going to the bathroom.

Talk about germs from other people.

   1) I don't eat or drink anything from another person.

   2) I don't share any of my food or drink with others.

   3) If I want to share some food, I have to cut with a clean table
      knife before anyone has eaten from it.

Role-play ways of saying "No, thank you."

On "Health and Safety" story page, write: I don't eat or drink anything from
   another person. I don't share any of my food or drink with others."

Physical Education
Stand/walk on tiptoes while music plays and stop when music stops.

Story
Becky's Christmas (Tasha Tudor): read first half
The Shepherd (Helga Aichinger)

Memory Verse
"Whoever shuts his ear to the cry of the poor will also cry himself and not
be heard." Prov. 21:13

WEEK 14   THURSDAY

Bible
Read/tell the story of Luke 2:17-20 (shepherds spread word and praise
God).
Review: What did the shepherds do after they saw Mary and Joseph and the
baby Jesus? (They spread the word; they told others) How did the
others react? (They were amazed)   How did Mary react? (She "treasured
up all these things and pondered them in her heart." Luke 2:19) What
did the shepherds do after telling others? (They returned, "glorifying and
praising God." Luke 2:20)
Make puppets of several other people - those told the Good News by
shepherds. Do you share the news of Jesus' birth with others?

Reading
Read a poem.
Rhyming: Child names words to rhyme with "kite," "key," "kept," "kin."
(Alone) Hand-eye coordination: Child traces with crayons over lines and
figures you've drawn on worksheet. Do several each of l - \ / O.
Kinesthetic: Using two fingers and repeating sound for K k, child traces
letter card, in the air, and on your back.

Music
Hark! The Herald Angels Sing
Joy to the World
Deck the Halls
O Come All Ye Faithful

Arithmetic
Using 25 counters (bread tags or other small item), have child count them
(with your help) into piles of 1.

God's World
Shapes in Nature
Talk about shapes of: icicles and snowflakes.
Look at under magnifying glass/microscope.
Continue looking at The Seeing Eye book.

Physical Education
Walk in circle without losing balance.

Story
Becky's Christmas (Tasha Tudor); finish from Wednesday.
Christmas Bear (Marie Colmont)
The Animals' Christmas Eve (Gale Wiersum); Golden Book.

Memory Verse
"Give, and it will be given to you... for with the same measure that you use, it will be the measure back to you." Luke 6:38

WEEK 14   FRIDAY

Bake bread together

Preparation for next week

General:
_____Read over lesson plans
_____List materials needed
_____Collect materials needed
_____Story pages etc., to notebook

Library:
_____Return books used this week
_____Check out books for week after next

Field Trips:
_____Reconfirm next Friday's trip
_____Thank you note for last trip
_____Set up trip for week after next

WEEK 15   MONDAY

Bible
Read/tell the story of Matt. 2:1-12 (visit of the magi).
Review: Who came asking about the baby born who was King of the Jews? (magi/wise men) What had they seen? (His star) What did they want to do? (worship Him) How did King Herod feel about this? (he was disturbed) How did the wise men find Jesus? (They followed the star. "The star they had seen in the east went ahead of them until it stopped over the place where the child was." Matt. 2:9c) How did they feel when they saw the star? ("they were overjoyed," Matt. 2:10b) When they saw Mary and the child, what did they do? (They bowed down and worshipped Him.) What did they give him? (respect and gifts: gold, incense, myrrh) Did they report back to Herod? (no) Why not? (they had been warned in a dream not to)
Make three wise men puppets.

Reading

Read a poem.

Introduce "L l" letter shape and sound letter makes. Child traces letter shape on card while repeating sound.

(Alone) Visual discrimination: Child sorts L and l cards from A-J and a-j cards; matches with L's and l's on the file folder.

Sequence and complete sentences: Child dictates story about baking bread last Friday.

Art

Make Christmas gift: Mom - noteholder made from spring-type clothespin with "wings" and feelers glued on to make butterfly. Glue all onto rock.

Arithmetic

Introduce number two and symbol 2. We are going to make a counting book of 2. (Use 3 pieces of construction paper folded in half.) On the outside of the cover write:

My
Counting Book
of
2
Name   Date

On paper plate with numeral 2 written in the middle of it, have child clip the correct number of clothespins to its edge.

Page 1: Have child color 2 shapes on worksheet you make; cut and mount object part to page 1.

Page 2: Have child glue numeral 2 and two object shapes to page 2.

Character Building

Hospitality: This is another part of sharing - sharing our home and friendship with others. Who can we share our home and friendship with? When people come, how can we make them comfortable? (offer food and comfortable chair; get to know them better; have peaceful home; no fighting; have clean home; toys and other things picked up)

On Character Building story page write: Hospitality is sharing my home and friendship with others.

Physical Education

Indoor bowling.

Story

<u>Christmas is a Time of Giving</u> (Joan Walsh Anglund)

Memory Verse

(be)"...given to hospitality." Rom. 12:13b

WEEK 15   TUESDAY

Bible

Read/tell the story of Matt. 2:13-18. (Escape to Egypt; Herod)

Review: Who appeared to Joseph in a dream? (an angel of the Lord) What did the angel tell Joseph to do? (Get up and take Jesus and Mary to Egypt. They were to stay there until the angel told them.) How did Joseph respond? (He got up and obeyed right away, during the night.) How did Herod feel when the wise men did not return to him to tell him where the baby was? ("he was exceedingly angry" Matt.2:16b) What did he do with his anger? (He ordered all baby boys two years old and younger who lived in Bethlehem and the surrounding areas to be killed.) Why do you think Herod was angry? (probably jealous and afraid)

Make a Herod puppet.

Reading

Read a poem.

Left-to-right eye movement: Child copies patterns of beads you've strung and laid on the table (knot at the left).

(Alone) Visual discrimination: Child matches crayons from two boxes (16 crayons each).

Speech: Child "reads" book, using pictures as guide, if necessary.

Music

Hot Cross Buns

Muffin Man

Christmas songs

Arithmetic

Show child a card with two dots on it. How many dots are there?

Write 2 on the chalkboard. Have child hold up correct number of fingers. Repeat with previous numbers.

Page 3: Have child use 2 strips of paper (1/2" x3") to make loops for chain. Glue ends together. Glue 2-loop chain to page 3.

Page 4: Have child put 2 stickers on it.

God's World

Introduce: There are four main groups of food that keep us healthy.

1) Bread/Cereal Group - needed for energy, protein (whole grain)

Read poem: "Pancakes"

    a. Read: j633.1 M683f   <u>From Grain to Bread</u> (Ali Mitgutsch); color drawings.

    b. This group includes all things made from grains - wheat, rye, oats, barley, corn flour, rice, breads, products made with flour(s), cereal.

    c. On construction paper write: 1. BREAD AND CEREAL GROUP. Cut out pictures of items from this group (try to have healthy food pictures available).

Physical Education

Beanbag toss

Story

Brambly Hedge - Winter Story (Jill Barklem)

Memory Verse

"But whoever has this world's goods and sees his brother in need, and shuts up his heart from him, how does the love of God abide in him?" I John 3:17

WEEK 15   WEDNESDAY

Bible

Talk about how Christmas is a celebration of Christ's birth. Does Satan want us to think of Jesus Christ and worship Him? (No!) How does he get us to think of other things on Christmas? (He wants to distract us from the true meaning of Christmas, so he tries to get us to focus on Santa Claus, on lots of things, on getting, and on being busy.) What can we do to counteract this and keep the true celebration of Christmas?

1) Think of the Christmas story and how much God loves us.
2) Use the holiday "season" as a time to do several special things as a family.
3) Give a gift to someone who may not otherwise get one (with a note that Jesus loves him).
4) Make your gifts instead of spending lots of money to buy things.
5) When people ask what you've asked Santa for, tell them that you are celebrating Jesus' birthday.
6) Bake a birthday cake for Jesus. Sing "Happy Birthday" to Him on Christmas. Have a birthday party.
7) Give a gift of yourself to Jesus this Christmas (one new good habit you want to add, a service project to help other people, etc.).
8) Pray for God's help to enable you to think about God's incredible love for us and of Jesus' birth.

Reading

Read a poem.

Auditory discrimination: Child repeats clapping patterns.

(Alone) Closure: Child fills in missing parts of 6-12 faces you drew on chalkboard.

Listening: Child repeats sequences after you say them.

wise men, Herod, jealousy	hospitality, sharing, kindness
celebration, angels, bells	star, love gift, meaning
birth, God, manger	thankfulness, sharing, giving
nutrition, food groups, steward	vegetables, bread, cereal
fruits, grains, oats	barley, wheat, rye
strawberries, raspberries, blueberries	celery, salad, lettuce
vitamins, minerals, carbohydrates	carrots, spinach, squash

Art

Make Christmas gift for Dad.

Arithmetic

Have child match card with numeral 2 on it with card that has two objects on it. (Have 4 of each.) Have numerals 0-1 (and their corresponding object cards) mixed in with them to do, too.

Page 5: Have child use two popsicle sticks to make design. Glue to page 5.

Page 6: Stamp two rubber stamp images to page 6.

Review pages so far. Write 2 at top of each page as you review with child how many items are on each page.

Health/Manners

Manners - Thank-you Notes

Talk about parts of a thank-you note:

1) Who gave the gift?

2) What did they give?

3) When? (what occasion?)

4) How is it special to you?

5) Thanks

6) Who from?

Practice with several situations (birthday, Christmas gifts). Write one or two thank-you notes depending on time, for actual Christmas gifts they received.

On "Manners" story page, write: I remember to send "thank-you" notes.

Physical Education

Balance on one foot while music plays.

Story

Karin's Christmas Walk (Susan Pearson)

Any of the Babar books (Laurent de Brunhoff)

Memory Verse

"Therefore receive one another…" Rom. 15:7a

WEEK 15   THURSDAY

Bible

Act out the Christmas story with the puppets the child has made:

Angel and Mary

Angel and Joseph

Mary and Joseph marry and travel to Bethlehem.

No room in the inn; Jesus born in manger

Angel and shepherds

Shepherds hurry to see Jesus.

Shepherds share the good news.

Wise men

Angel and Joseph; flee to Egypt.

Herod has baby boys killed.

ENJOY YOUR CHRISTMAS!

Reading
Read a poem.

Rhyming: Child names rhyming words for "late," "list," "lack," "led."

(Alone) Hand-eye coordination: Child colors coloring book page picture with crayons.

Kinesthetic: Using two fingers and repeating sound of letter, child traces letter "l" on the card, in the air, and on your back.

Music
We Wish You a Merry Christmas

Jesus Loves Me

Arithmetic
Using 25 counters, have child count them out into piles of 2.

Page 7: Punch 2 holes in paper. Mount to page 7. Write 2 at top of page.

Page 8: Cut and glue two objects from magazine. Write 2 at top of page.

Page 9: Color in correct amount on number line you've drawn. Punch holes through pages after reinforcing; tie.

God's World
2. Fruit/Vegetable Group

a. How many basic food groups are there? (four) What is the first one? (bread/cereal)

b. The next one is the fruit and vegetable group. They are needed for vitamins and minerals.

c. Have child dictate and list all the varieties (s)he can think of for fruit and vegetables.

d. Cut out pictures; glue to poster labeled 2. FRUIT AND VEGETABLES GROUP

Physical Education
Balance on balance beam/curbstone for 10 feet.

Story
Jamberry (Bruce Degen)

My Christmas Treasury (Gale Wiersum) Golden Book

Memory Verse
"While you are enriched in everything for all liberality..." II Cor. 9:11a

WEEK 15   FRIDAY

Make Christmas cookies together

Preparation for next week

General:
_____Read over lesson plans
_____List materials needed
_____Collect materials needed
_____Story pages etc., to notebook

Library:
_____Return books used this week
_____Check out books for week after next

Field Trips:
_____Reconfirm next Friday's trip
_____Thank you note for last trip
_____Set up trip for week after next

WEEK 16   MONDAY

Bible

Faith: what is it? Read Heb. 11:1 ("Now faith is the substance of things hoped for, the evidence of things not seen.") Give examples of faith in your life and from Bible characters (see Heb. 11 for examples). Tell several Bible stories to illustrate it.

On story page, write: Faith is being certain of something we hope for and cannot see.

Read Proverbs 30:5a: "Every word of God is pure." We can trust in what God says.

Reading

Read a poem.

Introduce letter shape and sound for "M m." Child says sound while tracing letter.

(Alone) Classifying: Child sorts M and m cards from A-L and a-l cards; matches with the M's and m's on the file folder.

Sequence and complete sentences: Child dictates story about baking Christmas cookies last Friday.

Art

Using watercolors, have child paint a picture of something he would like to do this new year.

Arithmetic

Introduce number three and symbol 3. We are going to make a counting book of 3. (Using 3 pieces of construction paper folded in half, write on the outside of the cover: My Counting Book of 3 with the child's name and date, using the same format as for previous books.)

On paper plate with numeral 3 written in the middle of it, have child clip the correct number of clothespins to its edge.

Page 1: Have child color 3 shapes on worksheet you make; cut and mount object part.

Page 2: Have child glue numeral 3 and three object shapes to page.

Character Building

Availability: God wants me to be available to serve the people in authority over me and to serve those I am responsible for. I need to take care of these responsibilities before I consider the needs of others. I need to be able to say, "no" to requests from others if it would take me away from doing my job and completing it all the way. Have child give examples of when he wanted to play or do something and Mom or Dad asked him to help in some way. What was his attitude?

Have child role-play right and wrong way to handle availability to our "chain of authority."

On Character Building story page write: God wants me to be available to serve my family.

Physical Education

Indoor bowling.

Story

Yesterday's Snowman (Gail Mack)

The Art of Colonial America (Shirley Glubok) j709.73G56a; look at pictures

Memory Verse

"...serving the Lord." Rom. 12:11c

"So Jesus answered and said to them, 'Have faith in God.'" Mark 11:22

"Now faith is the substance of things hoped for, the evidence of things not seen." Heb.11:1

WEEK 16   TUESDAY

Bible

Faith is for good times and bad. Review definition of faith (Hebrews 11:1; see Monday's lesson). It is a challenge during good times to remember it is GOD who has blessed us and we still need to depend on Him. It is a challenge during the bad/hard times to see the big picture and remember that God is in control and to remember that He is working to mold us and help us grow. (Ex.: a diamond -pieces have to be chipped away to get the beautiful, sparkling facets.) Give examples from the Bible of keeping faith during good times; it helps keep us humble and helps us retain important priorities. Give examples from the Bible of keeping faith during challenging time: Noah building the ark (no one outside of family believed him, cooped up during 40 days of rain on ship with animals).

On story page, write: Faith is for good times and hard times.
We need always to remember God's qualities: steadfast love and
   faithfulness and His promises to us ("I will never leave you nor forsake
   you... God will supply all your needs... The Lord is my Shepherd, I shall
   not want...").

Reading

Read a poem.
Left-to-right eye movement: Child copies pegboard patterns you have made,
   making sure that he begins on the left side.
Speech: Child "reads" book to you.

Music

Lavender's Blue

Arithmetic

Show child a card with 3 dots on it. How many dots are there?
Write 3 on the chalkboard. Have child hold up correct number of fingers.
   Repeat with previous numbers.
Page 3: Have child use 3 strips of paper (1/2" x 3") to make loops for chain.
   After gluing ends together, glue 3-loop chain to page.
Page 4: Have child put on three stickers.

God's World

3. Dairy Group
   a. Briefly review first 2 groups of food.
   b. Today we're going to learn about the third group of food - the dairy
      group. These foods are all made from milk (cow/goat): milk, cheese,
      yogurt, cottage cheese, cream cheese, ice cream.
   c. Why are they important? Calcium for bones and teeth; good source
      of protein.
   d. Read: From Grass to Butter (Ali Mitgutsch); j637M683f; color illus. of
      cow, butter
   e. Cut out pictures from this group. Glue to poster labeled 3. DAIRY
      GROUP.
   Resources:
   637.4M683f   From Milk to Ice Cream (Ali Mitgutsch)

Physical Education

Beanbag toss.

Story

Any of the Frances books (Russell Hoban)
Shadrach, Meshach and Abednego (illus. Paul Galdone); j224B585.

Memory Verse

"But he who trusts in the Lord will be prospered." Prov. 28:25b
"But whoever trusts in the Lord shall be safe." Prov. 29:25b
"Your faith has made you well." Luke 17:19c
"Jesus said to him, 'If you can believe, all things are possible to him who
   believes.'" Mark 9:23b

WEEK 16   WEDNESDAY

Bible
Faith is meant to be used. We can't just talk about being good and loving others. We must show it. Read/tell of James 2:14-17, 22. Talk about how we can use our faith each day (Ex.: help others who are needy; be a good friend; obey parents; have a cheerful heart).

On story page, write: Faith is meant to be used.

Reading
Read a poem.

Auditory discrimination: Child listens to sets of two words and tells you whether they have the same or different beginning sounds.

lamp, light	mother, memories
lady, individual	name, make
love, like	majesty, daddy
loyalty, joy	marker, mud
listening, forget	moss, night

(Alone) Classifying: Child sorts cards (wallpaper cut into shapes) by shapes. (10 each of 3-4 shapes)

Art
String popcorn and/or cranberry garland for outdoor tree, to feed the birds.

Arithmetic
Have child match card with numeral 3 on it with card that has three objects on it. (Have 4 sets of these.) Have numerals 0-2 sets mixed in with them.

Page 5: Have child use three popsicle sticks to make design. Glue to page.

Page 6: Stamp 3 rubber stamp images on page.

Review pages so far with child. Write 3 on top of each page as you review with child how many items are on each page.

Health/Manners
Talk about eye contact when speaking and listening.

Why do we need to look at others when we talk and listen?
1) Shows you are listening to other person.
2) Shows you are honest.
3) Shows you are concentrating on the conversation.
4) It is polite

Role-play with child, right and wrong ways.

On "Manners" story page, write: I always have eye contact when I speak and listen to others.

Physical Education
Hop while music is playing and stop when it stops.

Story
Noah and the Great Flood (illus. Warwick Hutton); j222.11H985n.

Listen to a Shape (Marcia Brown); shapes in nature

Memory Verse
"But be doers of the word, and not hearers only..." James 1:22a

WEEK 16   THURSDAY

Bible
Faith is meant to be shared. How can we share our faith?
  1) Pray for others.
  2) Talk to others about Jesus and how He loves us.
  3) Show faith to others by your life: values, caring for them, helping.
On story page, write: Faith is meant to be shared.
Have child think of one or more sentences of what Jesus means to him.
  Write this down as the last thought on story page.

Reading
Read a poem.
Rhyming: Child names rhyming words for "my," "mud," "mug," "more."
(Alone) Hand-eye coordination: Child laces yarn/shoelace through sewing
  card.
Kinesthetic: Using two fingers and repeating sound, child traces M m on the
  letter card, in the air, and on your back.

Music
Songs of your choice

Arithmetic
Using 25 counters, have child count them out into piles of 3.
Page 7: Punch 3 holes in paper. Mount to page. Write 3 at top of page.
Page 8: Cut and glue three objects from magazine. Write 3 at top of page.
Page 9: Color in correct amount on number line you've drawn.
Punch holes; reinforce; tie book together.

God's World
4. Meat/Protein Group
    a. Briefly review names of food groups 1, 2, 3.
    b. Today, we learn about the fourth group of foods - the meat/protein
       group. Protein is needed for our growth. There are four main types
       of food in this group: fish, meats/poultry, dried legumes (complimen
       tary proteins), eggs.
    c. Have child name as many varieties of each as you list them.
    d. Cut out pictures from this group. Glue to poster labeled 4. MEAT/
       PROTEIN GROUP

Physical Education
Walk in a circle without losing balance.

Story
Good News! (A Happy Day book)

Memory Verse
"Whoever confesses that Jesus is the Son of God, God abides in him, and he in God." I John 4:15
"Go, therefore and make disciples of all the nations…" Matt. 28:19a
"Only fear the Lord, and serve him in truth with all your heart; for consider what great things he has done for you." I Sam. 12:24

WEEK 16   FRIDAY

Visit grocery store.

Poem: "Counters" (Elizabeth Coatsworth)

Preparation for next week:

General:
_____Read over lesson plans
_____List materials needed
_____Collect materials needed
_____Story pages etc., to notebook

Library:
_____Return books used this week
_____Check out books for week after next

Field Trips:
_____Reconfirm next Friday's trip
_____Thank you note for last trip
_____Set up trip for week after next

WEEK 17   MONDAY

Bible
God likes order and wants us to plan. Review what God did when He created the earth:
        Day 1: light, day and night
        Day 2: sky
        Day 3: land and seas; vegetation (plants and trees)
        Day 4: sun, moon and stars
        Day 5: water creatures, birds
        Day 6: animals; man and woman
        Day 7: God rested
He has a plan and he does things in a certain order. God is not a god of chaos or disorder.
What happens when we don't have a plan? (We don't have a target to aim for; there will be time wasted; we will feel frustrated; we will miss out on accomplishing good things for God; we can't work calmly one step at a time.)

What happens when we or our rooms are disorganized or out of order? (We don't know where things are; we waste time; we feel frustrated; we worry; we are not good stewards of what God has given us; someone may get hurt when things are not in their places; we may forget to take important things with us; we do not feel as good about ourselves as we could; we feel guilty; we are not obedient.)

How did you feel when you reached your goal of (Ex.: stopping sucking thumb/catching a ball, etc.)? (happy; good inside) That's how God wants us to feel. He wants us to plan and be orderly.

On story page, write: God created the world in an orderly way. God does not like chaos and disorder.

Reading

Read a poem.

Introduce letter shape and sound for N n. Have child repeat sound while tracing shape with fingers.

(Alone) Classifying: Child sorts N n cards from other letter cards; matches with the N's and n's on file folder.

Sequence and complete sentences: Child dictates story of grocery store tour.

Art

Make food collage from magazine pictures cut out and glued to construction paper/butcher paper.

Arithmetic

Introduce number four and symbol 4. We are going to make a counting book of 4. (Using 3 pieces of construction paper folded in half, write on the outside of the cover: My Counting Book of 4 with the child's name and date, using the same format as for previous books.)

On paper plate with numeral 4 written on the middle of it, have child clip the correct number of clothespins to its edge.

Page 1: Have child color 4 shapes on worksheet you have made; cut and mount object part to page 1.

Page 2: Have child glue numeral 4 and four object shapes to page 2.

Character Building

Orderliness: What good things come from being orderly?
1) It shows good stewardship.
2) It takes less time to keep things clean and find things.
3) We and our things look better.

How can we help our home stay orderly?
1) By being a good steward; keep clean and picked up.
2) By putting things away in their right places.
3) By watching what we bring into our home.
4) By getting rid of things that are not needed and are cluttering.

On Character Building story page, write: When I keep my room orderly, it looks nice and it is easier to find things.

Physical Education

Indoor bowling.

Story
Bear Weather (Lillie D. Chaffin)
The Seven Days of Creation (illus. Leonard & Everett Fisher); j222.11F534s.

Memory Verse
"For God is not the author of confusion but of peace..." I Cor.14.33a

WEEK 17   TUESDAY

Bible
Orderliness: keeping ourselves clean and neat
Have child tell what (s)he does to keep herself clean and neat and then talk
    about the rest of the areas:
      Body: I wash my face and hands each day.
               I bathe regularly. I brush my teeth.
               I brush my hair. My fingernails are clean.
      Clothes: I wear clean clothes each day.
               I fold my clothes instead of throwing them on the floor.
               I don't play in my best clothes.
Have child draw picture of him/herself clean and neat.
On story page, write: I keep myself clean and neat.

Reading
Read a poem.
(Alone) Left to right eye movement: Child colors objects in horizontal rows
    on worksheet you've made (make 4-6 horizontal rows with 3-5 objects
    in each row). Make sure that child works lefts to right, top to bottom.
Visual discrimination: Hold up a group of several objects (bread tags of
    different colors, crayons). Child makes matching set with extra bread
    tags and crayons.
Speech: Child "reads" book to you.

Music
Songs of your choice

Arithmetic
Show child a card with four dots on it. How many dots are there? Write 4
    on the chalkboard. Have child hold up correct number of fingers.
Repeat with previous numbers (mix up sequence).
Page 3: Have child use 4 strips of paper (1/2" x 3") to make loops for chain.
    After gluing ends together, glue chain to page.
Page 4: Have child put on four stickers.

God's World
Processed, refined foods vs. whole, natural foods
Review 4 food groups by name. Go through each, one by one, and talk
    about differences in quality between processed, refined foods, and
    whole, natural foods. Tell child that food has become more processed
    and less nutritious in some ways over history.

I.   Bread/Cereal - Ask child how he/she would feel if someone gave him a wrapped gift, then took it all back except for the wrapping paper; he could keep that. That is what white, refined flour is like; the best, most nutritious part has been taken away. Whole wheat, whole grain, brown rice, and unsweetened cereal are best.

II. Fruit/Vegetables - Raw best; fresh best; lightly salted, unsweetened (Ex.: apple sauce).

III. Dairy - Fresh, whole product.

IV. Meat/Protein - Needs to be cooked; lightly salted; broiled better than fried.

The choice is yours. God asks us to be the best steward of our bodies we can be. It is up to you to make the best choices.

Resources:

j641 P655r	The Natural Snack Cookbook: 151 Good Things to Eat (Jill Pinkwater)
j638.f1 M683f	From Blossom to Honey (Ali Mitgutsch)
j633.64 L345s	Sugaring Time (Kathryn Lasky); photographs and story of family maple sugaring

Physical Education

Bean bag toss.

Story

Summer is... (Charlotte Zolotow)
The Creation (illus. Jo Spier); j222.1B58c.

Memory Verse

"My son, eat honey because it is good…" Prov. 24.13a
"Whatever your hand finds to do, do it with your might." Ecc. 9:10a

WEEK 17   WEDNESDAY

Bible

Orderliness: keeping our home, yard, and car clean and neat.

Have child tell what (s)he does to keep room clean and neat (pick up clothes, picks up toys, makes bed, dusts, empties wastebaskets, etc.).

What would happen if we did not take care of our home to keep it clean and neat? (It would be hard to move around because of the mess; it would be dangerous; it would smell bad because the garbage would not be taken out; it would not be a relaxing, pleasant place to live; we would not be good stewards of the home God has given us.)

How about toys and books? Are they tossed on the floor or broken, or are they handled gently and put away each time you use them?

How about the yard? (Messy, long grass is not pretty; we would not be good stewards.) The car? (It would be messy; it might be dangerous if it did not have proper maintenance; it would not be pleasant to ride in; we would not be good stewards.)

On story page, write: I help keep our home, yard, and car(s) neat and clean.

Have child draw a picture of his (her) room neat and clean.

Reading

Read a poem.

Auditory discrimination: Child repeats your clapping patterns.

(Alone) Closure: Child fills in missing parts on the shapes you've drawn in rows on a worksheet. (Ex.: part of circle missing, etc.)

Listening: Child repeats sequence you say.

planning, order, Creation	steward, organize, easy
timesaving, clean, comfortable	us, clothes, shoes
yard, home, car	blessing, stewardship, God
processed, natural, refined	fiber, vitamins, wholegrain
choice, decision, health	directions, right, left
up, down, sideways	skipping, balanced, bowling
newspaper, press, machine	edition, reporting, periodical
communication, read, journalism	

Art

Popcorn "snow" glued to construction paper winter scene.

Arithmetic

Have child match card with numeral 4 on it with card that has four objects on it. (Have 4 sets of these.) Have numerals 0-3 sets mixed in with them.

Page 5: Have child use four popsicle sticks to make design. Glue to page.

Page 6: Stamp 4 rubber stamp images on page.

Review pages so far with child. Write 4 at top of each page as you review with child how many items are on each page.

Health/Manners

Teaching child new jobs around home

Besides what their responsibilities are, teach them the correct ways of doing increasingly more difficult jobs.

On "Personal Responsibility" story page, write: I cheerfully do my chores each day. My work is important in helping our family.

Physical Education

Skip while music is playing and stop when music stops.

Story

The Berenstein Bears and the Messy Room (Stan and Jan Berenstein)

Choo-Choo- The Story of a Little Engine Who Ran Away (Virginia Lee Burton)

Memory Verse

"And whatever you do, do it heartily, as to the Lord and not to men." Col. 3:23

"He who is slothful in his work is a brother to him who is a great destroyer." Prov. 18:9

WEEK 17 THURSDAY

Bible

Develop good stewardship habits. Review areas of orderliness from Tuesday (ourselves) and Wednesday (our home, yard, and car). Have child tell areas in which he is already a good steward and areas he needs to do better. (Make a list of up to three things you and child decide he needs to work on.)

On story page, write: I am beginning to work on (specific areas). (Ex.: brushing my hair each day, not throwing my clothes on the floor, picking up my toys 10 minutes before bedtime each evening.) Then write: I am becoming a better steward of all that God has given me.

Reading

Read a poem.

Rhyming: Child names rhyming words for "name," "night," "nap," "noon."

(Alone) Hand-eye coordination: Child does puzzle(s).

Kinesthetic: Using two fingers and repeating the letter sound, child traces shape of N n on letter cards, in the air, and on your back.

Music

Song of your choice

Arithmetic

Using 25 counters, have child count them out into piles of 4.

Page 7: Punch four holes in paper. Mount to page. Write 4 at top of page.

Page 8: Cut and glue four objects from magazine. Write 4 at top of page.

Page 9: Color in correct amount on number line you've drawn.

Punch holes; reinforce, tie book together.

God's World

Introduction to directions.

Have child lead you through house blindfolded by verbal directions (turn left/right; walk three steps, etc.)

Physical Education

Balance on balance beam/curbstone for 10 feet.

Story

The Shoelace Book (Elizabeth Winthrop) Golden Book

A Roundabout Turn (Robert H. Charles)

Memory Verse

"And let us not grow weary while doing good..." Gal. 6:9a

WEEK 17   FRIDAY

Tour newspaper office.

Preparation for next week:

General:
_____Read over lesson plans
_____List materials needed
_____Collect materials needed
_____Story pages etc., to notebook

Library:
_____Return books used this week
_____Check out books for week after next

Field Trips:
_____Reconfirm next Friday's trip
_____Thank you note for last trip
_____Set up trip for week after next

WEEK 18   MONDAY

Bible

Goals: Ask the child: Do you know what a goal is? (It is something to be, do, or have.) Some examples: "be" -an obedient daughter, a doctor; "do" -learn to read, not suck thumb; "have" -a garden, a horse.

After we decide what it is we want, then we need to decide if God would think it would be good for us; if not, we need to forget that and choose another goal. We need to choose only goals that would make God happy. We also need to make sure we have the goal for the right reason - not to be greedy or to compare and covet something someone else has/is/does. That might mean a good goal, but for the wrong reason. So, we would need to choose another goal.

Some goals we can reach in a short time; others take longer.

On story page, write: A goal is something I want to be, to do, or to have. It needs to be pleasing to God.

What goals have you reached?

Reading

Read a poem.

Introduce letter shape and sounds (ah, oh, ooh) for O o. Child traces letter shape on card while repeating three sounds.

(Alone) Classifying: Child sorts O and o cards from other letter cards; then matches with O's and o's on the file folder.

Sequence and complete sentences: Child dictates story about visit to newspaper office.

Art
Chalk Pictures. (Colored chalk)

Arithmetic
Introduce number five and symbol 5. We are going to make a counting book of 5. (Using 3 pieces of construction paper folded in half, write on the outside of the cover: "My Counting Book of 5" with the child's name and date, using the same format as for previous books.)

On paper plate with numeral 5 written in the middle of it, have child clip the correct number of clothespins to its edge.

Page 1: Have child color five shapes on worksheet you've made; cut and mount object part.

Page 2: Have child glue numeral 5 and five object shapes to page.

Character Building
Planning, determination: God wants us to plan and to be determined to reach our goals by taking the necessary action.

Give an example of a family wanting to take a trip across the country by car. What would be missing if they forgot to bring their clothes and food? (They hadn't planned enough and hadn't broken the goal down in to parts.) What would happen if they got impatient or tired of being in the car, driving from one place to their next stop? (They'd be giving up and not following through on their goal.) What would happen if when they stopped at a town someone asked them to stay two extra weeks and to visit Canada with them? (They would be getting sidetracked and wouldn't be able to complete their goal.)

What do we need to remember about goal-planning?
1. Break goal down into parts ("Inch by inch, it's a cinch.")
2. Use what energy and time you need to complete the goal; follow-through.
3. Don't get sidetracked. Keep your eyes on the goal. (Tell child about purpose of blinders for horses: Keeps them looking only at where they are going.)

On the Character Building story page, write: Once I have set a goal, I will break it down, do the work, and refuse to get sidetracked.

Physical Education
Indoor bowling.

Story
Hare and Tortoise (Aesop; illus. Paul Galdone)
Any of the books by Tasha Tudor

Memory Verse
"Cause me to know the way in which I should walk..." Ps. 143:8c
"But seek first the kingdom of God and His righteousness, and all these things shall be added to you." Matt. 6:33

WEEK 18   TUESDAY

Bible

What must we do to reach our goal?

1. Choose a goal that is pleasing to the Lord Jesus Christ.
2. Really desire it. Think of yourself reading, giving away flowers to others from your garden. But realize you can't depend on it (your goal) for happiness. And it can't become your "god."
3. Set a plan to follow - steps to reach your end result. Ask Mom and Dad to help you break it down into little parts and concentrate on one step at a time.
4. Act on your plan. Follow through. Do your best work (Ecc. 9:10a,b). Realize that at no times are all conditions right. Satan may try to discourage you and make you fail.
5. Commit your work to the Lord (Prov. 16:3). Give God the glory for your successes. All blessings come from God.

On story page, write: I need to desire my goal, to write it down, to have a plan to reach it, to act on my plan, and to commit my work to the Lord.

What will God do for us if we trust Him? He will guide our steps. He will lengthen our days and help us accomplish more. He will give us wisdom. He will give us peace. He will help us choose right goals.

On story page, add: God will guide my steps and give me wisdom.

Reading

Read a poem.

(Alone) Left-to-right eye movement: Child draws lines on worksheets you've made from animals and people on the left to their homes on the right.

(Alone) Visual discrimination: Child sorts beans and seeds into egg carton segments.

Speech: Child "reads" book to you.

Music

Songs of your choice.

Arithmetic

Show child a card with five dots on it. How many dots are there?

Write 5 on the chalkboard. Have child hold up correct number of fingers. Repeat with previous numbers. (Mix up sequence.)

Page 3: Have child use five strips of paper 1/2x3" to make five loop chain. Glue to page.

Page 4: Have child put five stickers on it.

God's World

Directions

There are four words people use to give directions, no matter where you are in the world: north, south, east, west.

We can find them on a map or a globe. (Show them.)

Physical Education

Bean bag toss.

Story
> Little Red Hen
> Children of the Northlights (Ingri and Edgar D'Aulaire)

Memory Verse
> "Commit your works to the Lord, and your thoughts will be established."
> Prov. 16:3

WEEK 18   WEDNESDAY

Bible

Our goals and others. There are two things we need to keep in mind about our goals and other people. First, accountability is a way to help each other in reaching goals. It means having to answer to the other person after we have told him what our goal is and what we plan to do on it. Ecclesiastes 4:9-10 says that two are better than one because if one falls down, the other can pick him up. I Thessalonians 5:11 tells us to "encourage one another and build each other up."

The second thing we must remember about other people and our goals is that we cannot compare. Our possessions, goals, talents, abilities are different from those of anyone else. God says coveting, or wanting what someone else has/is/does, is wrong. Everyone's goals and timetables are individual. They all differ. God made us each unique and special. He wants us to have the right motives.

On story page, write: I must not compare myself with others. God made me special - with unique talents and abilities. I need to do my best. I can help others reach their goals by encouraging them in God-pleasing goals.

Reading

Read a poem.
Auditory discrimination: Child listens and tells you whether the beginning sounds for each set of two words is the same or different:

note, mope	otter, at
nothing, name	octopus, ostrich
magnet, nickel	umbrella, other
number, nice	improve, old
nutshell, nail	oblong, aluminum

(Alone) Closure: Child matches cards with missing parts to cards with the object (10-20).
Listening: Child repeats sequences after you:

goals, planning, follow through	puppy, fish, hamster
commitment, Lord, guidance	cat, turtle, bird
accountability, help, partner	compare, covet, bitterness
blessing, direction, loyalty	directions, map, home
north, south, compass	east, west, lost
globe, round, world	map, flat, atlas
orient, follow, navigate	pets, responsibility, job

Notes

Art
Draw picture of newspaper office and send it with a thank you note to them.

Arithmetic
Have child match card with numeral 5 on it with card that has five objects on it. (Have 4 sets of these.) Have numerals 0-4 sets mixed in with them.

Page 5: Have child use five popsicle sticks/toothpicks to make design. Glue on.

Page 6: Stamp 5 rubber stamp images to page.

Review pages so far with child. Write 5 on at of each page as you review with child how many items are on each page.

Health/Manners
Taking Care of Pets

If you have a pet, talk over specifics in caring for it. If you don't, talk in terms of a hypothetical situation.

Example: Pet dog - food and water, exercise, play with him, brush, take to vet for shots, etc.

Talk about what would happen to pet if it was neglected and its basic needs were not met. Draw a picture of pet.

On "Personal Responsibilities" story page, write: I care for our pet(s) each day.

Resources:

j6362819G	Great Pets: An extraordinary guide to usual and unusual family pets (Sara Stein)
j636.7	Puppies (Judith E. Rhard) National Geographic
j636.7H52al	Album of Dogs (Marguerite Henry); good for large color paintings
j636.73F755d	Dogs Working for People (Joanna Foster) Natural Geographic
j636.8C77b	The Big Book of Cats (Gladys Emerson Cook); good for large color illus.

Physical Education
Jump/hop while music is playing and stop when music stops.

Story
Katy and the Big Snow (Virginia Lee Burton)
The Little Engine That Could (Watty Piper)

Memory Verse
"A man's heart plans his way, but the Lord directs his steps." Prov. 16:9

WEEK 18   THURSDAY

Bible
Go over the 7 areas of goal setting - with examples of each:
1. Spiritual (attend Sunday School each week; learn Psalm 23)

2. Personal Growth (habits, attitudes: cheerfulness, encouragement to others, obedience)
3. Physical (standing up straight)
4. Intellectual (learning reading, learning some new part of arithmetic)
5. Monetary (having a certain $ level in a savings account)
6. Service (choosing a project to do for someone else)
7. Family (helping Mom with a job without being asked each day)

List these on a separate poster.
Have child contribute ideas for each area.

Reading

Read a poem.
Rhyming: Child names words to rhyme with: "over," "ow," "old."
(Alone) Hand-eye coordination: Child strings beads onto shoelace.
Kinesthetic: Child, using two fingers and repeating three sounds, traces O o
on the card, in the air, on your back.

Music

Songs of your choice

Arithmetic

Using 25 counters, have child count them out into piles of 5.
Page 7: Punch 5 holes in paper. Mount to page. Write 5 at top of the
page.
Page 8: Cut and glue five objects from magazine. Write 5 at top of page.
Page 9: Color in correct amount on number line you've drawn.

God's World

Directions
Review N-S-E-W. What are the 4 directions on a map? (N S E W) Show a
globe and flat map. Talk about differences and likenesses (can show
same area).
Tell what a compass does (helps us find our way; shows us directions).
Skim through with child:

j912 H24wo   The World Atlas (Hammond, Inc.)
j912 N277n   Picture Atlas of Our World (National Geographic)
j912.014K7m   Maps and Globes (Jack Knowlton)

Physical Education

Walk in circle without losing balance.

Story

Lentil (Robert McCloskey)
North, South, East and West (Franklyn M. Branley)

Memory Verse

"Trust in the Lord with all your heart, and lean not on your own
understanding; In all your ways acknowledge Him, and He shall direct
your paths." Prov. 3:5,6

WEEK 18   FRIDAY

Visit animal shelter

Preparation for next week:

General:
_____Read over lesson plans
_____List materials needed
_____Collect materials needed
_____Story pages, etc. to notebook

Library:
_____Return books used this week
_____Check out books for week after next

Field Trips:
_____Reconfirm next Friday's trip
_____Thank you note for last trip
_____Set up trip for week after next

WEEK 19   MONDAY

Bible

Actual goal setting - Have child select one area and set goal for himself/
  herself, following these steps:
1. Select a goal desired.
2. Analyze.
3. Write the goal down.
4. Work out a plan and set up rewards for small steps.
5. Commit work to the Lord.
Then have him/her begin.

Reading

Read a poem.
Introduce letter shape and sound for P p. Child repeats sound while
  tracing letter card.
(Alone) Classifying: Child sorts P and p cards from other letter cards; then
  matches with the P's and p's on the file folder.
Sequence and complete sentences: Child dictates story about trip to the
  animal shelter.

Art

On blue construction paper, glue green ground/white snow. Then have
  child, using toothpick/Q-tip dipped into glue, put little drops of glue in
  the "sky" part of the picture. Cover with glitter; shake off excess
  (newspapers down first!).

Arithmetic

Introduce number six and symbol 6. We are going to make a counting book of 6. (Using 3 pieces of construction paper folded in half, write on the outside of the cover: "My Counting Book of 6" with the child's name and date, using the same format as for previous books.)

On paper plate with numeral 6 written on the middle of it, have child clip the correct number of clothespins to its edge.

Page 1: Have child color 6 shapes on worksheet you have made; cut and mount object part to page 1.

Page 2: Have child glue numeral 6 and six objects to page.

Character Building

Keeping your promise and having endurance: Tell how important it is to God for us to keep our word/promise.

We need to resist what would break us down from meeting our goal or keeping our promise. We need to know what resources are available to build us up/help us keep our promises. We need to stick together with others who have the same promises (Ex. - loving God, respect family, never take drugs, say good things).

On Character Building story page, write: Keeping my promises is very important to God.

Physical Education

Bounce and catch ball.

Story

Down, Down the Mountain (Ellis Credle)

Stories That Never Grow Old: Best Loved Stories (retold by Watty Piper); j398P665; read one today.

Memory Verse

"Vows made to You are binding upon me, O God." Ps. 56:12a

WEEK 19 TUESDAY

Bible

Now what??? Since I've begun,...

1. Following through - keep your promise to yourself. There will be setbacks, unexpected frustrations. Resolve to continue. The Bible tells us to keep our word.

2. How do you keep track? Make a chart. Have stickers, etc.

3. Continue to learn more about God.

4. Realize that before you reach this goal, set another goal so you keep making progress.

Reading

Read a poem.

(Alone) Left-to-right eye movement: Child uses crayons to connect rows of dots going horizontally across worksheet (10-12 rows of dots).

Visual discrimination: Child matches like cards - patterns of letters (2 each of fg, fh, hi, hj, ik, il, jm, jn, ko, kp, la, lb, mc, md, ee). May need to have child use only half of the matching sets at first.

Music

America the Beautiful
Yankee Doodle

Arithmetic

Show child a card with six dots on it. How many dots are there?
Write 6 on the chalkboard. Have child hold up correct number of fingers. Repeat with previous numbers learned (mix up the sequence).
Page 3: Have child use six strips of paper (1/2x3") to make loops for chain. After gluing together, glue to page.
Page 4: Have child put six stickers on it.

God's World

Directions - USA Map
Look at map of the USA. Have child show parts that border water (east coast by Atlantic Ocean; west coast by Pacific Ocean; south by Gulf of Mexico). Show north, south, east and west on map. Show state and city/town where you live. Tell child there are 50 states. They are each part of the United States of America. Show Washington, D.C. This is where the laws for our country are made. Talk about climate differences depending on location in USA (snow in north; hot, sunny weather in south). This affects what crops people grow, how they make a living. Show main roads on map.

Physical Education

Simon Says.

Story

Baby Susan's Chickens (J. H. Berg); Golden Book
Stories That Never Grow Old; read another story today.

Memory Verse

"Let your eyes look straight ahead...". Prov. 4:25a

WEEK 19   WEDNESDAY

Bible

Review of unit: God likes order and wants us to plan.
On story page, under subsection of goals, add: Once I begin, I need to follow through on my actions.
Reread entire story page. Review child's goal, action plan, chart for keeping track, and reward system.

Reading

Read a poem.
Auditory discrimination: Child repeats your clapping patterns.

(Alone) Maze: Child races matchbox car through maze on cardboard.
Listening: Child repeats sequences after you:

promises, vow, keeping	help, self-esteem, love
spiritual, goal, growth	attitude, habit, physical
intellectual, money, service	family, priorities, visualizing
chart, short-term, long-term	follow through, on track, blessings
effort, order, planning	U.S.A., fifty, continent
N. America, Mississippi, oceans	Pacific, Atlantic, Canada
Mexico, Gulf of Mexico, land	Washington D.C., nation, capitol
elderly, respect, honor	

Art

Make telephones from toilet paper rolls and string.
Paint front of pretend store.

Arithmetic

Have child match card with numeral 6 on it with card that has six objects on it. (Have 4 sets of these.) Have numerals 0-5 sets mixed in with them.
Page 5: Have child use six popsicle sticks/toothpicks to make design. Glue to page.
Page 6: Stamp 6 rubber stamp images on page.
Review pages so far with child. Write 6 at top of each page as you review with child how many items are there.

Health/Manners

We help elderly people
What changes happen to people as they get older? Have child name as many as (s)he can, then give clues: may not see as well (reading and driving); may have less energy; may have less strength (not as self-sufficient); may not hear as well (phone, not hear conversations, talks loudly); may be afraid of changes and death; may feel lonely; may not be able to drive car; may have had many friends die; may not be treated as well as when they were younger (less respect); may be shaky (writing, walking); may talk loudly; may not feel as well (medicated, cross); may not feel useful, appreciated.
Have child think of as many ways as he can to help an older person. Choose one or two ways and begin to do it.
On "Personal Responsibilities" story page, write: I am polite and helpful to people older than myself.
Grandpa and Me - We Learn about Death (Marlee & Ben Alex); Bethany House Pub., 1982.
It Must Hurt Alot (Doris Sanford) Multnomah Press, 1985.
The Tenth Good Thing About Barney (Judith Viorst) Atheneum, 1971

Physical Education

Tiptoe while music is playing and stop when music stops.

Story

The Old Woman and Her Pig and 10 Other Stories (Anne Rockwell); j398.208R684o; read one story today.

Stories That Never Grow Old (read a third story today from this book).

Memory Verse

"But let your `Yes' be `Yes,' and your `No,' `No,' lest you fall into judgment."

WEEK 19   THURSDAY

Bible

God loves us and wants us to grow. He wants us to grow in wisdom - making right choices and learning about Him. How? We need to know what he wants for us:

1. Wisdom from Dad and Mom.
2. Sunday School and church.
3. Listen to cassette tapes that talk/sing about God.
4. Have Dad and Mom read Bible stories to you.
5. Pray to God each day.

God wants us to recognize and avoid wrong teachings. By learning more of what God likes and wants, we can know what God hates and wants us to stay away from. Anything that goes against what you've learned in Sunday School or what your parents have taught you, check with them before you even begin doing it, no matter who tries to talk you into it!

On new story page, entitled: "God loves me and wants me to grow," write: God wants me to learn more about Him. He wants me to stay away from wrong teachings and ideas.

In large circle cut out of construction paper, find/draw picture of someone trying to get someone else to do/say/think something wrong. Draw a diagonal line through it with dark-colored marker.

Reading

Read a poem.

Rhyming: Child names rhyming words for "pen," "put," "page," "paw."

(Alone) Hand-eye coordination: Child makes collage using scissors, glue, and colored construction paper.

Kinesthetic: Using two fingers and repeating sound "p" child traces P p on letter card, in the air, on your back.

Music

Star-Spangled Banner

Review Tuesday's songs.

Arithmetic

Using 25 counters, have child count them out into piles of 6.

Page 7: Punch 6 holes in paper. Mount to page. Write 6 at top.

Page 8: Cut and glue six objects from magazine. Write 6 at top.

Page 9: Color in correct amount on number line you've drawn.

Punch holes; reinforce; tie book together.

God's World
Directions - State map
How many States in the USA? (50) Our state is (have child name it). Show map of state. Have child find north, south, east, and west. Note any geographic features, boundaries. Show your town. Show main roads. Have child travel (with finger) from one place to another by following roads. Look at map legend and point out several items of interest from this "code."

Physical Education
Somersaults; head stands.

Story
The Old Woman and Her Pig (read a second story from this book)
Stories That Never Grow Old (read a fourth story from this book)

Memory Verse
"The Lord will perfect that which concerns me..." Ps. 138:8a

WEEK 19   FRIDAY

Field trip of your choice.

Preparation for next week:

General:
_____Read over lesson plans
_____List materials needed
_____Collect materials needed
_____Story pages, etc. to notebook

Library:
_____Return books used this week
_____Check out books for week after next

Field Trips:
_____Reconfirm next Friday's trip
_____Thank you note for last trip
_____Set up trip for week after next

WEEK 20   MONDAY

Bible
God tells us to stay away from wrong attitudes (Gal.5:19-21). He does not want us to fight. Take photo/find picture of two people fighting. Mount on construction paper circle, and draw diagonal line through it. Does fighting show love to each other? (No) Does fighting build us up? (No) Does fighting show obedience to God and parents? (No) What are some consequences of fighting? (Anger, harsh words, discord,

disobedience, someone getting hurt)

On story page write: God doesn't want me to fight.

Reading

Read a poem.

Introduce letter shape and sound for "Qu qu." Explain that Q is not a sound by itself and it is not used except with u. Have child say sound (kwuh) while tracing letter shape.

(Alone) Classifying: Have child sort Qu and qu cards from other letter cards; match with the Qu's and qu's on the file folder.

Sequence and complete sentences: Have child dictate story about field trip.

Art

Cut out, decorate, and glue buildings, etc., to "cityscape" on butcher paper/ construction paper (train, roads, river, buildings, bridges, etc.).

Arithmetic

Introduce number seven and symbol 7. We are going to make a counting book of 7. (Using 3 pieces of construction paper folded in half, write on the outside: "My Counting Book of 7" with the child's name and date, using the same format as for previous books.)

On paper plate with numeral 7 written on the middle of it, have child clip the correct number of clothespins to its edge.

Page 1: Have child color seven shapes on worksheet you have made; cut and mount object part to page.

Page 2: Have child glue numeral 7 and seven object shapes to page.

Character Building

Courage: Read, <u>Michael is Brave</u> (Helen E. Buckley); Michael overcomes his fears by helping a girl overcome hers.

To be courageous/brave, we need to use our available resources in creative ways; we need to face danger without thinking of giving up; and we need to face up to an opponent knowing that we will, in the end, succeed.

Give example of David and Goliath. Show how David used available resources, faced danger, and had confidence he (with God's help) would succeed.

On Character Building story page, write: Courage means choosing not to be afraid.

Physical Education

Bounce and catch ball.

Story

<u>Stopping by Woods on a Snowy Evening</u> (Robert Frost; illus. Susan Jeffers)

<u>Courage</u> (Jane Belk Moncure); j179.6M739c.

Memory Verse

"Test all things; hold fast what is good. Abstain from every form of evil." I Thess.5:21,22

"Watch, stand fast in the faith, be brave, be strong." I Cor.16:13

WEEK 20   TUESDAY

Bible

God doesn't want me to be jealous or to envy other people. What does envy mean? (resentful awareness of advantage enjoyed by another person and desire to possess the same advantage) What does it mean to be jealous? (being unfriendly towards someone you envy) What happens when you are jealous? (not happy; feel angry/unfriendly with the other person; not thankful for what you have; may get angry with God; not content) These are wrong attitudes and wrong actions.

Find picture of one person looking at another's things longingly. Put in construction paper circle and draw diagonal line through it.

On story page, write: God doesn't want me to be jealous.

Reading

Read a poem.

Left-to-right eye movement: Put five (and then more rows as skill increases) colored picture cards in a row in front of the child. Child reads the cards by naming them, beginning at the left.

(Alone) Visual discrimination: Dominos - child sees how long a line he can make with the cards by matching the pictures.

Speech: Child "reads" book to you.

Music

Star-Spangled Banner

Yankee Doodle

Arithmetic

Show child a card with seven dots on it. How many dots are there?

Write 7 on the chalkboard. Have child hold up correct number of fingers. Repeat with previous numbers, mixing up sequence.

Page 3: Have child use 7 strips of paper (1/2x3") for paper chain. Glue together and to page.

Page 4: Have child put seven stickers on it.

God's World

Directions - city map

Show map of your (or nearby) city. Have child show N-S-E-W and locate geographic features (river, etc.)

Locate three or four landmarks on map (library, city hall, any rivers, bus/train lines, Dad's office, church).

Have child travel from one point to another on map, following roads (using finger).

Physical Education

Simon Says.

Story

Story of your choice

Memory Verse
"And a servant of the Lord must not quarrel but be gentle to all..." II
Tim.2:24a

WEEK 20   WEDNESDAY

Bible
God doesn't want me to be angry. How do you feel when you are angry at
someone? (unfriendly, unloving, unpleasant, feel hot inside, feel like
stomping around, feel like hitting that person)

Are those feelings that build you up? (No) Do they build up the other
person? (No) What can we do with those angry feelings that everyone
feels sometimes? (punch a pillow, pound on clay, make an "angry"
picture with crayons) After we don't feel so angry, what can we do?
(pray - ask God to help us forgive the other person and ask God to
forgive us for being angry; ask other person to forgive us for what we
did)

Find/draw picture of someone angry. Mount on construction paper circle;
draw diagonal line through it.

On story page, write: God doesn't want me to be angry.

Reading
Read a poem.

Auditory discrimination: Child tells whether beginning sounds are the same
or different:

pen, when	queen, quiet
pig, permission	riddle, quite
dump, penny	question, quick
top, pet	candle, quack
parents, pleasant	quarter, communion

(Alone) Closure: Child puts missing parts on 8-10 faces you've drawn on a
worksheet.

Listening: Child repeats sequences after you:

growth, courage, blessings	patient, loving, small
teachings, choices, choose	city, metropolitan, town
wrong, fighting, anger	library, church, buildings
envy, jealousy, selfishness	helpers, policemen, firemen
sad, problems, disobedience	business, residential, parks
bravery, action, helper	babies, gentle, soft
tummy, neck, gurgle	burping, feeding, changing
rock, cuddle, kindness	

Art
Complete cityscape from Monday.

Arithmetic
Have child match card with numeral 7 on it with card that has seven objects
on it (have 4 sets of these). Have numerals 0-6 sets mixed in with them.

Page 5: Have child use seven popsicle sticks/toothpicks to make a design.
Glue to page.

Page 6: Stamp seven rubber stamp images on page.
Review pages so far with child. Write 7 at top of each page as you review
with child how many items are on them.

Health/Manners

We are Careful with Babies
Have child look at his/her baby pictures and think about what baby's needs
are and what they are able to do. They sleep, eat, cry, smile; later they
hold things, crawl, and talk. Needs: love, food, clothing (dry and
warm), shelter, protection, sleep.
Show how to:
1. Hold baby carefully, head and neck supported; hold close.
2. Change disposable diaper.
3. Hold when feeding bottle.
4. Wrap in blanket.
5. Put down in crib.
Practice with dolls.
On "Personal Responsibility" story page, write: I am careful and loving to
babies and children younger than myself.

Physical Education

Walk in circle while music is playing and stop when music stops.

Story

It Could Always Be Worse (Margot Zemach)
Looking Out the Window (Miss Frances); Golden Book
Any of the Robert McCloskey books

Memory Verse

"He who is of a proud heart stirs up strife..." Prov. 28:25a

WEEK 20 THURSDAY

Bible

God doesn't want us to be selfish. What does selfish mean? (being
concerned with yourself without thinking of others) Can you think of
any time you or someone in a story was selfish? (interrupting; not
sharing toys or equipment; not being thoughtful of others; not obeying)
How do you think God feels when we are selfish? (Unhappy and sad;
He wants us to think of others more than ourselves. He wants us to be
kind and thoughtful and obedient.)
Find/draw picture of someone being selfish; mount on construction paper
circle. Draw diagonal line through it.
Write on story page: God doesn't want me to be selfish.

Reading

Read a poem.
Rhyming: Child names rhyming words for "queen," "quick," "quill."
(Alone) Hand-eye coordination: Child traces with crayon over lines and
figures you've made on a worksheet: | - / \ o.

Kinesthetic: Using two fingers and repeating sound, trace Qu qu on letter cards, in the air, and on your back.

Music
America the Beautiful

Arithmetic
Using 25 counters, have child count them out into piles of 7.
Page 7: Punch seven holes in paper; mount to page; write 7 at top of page.
Page 8: Cut and glue seven objects from magazine. Write 7 at top of page.
Page 9: Color in correct amount on number line you've drawn.
Punch holes; reinforce; tie book together.

God's World
What is a city?
Define: A city is an inhabited place of greater size or population than a town or village.
Basic services: police, fire, public education, water.
Read Busy City (Joe Mathieu); Golden Book

Physical Education
Somersaults, head stands

Story
The Story of An English Village (John S. Goodall)
Apt.3 (Ezra Jack Keats)

Memory Verse
"Be angry and do not sin: do not let the sun go down on your wrath."
Eph. 4:26

WEEK 20   FRIDAY

Field trip of your choice.

Preparation for next week:

General:
_____Read over lesson plans
_____List materials needed
_____Collect materials needed
_____Story pages, etc. to notebook

Library:
_____Return books used this week
_____Check out books for week after next

Field Trips:
_____Reconfirm next Friday's trip
_____Thank you note for last trip
_____Set up trip for week after next

WEEK 21 MONDAY

Bible

God doesn't want me to be proud. What does it mean to be proud? (to think you are better than others) Do you know how God feels about pride/being proud? (He hates it!) How does He want us to feel toward others? (He wants us to think more of others than ourselves. He wants us to build others up by our actions and attitudes, not tear them down.)

Find/draw picture of someone showing pride (Ex.: one person real big, other very small). Mount on construction paper circle; draw diagonal line through it.

On story page, write: God doesn't want me to be proud.

Reading

Read a poem.

Introduce letter shape and sound for R r. Child traces letter card while repeating sound.

(Alone) Classifying: Child sorts R and r cards from other letter cards; then matches them to R's and r's on the file folder.

Sequence and complete sentences: Child dictates story about last week's field trip.

Art

Make picture of different parts of hospital on butcher paper or construction paper (emergency room, patient room, waiting room, etc.).

Arithmetic

Introduce number eight and symbol 8. We are going to make a counting book of 8. (Using 3 pieces of construction paper folded in half, write on the outside of the cover: "My Counting Book of 8" with the child's name and date, using the same format as for previous books.)

On paper plate with numeral 8 written on the middle of it, have child clip the correct number of clothespins to its edge.

Page 1: Have child color 8 shapes on worksheet you have made; cut and mount on page.

Page 2: Have child glue numeral 8 and eight objects to page.

Character Building

Joyfulness: Being joyful and cheerful and happy is a choice. Sometimes it would be easier to be grumpy or pouty or sad. But no matter what happens to us or to those around us, God wants us to choose to be joyful. God wants us to be happy. He will help us, when we choose to be happy.

When we are joyful, how does it affect others? (It builds them up.) We can give love and smiles and encouragement to others when we are joyful, easier than when we are sad or grumpy.

On Character Building story page write: Joyfulness means choosing to be bubbling with happiness.

Physical Education
Roll and catch a ball.

Story
It's Mine! (Leo Lionni)

Memory Verse
"Let us not become conceited, provoking one another, envying one another." Gal. 5:26
"Rejoice always," I Thess.5:16

WEEK 21   TUESDAY

Bible
God wants us to guard what we see, hear, think, say, and do. He doesn't want us to say, do, or think wrong/bad things. He doesn't want us to see or hear wrong/bad things. What you think about, you bring about. Why does God want us to guard ourselves? (He wants to fill us up with good things; He wants to build us up, not break us down. He wants to feed our mind strong, good information, not bad.)

Put funnel on top of child's head. God wants us to be putting good thoughts, good pictures, good words into this machine/bank account... YOU! What is put in - by yourself and by others - is what you will get out, in what you say (words) and what you do (actions).

When you say or do things that God doesn't want you to, does that please God? (No) Does it build you up? (No) How can you be careful about your words and actions? (Ask God to help you to make the right choices; watch carefully what you see in books, magazines, TV, movies), and what you listen to (conversations, TV, radio, records/tapes). If you don't think it would make God happy to know you were seeing/hearing it - then don't!

Find picture of someone watching TV; mount in circle; draw diagonal line through it.

On story page, write: God doesn't want me to say or do wrong things.

Reading
Read a poem.

Left-to-right eye movement: Child "reads" row of five color shapes in row in front of him (left to right). (Ex.: "red circle, blue triangle," etc.)

(Alone) Visual discrimination: Child matches halves of pictures (match set of 20 pictures together).

Speech: Child "reads" book to you.

Music
Sweet Betsy from Pike
Down in the Valley

Arithmetic
Show child a card with eight dots on it. How many dots are there?
Write 8 on the chalkboard. Have child hold up correct number of fingers.

Repeat with previous numbers learned, mixing up the sequence.
Page 3: Have the child use eight strips of paper (1/2x3") to make chain; glue to page.
Page 4: Have child put eight stickers on it.

God's World
What is a city? (cont'd.)
j307 A752w   What is a Community (Caroline Arnold); FW; 1982.
Talk about differences between a large city, a small city, a town, a rural area/community: relationships, travel, services, recreation/entertainment.

Physical Education
Climb on inclined board.

Story
The Valentine Bears (Eve Bunting)

Memory Verse
"Pride goes before destruction," Prov.16:18a
"Do not be wise in your own opinion." Rom.12:16d

WEEK 21   WEDNESDAY

Bible
Review circle pictures (with diagonal lines). (God doesn't want us to listen to wrong teachings. He doesn't want me to fight... to be jealous... to be angry... to be selfish... to be proud... to say or do wrong things.)
How does God want you to act then? He tells us in Gal. 5:22-23a. There are nine "fruits," or results, of being filled with the Holy Spirit of God. For the next two weeks, we are going to be learning about them. The very first characteristic is love. Who can we love? (God, others, ourselves) How can we show love for God? (obey Him, worship Him) How can we show our love for others? (obey parents; be kind to others; do nice things for others - treat them special) How can we show love for ourselves? (take care of our bodies and minds; follow God's loving rules for us)
Cut out of brown/black construction paper (several sheets needed) a trunk and nine branches. You and child will be putting one "Fruit of The Holy Spirit" picture on each branch. Cut heart from pink construction paper. On it, glue picture of Jesus on top, family picture in middle, and picture of child on bottom. Write LOVE on it. Attach this to a branch of the poster tree. (Note: the individual characteristics pages will be taken off "tree" at the end of two weeks and put into notebook.)

Reading
Read a poem.
Auditory discrimination: Child repeats your clapping pattern.
Memory: Child looks at a tray of 4-6 objects; closes eyes; you take one or two away; he names missing object(s). Increase number of items as skill increases.

Listening: Child repeats sequences of words after you:

selfishness, pride, rebellion	wild flowers, animals, space
consequence, disobedience, sad	land, tree house, rural
happiness, joy, obedience	farther, commuting, commitment
blessings, Holy Spirit, fruit	pleasant, starlit, sweet-smelling
joyfulness, smile, pleasantness	choice, day-by-day, trying
good, habits, attitude	city, pollution, crime
congestion, hustle-bustle, visit	cultural, museums, shopping
construction, visitor, resident	country, peaceful, nature

Art

Make valentines (doilies, lace, construction paper, scissors, glue, markers, rubber stamps, crayons)

Arithmetic

Have child match card with numeral 8 on it with card that has eight objects on it (have 4 sets of these). Have numerals 0-7 mixed in with them.

Page 5: Have child use eight popsicle sticks/toothpicks to make design. Glue to page.

Page 6: Stamp eight rubber stamp images on page.

Review pages so far with child. Write 8 at top of each page as you review with child how many items are on each one.

Health/Manners

Safety Inside

Room by room, talk briefly about different safety habits.

Some examples by room are:

Kitchen - sharp knives away, wipe up spills, stay away from the stove, and no hot water.

Bathroom - be careful of hot water, wipe up spills, don't touch anything wet and touch electric appliance at the same time.

Stairs - keep things off stairway, keep toys picked up and put away.

All rooms - stay away from electrical outlets.

On "Personal Health and Safety" story page, write: I help keep our home safe.

Physical Education

Walk on tiptoes while music plays and stop when music stops.

Story

Town and Country (Alice and Martin Provensen); differences
When I Was Young In the Mountains (Cynthia Rylant)

Memory Verse

"Let the words of my mouth and the meditation of my heart be acceptable in Your sight, O Lord, my strength and my Redeemer." Ps.19:14

WEEK 21   THURSDAY

Bible
God wants me to be filled with joy! What is joy? (being filled with happiness) How can we show joy? (by smiling, by having a "smile in our voice") Does joy build us up or break us down? (builds us up) How do you feel when you are around someone who's happy and kind and whose eyes are twinkling? (feel happy, too) On yellow construction paper, draw circle; cut out. Put the word JOY at the top of the circle and draw a big smile face on it; attach it to a "branch."

Reading
Read a poem.

Introduce letter shape and sounds for S s (ss, zz). Child repeats sounds while tracing letter shape.

(Alone) Classifying: Child sorts S and s cards from others; then matches with the S's and s's on the file folder.

Sequence and complete sentences: Child dictates story about making and delivering Valentine cookies.

Music
Home on the Range

I Love the Mountains

Arithmetic
Using 25 counters, have child count them out into piles of 8.

Page 7: Punch eight holes in paper; mount to page; write 8 at top.

Page 8: Cut and glue eight objects from magazine. Write 8 at top of page.

Page 9: Color in correct amount on number line you've drawn.

Punch holes; reinforce; tie book together.

God's World
Country/Rural

Show pictures of some rural areas.

Talk about differences in priorities, jobs, personal preferences, services, and benefits (less traffic, see/hear more wild animals, see more wild flowers, have more space to play in, explore, "feel" seasons more because see more changes, able to plant large garden, able to walk along roadway, cleaner air, clearer sky, quieter).

j570 H951   Let's Go to the Woods (Harriet E. Huntington); b&w photos.

Physical Education
Rolls and somersaults.

Story
The Little House (Virginia Lee Burton)

Over in the Meadow (John Lanstaff)

Memory Verse
"Beloved, let us love one another, for love is of God..." I John 4:7a

WEEK 21   FRIDAY

Make and Deliver Valentine Cookies.

Preparation for next week:

General:
_____Read over lesson plans
_____List materials needed
_____Collect materials needed
_____Story pages, etc. to notebook

Library:
_____Return books used this week
_____Check out books for week after next

Field Trips:
_____Reconfirm next Friday's trip
_____Thank you note for last trip
_____Set up trip for week after next

WEEK 22   MONDAY

Bible

God wants me to be filled with peace. What is peace? (calmness, quietness, getting along with others) How do we act when we're peaceful? (not angry or loud or fighting; quiet, calm, friendly) Does peace build us up or break us down? (build us up) How do you feel when you're around someone who's friendly and calm? (feel friendly, calm, and happy, too) God wants us to be at peace with Him, with others, and with ourselves. Peace reminds many people of a calm river, so let's make our "peace picture" blue. (Out of blue construction paper, cut gently wavy lines across the paper halfway up. Write PEACE on the top of it; attach to a "branch.")

Reading

Read a poem.
Left-to-right eye movement: Child takes different steps (giant, medium, baby) to the right and left that you direct him to.
(Alone) Visual discrimination: Child matches wallpaper sample patterns on card (2 each of 20 patterns).
Speech: Child "reads" book to you.

Art

Valentine picture designs - draw design/shape on paper. Put it on top of white construction paper, which is on top of magazines. Hold tape in place so paper doesn't slip. Prick design with pin, making sure to go through first two layers. Untape. Mount white pin-pricked paper onto red construction paper.

Arithmetic

Introduce number nine and symbol 9. We are going to make a counting book of 9.

(Using 3 pieces of construction paper folded in half, write on the outside of the cover: "My Counting Book of 9" with the child's name and date, using the same format as for previous books.)

On paper plate with numeral 9 written on the middle of it, have child clip the correct number of clothespins to its edge.

Page 1: Have child color nine shapes on worksheet you have made; cut and mount object part to page 1.

Page 2: Have child glue numeral 9 and nine objects to page.

Character Building

Patience: Sometimes it is hard to wait for something we want very badly. What happens when we get impatient (when we're not waiting very well)? (We get grumpy and disrespectful and disobedient easily.) What would happen if we got all we wanted exactly when we wanted it? (We'd be greedy and demanding - very selfish.)

Sometimes God wants us to wait:

1. to learn to be thankful for what we have/get.
2. to learn that we can't be selfish and think only of our wants and needs.
3. to remember that God will allow everything to happen in its right time.
4. to be ready for it.

On the Character Building story page, write: "Patience means being content while I'm waiting for something."

Physical Education

Bounce and catch ball.

Story

The Happy Day (Ruth Krauss); animals come out of hibernation and see flower growing.

Memory Verse

"A merry heart does good like medicine." Prov.17:22a

WEEK 22   TUESDAY

Bible

God wants me to be patient. What does it mean to be patient? (to be pleasant and calm while you wait for something) Does this build you up or break you down? (build you up) When you are patient (pleasant, calm while you wait) does it make life easier or harder for those around you? (easier) What is an example of when you have been patient? (waiting to say something, get something, do something, or reach a goal) Even grown-ups need to be patient many times. Sometimes it's easy, sometimes it seems hard. Each time you are patient, you are practicing to make the next time easier.

(On a brown piece of construction paper, cut out a triangle. Talk with the child about the pyramids built many, many years ago in Egypt. The people there did not have modern machines like we do today. Each part of the building of the tall, huge structures took lots of time. The people had to be <u>patient</u>. On the triangle, write PATIENCE; attach it to a "branch."

Reading

Read a poem.

Auditory discrimination: Child tells if the beginning sounds for the two words is the same or different:

rake, wake	servant, selfish
rabbit, yes	salvation, such
running, reverence	seedlings, zoo
well, rent	zebra, sudsy
rural, really	silver, spiritual

(Alone) Closure: Child completes 10-12 faces with parts missing drawn by you on the chalkboard.

Listening: Child repeats sequence of words after you:

joyful, peaceful, patient	appreciate, conserve, stewardship
kindly, filled, Holy Spirit	citizens, voting, opinion
guidance, others, ourselves	Constitution, Declaration of
God, spilling, over	Independence
positive, desirable, character	godly, blessing, patriotic
founding, freedoms, responsible	United States, country, 1776
anthem, heritage, sacrifice	"In God we trust," motto, standard
quality, standard of living	century, growth, expansion

Music

If you're Happy
Peace like a River

Arithmetic

Show child a card with nine dots on it. How many dots are there? Write 9 on the chalkboard. Have child hold up correct number of fingers. Repeat with previous numbers learned, mixing up the sequence.

Page 3: Have child use nine strips of paper (1/2" x3") to make loops for chain. Glue together and glue to page.

Page 4: Have child put nine stickers on it.

God's World

U.S.A. Review:

1. What is it? (group of 50 states united by government)
2. Where is it? (in North America)
3. How many states are united? (50)
4. What makes our country so special? (a. Our freedoms: free speech, press, religion, bear arms, etc.; b. one language; c. individual government of states within federal guidelines; and d. country begun by pursuing religious freedom.)
5. How did we get our freedoms? (stated in document: Constitution of the United States of America)

Find pictures showing several of our freedoms; make poster.

Physical Education
Jump forward and backward over line; stand on tiptoes.

Story
Norman Rockwell's Americana ABC (George Mendoza)
Stone Soup (Marcie Brown) j398B878
A Book of God's Gifts (Golden Book)

Memory Verse
"...have peace with one another." Mark 9:50d
"and the peace of God, which surpasses all understanding, will guard your
    hearts and minds through Christ Jesus." Phil. 4:7

WEEK 22   WEDNESDAY

Bible
God wants me to be kind. What does it mean to be kind? (to care about
    others and to be helpful) What are some ways we can show kindness?
    (to do nice things to help others or to make things easier for others)
    Have child give examples. If you had some oranges you just got at the
    store with your Mom and on the way home you saw someone that
    looked hungry, what could you do? (give him an orange) Let's make a
    big round orange to remind us that God wants us to be filled with
    kindness toward other people. (Cut circle from orange construction
    paper, write KINDNESS on it, and attach it to a "branch.")

Reading
Read a poem.
Rhyming: Child names words to rhyme with "rod," "rope," "rode," "rub."
(Alone) Hand-eye coordination: Child colors coloring-book picture.
Kinesthetic: Child traces letter shape (using two fingers and repeating
    sound) of "R" "r" on letter card, in the air, and on your back.

Art
Crayon-resist picture. Use brightly colored crayons (pressing rather hard)
    to make picture/design. Paint over with watercolors.

Arithmetic
Have child match card with numeral 9 on it with card that has nine objects
    on it (have 4 sets of these). Have numeral 0-8 sets mixed in with them.
Page 5: Have child use nine popsicle sticks/toothpicks to make design.
    Glue to page.
Page 6: Stamp nine rubber stamp images on page.
Review pages so far with child. Write 9 on top of each page as you review
    with child how many items are on each page one.

Health/Manners
Safety Outside:
1. Stay away from lawn mowers and other equipment.
2. Stay away from the street.

3. Stay away from strange dogs.
4. Do not talk to strangers.
5. Do not play in, around or under a car.
6. Obey your parents' rules for your yard.
Draw picture showing her/himself being safe outside.
On "Health and Safety" story page write: "I am careful outside."

Physical Education
Move to music and stop when music stops.

Story
The Big Book of Cowboys (Sydney E. Fletcher); J917.8F61.
All for Love (Tasha Tudor); J808.8A416; pictures.

Memory Verse
"Be patient in tribulation." Romans 12:10-12b

WEEK 22   THURSDAY

Bible
God wants me to be filled with goodness. What does goodness mean? (to be virtuous, to follow God's rules) Does being good build you up or break you down? (build you up) Does this make God happy or sad? (happy) How does it make you feel to know you're obeying? (happy) Does God reward His followers for obeying? (yes) Let's make a purple crown to help us remember that God wants us to be filled with goodness, to choose to be good. (Cut crown out of purple construction paper; write GOODNESS on it; attach to a "branch.")

Reading
Read a poem.
Rhyming: Child names rhyming words for "swim," "sum," "say," "stir."
(Alone) Hand-eye coordination: Child laces shoelace through sewing card(s).
Kinesthetic: Using two fingers and repeating two sounds of "s," child traces "S s" on the card, in the air, and on your back.

Music
Songs of your choice

Arithmetic
Using 25 counters, have child count them out into piles of 9.
Page 7: Punch 9 holes in paper. Mount to page; write 9 at top of page.
Page 8: Cut and glue nine objects from magazine; write 9 at top of page.
Page 9: Color in correct amount on number line you've drawn. Punch holes; reinforce; tie book together.

God's World
U.S.A., (continued)
1. When did our country declare its independence? (July 4, 1776)

2. What can we do for it to help it be strong? (build it up, not break it down, in actions and words; pray for country and leaders)
3. What made our country strong and will continue to bless it? (it is shown on our money, "In God We Trust")
4. What is our symbol? (bald eagle)
5. What is our national anthem? Read <u>The Star-Spangled Banner</u> (Peter Spier); j784S795s; illus.

Resources:

j929.9B59f	<u>Flags of the U.S.</u> (Geoffrey Biggs); b&w colored illus. of all states' flags and little interpretation of each flag
j929.9 G350	<u>Our Country's Flag</u> (Nicholas Georgiady and Lois Romano)
j917.53 S35t	<u>This is Washington, D.C.</u> (M. Sasek); large color illus, with easy text

Physical Education

Walk in circle without losing balance.

Story

<u>Fire! Fire!</u> (Gail Gibbons)
<u>Watch the Stars Come Out</u> (Riki Levinson); girl and brother travel to New York City

Memory Verse

"But he who honors Him has mercy on the needy." Prov.14:31b
"Blessed is the nation whose God is the Lord, and the people whom He has chosen as His own inheritance." Ps.33:12

WEEK 22   FRIDAY

Visit Fire Station:

Resources:

j363.37B942f	<u>The Fire Station Book</u> (Nancy Bundy); photos
j371.425P484f	<u>Careers with a Fire Department</u> (Johanna Peterson)

Preparation for next week:

General:
_____Read over lesson plans
_____List materials needed
_____Collect materials needed
_____Story pages, etc. to notebook

Library:
_____Return books used this week
_____Check out books for week after next

Field Trips:
_____Reconfirm next Friday's trip
_____Thank you note for last trip
_____Set up trip for week after next

WEEK 23   MONDAY

Bible

God wants me to be faithful. What does it mean to be <u>faithful</u>? (to be full of faith, to be loyal to God) Does this build you up or break you down? (build you up) Does this make God happy? (yes) After the leaves have fallen in autumn is God faithful in making new leaves? (yes) Let's make a green leaf to remind us to be faithful. (Cut leaf shape out of green construction paper; write FAITHFULNESS on it; attach to a "branch.")

Reading

Read a poem.

Introduce the letter shape and sound for "T t." Child repeats sound while tracing letter shape.

(Alone) Classifying: Child sorts T and t cards from other letter cards, then matches with the T's and t's on the file folder.

Sequence and complete sentences: Child dictates story about visit to the fire station.

Art

Draw and color/paint fire station picture; send it with thank-you note to the fire station.

Arithmetic

Introduce number ten and symbol 10. We are going to make a counting book of 10. (Using 3 pieces of construction paper folded in half, write on the outside of the cover: "My Counting Book of 10" with the child's name and date, using the same format as for previous books.)

On paper plate with numeral 10 written on the middle of it, have child clip the correct number of clothespins to its edge.

Page 1: Have child color ten shapes on worksheet you have made; cut and mount to page.

Page 2: Have child glue numeral 10 and ten objects to page.

Character Building

Self-Control: Have child roleplay several situations that show someone controlling himself and showing no control. How did your actions affect the other person?

On Character Building story page, write: "I need to tell myself `NO' when I'm tempted to do or say the wrong thing."

Physical Education

Roll and catch ball.

Story

<u>The Little Fireman</u> (Margaret Wise Brown)
Any other book by Margaret Wise Brown

Memory Verse

"You who love the Lord, hate evil!" Ps.97:10a
"Do what is good..." Romans 13:3c

WEEK 23   TUESDAY

Bible

God wants me to be filled with gentleness. What does <u>gentle</u> mean? (soft, mild, kind) How can we be gentle? (to speak softly and kindly, to be mild-tempered, not stormy and pouty and "screamy," to act gently, touch others in a soft, kind way, not hit or grab) Does gentleness build us and others up or tear down? (build up) When I think of gentleness, I think of a lamb, soft and mild. We are God's lambs too; He is our Shepherd. Let's make a soft white lamb to remind us to be filled with gentleness. (Cut out lamb shape from white construction paper, put on eye and mouth. On top write GENTLENESS; paint rest with a solution of half white glue and half water; cover with cotton balls/pieces; attach to "branch.")

Reading

Read a poem.

Left-to-right eye movement: Make patterns of beads on string, laying knot at the left side. Child copies pattern of beads on another string.

(Alone) Visual discrimination: Child matches colors of crayons in 3 boxes of 16 crayons.

Speech: Child "reads" book to you.

Music

Songs of your choice

Arithmetic

Show child a card with ten dots on it. How many dots are there? Write 10 on the chalkboard. Have child hold up the correct number of fingers. Repeat with previous numbers learned, mixing up the sequence.

Page 3: Have the child use ten strips of paper (1/2" x 3") to make a chain; glue to page.

Page 4: Have child put ten stickers on.

God's World

Temperature: Heat/cold measured in air, water, people, meat roasting, ovens, etc., by thermometer. Show several different kinds of thermometers.

Three forms of matter: Solid, liquid, gas.

Show: Water at 32 degrees = solid (ice)

       Water at 32 degrees = liquid (water)

       Water at 212 degrees (boiling point) = gas (steam)

Physical Education

Climb on inclined board

Story

<u>Fire Engine Book</u> (Tibor Gergely); illus.; Golden Book

<u>I Like Butterflies</u> (Gladys Conklin)

Memory Verse
"I have chosen the way of truth..." Ps.119:30a

WEEK 23   WEDNESDAY

Bible
God wants me to be filled with self-control. What is self-control? (to have power over our emotions, our desires-what we want, and what we think WE want to do) Who knows what is better for us, God or us? (God!) Do we always act in the best way, by ourselves? (no) We sometimes feel pouty or want to do things that we shouldn't. What can we tell ourselves when we feel that feeling coming on? (STOP!) Then we can GO with the right action, choice, or attitude. To help us remember that God wants us to be filled with self-control, let's make a red stop sign so we can think, "Stop!" (Cut 8-sided stop sign from red construction paper; write SELF-CONTROL on it; attach to a "branch.") Review all nine fruits/products of the Holy Spirit of God.

Reading
Read a poem.
Auditory discrimination: Child repeats clapping patterns you make.
(Alone) Classifying: Child sorts wallpaper shapes into triangle, heart, circle, and square piles (10 of each shape).
Listening: Child repeats sequences of words after you:

goodness, faithfulness, nice	self-control, temper, will
gentleness, lamb, softness	Holy Spirit, helper, guiding
heat, temperature, thermometer	matter, forms, three
solid, liquid, gas	ice, water, steam
sounds, noises, pleasant	wanted, unwanted, shrieking
learning, practice, patience	safety, sharp objects, matches
inclined, rolling, catching	emergency, cautious, obedient
heat, coldness, changing	

Art
Make pussy willow picture with cut-off ends of Q-tips, brown pipe cleaners, construction paper.

Arithmetic
Have child match card with numeral 10 on it with card that has ten objects on it. (Have four sets of these.) Have numerals 0-9 sets mixed in with them.
P.5: Have child use ten popsicle sticks-toothpicks to make design. Glue to page.
P.6: Stamp 10 rubber stamp images on page.
Review pages so far with child. Write 10 on top of each page as you review with child how many items are on each page.

Health/Manners
Safety of Medicine, Sharp Objects, and Matches
Sometimes one of us has to take medicine to get over an illness. If Dad has

medicine does Mom take some of it? (no) That's right. We don't take anyone else's medicine. And we only take the amount the doctor prescribed for us; we don't take more than we were supposed to. That would be abusing it, using it in a way it was not meant to be used. Is that being a good steward of our bodies? (no) So how should we treat medicine? (carefully)

How about sharp knives or other sharp tools? What if you found one lying on the edge of the counter, where you could reach it? Would it be best to play with it or tell Mom about it being there? (tell Mom) Can sharp objects hurt you? (yes) How? (they can cut you easily or poke you and hurt you)

How about matches? What are they used for? (to start a fire) When have you seen them used? (to start a campfire, to begin woodstove/fireplace fire) Are they toys to play with? (no!) What if you and a friend were playing at our home and you found matches on the table from when the woodstove fire was started and your friend said, "Let's sneak outside and try them!" What would you do? (Say, "NO!" Get the matches from him and tell your mother/father) What could happen from being careless with matches? (start a house fire; start a forest fire; other people might get hurt/burned/killed; you might get hurt/burned/killed)

On "Personal Health and Safety" story page, write: "I am careful with medicine. I don't touch sharp objects. I don't play with matches."

Physical Education
Skip while music plays and stop when music stops.

Story
Wait Till the Moon is Full (Margaret Wise Brown)
The Wonder Book of Firemen and Fire Engines (Lisa Peters); Golden-type book

Memory Verse
"Let your gentleness be evident to all men." Phil.4:5a

WEEK 23   THURSDAY

Bible
Introduction to: "God wants me to obey and make the right decisions."
What is obedience? (God asked Noah to build a boat of a certain size, to collect two of each kind of animal and to get the animals and his family in the boat at the right time. Noah obeyed, even though it was not raining) What are some rewards/blessings for obedience?
On story page write: "God wants me to obey and make the right decisions. To obey means to do what God wants me to do, to follow God's rules. It is important to God that I obey. He will bless me for my obedience."

Reading
Read a poem.
Rhyming: Child names rhyming words for: "top," "toy," "tube," "toot."
(Alone) Hand-eye coordination: Child does puzzle(s).

Kinesthetic: Using two fingers and repeating the "t" sound, child traces "T t" on the letter card, in the air, on your back.

Music

The Wise Man and the Foolish Man

Arithmetic

Using 25 counters, have child count them out into piles of 10.
Page 7: Punch 10 holes in paper; mount to page; write 10 at top.
Page 8: Cut and glue ten objects from magazine; write 10 at top.
Page 9: Color in correct amount on number line you've drawn. Punch holes; reinforce; tie book together.

God's World

Sounds/Noises: A sound is made by something moving back and forth in the air; vibrations in air=sound waves.
Megaphones, amplifiers: make sounds louder.
Echos: sounds bouncing off surface.
What makes sounds? (people's voices and movements; animals; musical instruments; machines; nature: wind, ocean)
Noise: Loud, confused or unwanted sound(s). Examples: screaming, pounding on piano, loud machine, traffic (man-made)

Physical Education

Stand on one foot and then the other, balancing.

Story

Blue Sea (Roibert Kalan)
5 Pennies to Spend (Miriam Yound); Golden Book

Memory Verse

"Whoever has no rule over his own spirit is like a city broken down, without walls."

WEEK 23   FRIDAY

Tour emergency communication center or visit ambulance station.

Preparation for next week:

General:
_____Read over lesson plans
_____List materials needed
_____Collect materials needed
_____Story pages, etc. to notebook

Library:
_____Return books used this week
_____Check out books for week after next

Field Trips:
_____Reconfirm next Friday's trip
_____Thank you note for last trip
_____Set up trip for week after next

WEEK 24   MONDAY

Bible

Rebellion: what is <u>rebellion</u>? (choosing not to obey) How did Adam and Eve rebel/disobey? (God had told them not to eat from a certain tree. They chose to listen to temptation and do what God asked them <u>not</u> to do) How did God feel? (He was sad) What are some consequences of disobedience?

On story page write: Rebellion means to choose to disobey God. God would hate it if I would disobey/rebel. There are consequences to rebellion.

Reading

Read a poem.

Introduce letter shape and sounds for "U u" (uh, you, u - as in put). Child repeats three sounds as he traces letter shape.

(Alone) Classifying: Child sorts U and u letter cards from others; then matches with the U's and u's on the file folder.

Sequence and complete sentences: Child dictates story about the tour to the emergency communications center (or ambulance station).

Art

Draw and color or paint picture of himself doing something obedient (picking up, being kind, helping others).

Arithmetic

Read <u>A Golden Sturdy Book of Counting</u> (H. Federko)

Begin making My COUNTING TO TEN Book. On cover write: "My Counting to Ten Book" with child's name and date, using the same format as for previous books. Using one page per number and writing numeral at top of page, stamp the correct number of rubber stamp images on pages for 0,1,2,3,4.

Character Building

Obedience, decisiveness. Talk about:
1. Refusing to be tempted to question something you know is best/right.
2. Making commitments now so there will be a structure to prevent future problems (Example: commitment never to take drugs).
3. Not getting sidetracked from obeying.

On Character Building Story page write: If I am tempted to disobey, I will not listen. I can make commitments to help me avoid problems later. I will not get sidetracked from doing what I know is right.

Physical Education

Bounce and catch ball.

Story
Angus and the Ducks (Marjorie Flack)
Peter Rabbit (Beatrix Potter)

Memory Verse
"If you love Me, keep My commandments." John 14:15

WEEK 24   TUESDAY

Bible
There will be times when other people will try to talk us into disobeying. How would they encourage us to disobey?
1. Cause doubts as to what the rules really are.
2. Cause doubts as to whether there would be consequences.
3. Make the disobedient act sound fun/good.
4. Cause us to question authority.

Temptation is sneaky and evil. The devil wants to destroy us and our relationship with God. We must not listen to temptation. We must not tempt others to disobey what they know is right. Read II Thessalonians 3:3, "But the Lord is faithful and he will strengthen and protect you from the evil one."

We need to focus on God and what He wants us to do. We need to ask ourselves if an act/word would please God or hurt Him. We need to say "no" to any influence that encourages us to go away from what we believe is right.

On story page write: The devil wants to destroy me and destroy my relationship with God. I need to focus on God and what He wants so I will not be tempted to disobey. II Thessalonians 3:3 says that God is faithful and He will strengthen and protect me from the evil one.

Reading
Read a poem.
Left-to-right eye movement: Child copies pegboard pattern you've made (left-to-right).
(Alone) Visual discrimination: Child sorts colored picture cards into matching pairs (2 each of 15-20 pictures/stamped designs).
Speech: Child "reads" book to you.

Music
"Fairest Lord Jesus"

Arithmetic
Read When We Went to the Park (Shirley Hughes); what she and Grandpa saw 1-10 or other counting book.

God's World
Music/Pleasant sounds
What can make music? (voices and instruments; talk about different kinds) Why do we make music? (to express emotions) Listen to cassette/record of classical music.

Physical Education
Jump forward and backward over line; hop on one foot at a time.

Story
Crash! Bang! Boom! (Peter Spier)

Memory Verse
"Then the Lord saw that the wickedness of man was great in the earth...and the Lord was sorry that He had made man on the earth and He was grieved in His heart." Gen.6:5a,6

WEEK 24   WEDNESDAY

Bible
How does my obedience affect me? (I am blessed by it from God) How does my obedience affect others? (It makes my parents joyful; it shows a good example and faith in action to others. It shows I do not follow wrong actions.)

On story page write: When I obey, it makes my parents glad and sets a good example to others.

Reading
Read a poem.

Auditory discrimination: Child listens to sets of two words and tells you whether beginning sounds are alike or different:

touch, deliver	up, over
tall, tomorrow	acrobat, unto
doctor, toenail	offer, ultimate
telling, truth	umbrella, office
topmost, down	under, uplift

(Alone) Closure: Child draws missing parts of shape (on worksheet of 10-20)

Listening: Child repeats sequences of words after you:

decisions, right, obedience	practice, lessons, commitment
rebellion, hating, consequence	jubilant, happy, songs
focus, God, pleasing	instruments, notes, orchestra
temptation, resist, no!	G-clef, whole notes, piano
example, leader, joyful	xylophone, recorder, humming
obedience, peers, parents	habit, benefits, blessings
music, heartfelt, joyous	praises, emotions, tempo
dancing, expressive, ballet	

Art
Make pinwheels (paper, stick/plastic straw, pin).

Arithmetic
Read Count and See (Tana Hoban).

Have child stamp correct number of rubber stamp images on pages for numbers nine and ten. Punch holes; reinforce; tie book together.

Match 0-10 numeral cards with 0-10 numerals on file folder.

Health/Manners

Physical safety in cars and away from home (at a friend's home, grandparents', store).

God wants us to be wise and use common sense. Some common sense safety rules to be used away from home are:

In car: Don't bother driver; he/she has to respond quickly and pay attention to the road. Wear your seatbelt all the time.

Away from home: Know your parents' names, your address and phone number. If visiting/traveling with grandparents, know their name and their address in case of accident. Remember to obey your family's safety rules and manners even when you're away from home.

Review child's parents' names, phone number and address. Review grandparents' names.

On "Personal Health and Safety" story page write: I always wear my seat belt. I know my parents' names and our address and phone number.

Physical Education

Walk while music plays and stay still as a statue when music stops.

Story

Spring Story (Brambly Hedge, Jill Barklem)
Jonah and the Great Fish (Clyde Robert Bulla); j224B59j

Memory Verse

"My son, if sinners entice you, do not consent." Prov.1:10,15b
"I delight to do Your will, O my God." Ps.40:8a

WEEK 24   THURSDAY

Bible

Obedience shows thankfulness. How does obedience show thankfulness? (It shows we are thankful to God for His control, His leadership, His power. It shows thankfulness for our talents. It shows we are thankful for each day. It shows we are thankful to be able to be of service to Him.)

On story page write: My obedience shows thankfulness to God.
Review section on obedience.

Reading

Read a poem.
Rhyming: Child names rhyming words for "up," "un."
(Alone) Hand-eye coordination: Child strings beads on shoelace.
Kinesthetic: Using two fingers and repeating three sounds for "u" child traces U's on cards, in the air, and on your back.

Music

"Skip to my Lou"

Arithmetic
Read his "My Counting to Ten" book.
Match 0-10 numeral cards with 0-10 dots on file folder.
Match 0-10 dot cards with 0-10 numerals on file folder.

God's World
Dance
Read:
j793.3 A542d   <u>Dancing is</u> (George Ancona); b&w photos; easy text
Resources:
j793.3 M29   <u>First Steps in Ballet: Basic Barre</u> (Thalia Mara); examples for home practice
j792.8 W181b   <u>Ballet for Boys and Girls</u> (Kathrine S. Walker & Joan Butler); b&w photos, ref.

Physical Education
Aerobics - run; continue to move to music.

Story
<u>A Whistle for Willie</u> (Ezra Jack Keats)
<u>The Dancing Man</u> (Ruth Bornstein)

Memory Verse
"Do everything without complaining or arguing." Phil.2:14
"Depart from evil, and do good; seek peace, and pursue it." Ps.34:14

WEEK 24   FRIDAY

Visit a police station.

Resources:
j363.2M381D   <u>A Day in the Life of a Police Cadet</u> (Troll Assoc.)
j352.2R263c   <u>Careers in a Police Department</u> (Joanne Ray)

Preparation for next week:

General:
_____Read over lesson plans
_____List materials needed
_____Collect materials needed
_____Story pages, etc. to notebook

Library:
_____Return books used this week
_____Check out books for week after next

Field Trips:
_____Reconfirm next Friday's trip
_____Thank you note for last trip
_____Set up trip for week after next

WEEK 25   MONDAY

Bible

God gives us the Ten Commandments. What are <u>commandments</u>? (Rules we must follow) The Ten Commandments are ten rules we must follow; they are a plan for right living. Why did God give us the Ten Commandments? (to glorify Him, to help us - give us a plan to follow)

Read story of Moses receiving the Ten Commandments from God (Exodus 19:9-20:21)

On new story page entitled "The Ten Commandments," write: God gave us ten rules to follow: The Ten Commandments - to glorify Him and to give us a plan to live right.

Reading

Read a poem.

Introduce letter shape and sound of V v. Child traces letter shape while repeating sound.

(Alone) Classifying: Child sorts V and v letter cards from others, then matches with the V's and v's on the file folder.

Sequence and complete sentences: Child dictates story about tour of police station.

Art

Draw and color/paint picture of police station. Mail with thank-you note to police station.

Arithmetic

Introduce concepts of many/few; more/less/equal.

On the table using beans/bread tags/crayons, have a pile of many and a pile of few. Talk about the difference with child.

For child's MORE AND LESS book, make cover using previous format.

For page 1 of book, have child stamp lots of rubber stamp images on one index card and a few on another. Mount both on first page and write on top of page: Many and Few.

Character Building

Reverence: Respecting God's holiness so much that we do all we can to build God up to others and treat Him with honor.

How would we treat a king? (say only nice, respectful things to him; do all we can to make him happy; serve him) That's what we need to do for God.

Physical Education

Roll and catch ball.

Story

<u>Wee Gillis</u> (Munro Leaf); choices, making decisions

<u>The Poky Little Puppy</u> (Janette Sebring Lowrey)

Any of Beatrix Potter's books

Memory Verse
"But sanctify the Lord God in your hearts..." I Pet.3:15a
"Worship God." Rev.22:9e

WEEK 25   TUESDAY

Bible
Read Commandments I and II.
I. "I am the Lord your God...you shall have no other gods before Me."
     (Ex.20:1-3) We must put God first in our lives.
II. "You shall not make for yourself any carved image." (Ex.20:4-6). We are
     to love the Lord our God with all our heart, soul, mind, and strength.
Copy these commandments on story page.

Reading
Read a poem.
(Alone) Left-to-right eye movement: Make worksheet with shapes in a row
     (6 rows). Child colors, working from the left to right.
Visual discrimination: You hold up several sets of objects (Ex: 3 red bread
     tags, 2 purple crayons, 4 paper clips). Child makes identical set.
Speech: Child "reads" book to you.

Music
White Coral Bells
Jesus Wants Me for a Sunbeam

Arithmetic
On flannelboard, have child put many circles on and put a few squares on.
     Repeat with other shapes.
For page 2 of book, have child lick many gummed stickers of a certain
     shape to a page and a few of another shape.

God's World
Plants - Structure
There are main parts in every plant:
     1. Roots - underground support, anchor plant firmly to ground, soak up
         moisture from ground.
     2. Stems - Hold leaves, branches up to fresh air and sunshine. Hold
         special cells that are like pipelines to carry water and minerals and
         food up and down.
     3. Leaves
     4. Flowers
     5. Seeds
Resource:
j581 Z72   <u>What's Inside of Plants</u> (Herbert S. Zim); color drawings; parts
         of plants: leaf, stem, root, flower, fruit, seed

Physical Education
Climb on inclined board.

Story
The Tiny Seed (Eric Carle)
The Noah's Ark Book (illus. Tibor Gergely); Golden Book

Memory Verse
"The fear of the Lord leads to life, And he who has it will abide in satisfaction; He will not be visited with evil." Prov.19:23

WEEK 25   WEDNESDAY

Bible
III. "You shall not take the name of the Lord your God in vain." (God's name is holy. We are to honor Him by honoring His name) What are some names for God? (God, Jesus Christ, Lord, Father, Holy Spirit, Son of God) No matter if others say these or other names for God in a bad or joking way, we are not to do this.
Copy commandment III on story page.

Reading
Read a poem.
Auditory discrimination: Child repeats clapping patterns you make.
(Alone) Closure: Child connects missing parts to his pictures (set of 20).
Listening: Child repeats sequences of words after you:

obedience, thankfulness, loyalty	commitment, humility, habit
Ten Commandments, Moses, tablets	mountain, representative, leader
reverence, holy, Lord	idols, name of God, humility
heart, mind, soul	Father, Jesus Christ, Holy Spirit
fire drill, practice, escape	firefighters, mask, helper
outside, quickly, safety	dangerous, hiding, waiting
plants, seeds, roots, growth	stem, leaves, flowers
propagation, vegetables, beet	air, water, sunshine, dirt

Art
Make "spring blossoms" picture: glue green stems (pipe cleaners or construction paper) onto construction paper background. Crumple small pieces of colored tissue paper and glue onto "stems" to make the blossoms.

Arithmetic
More/less
Put four shapes/objects on the table. Child closes eyes and you take one object away; open eyes; are there more/fewer?
Worksheet: put x on group of objects that shows less (4-6 rows of two sets of objects in each - a "more" group and a "less" group).

Health/Manners
Fire Drill
Review procedure from Wednesday, Week 4.

Physical Education
Balance on balance beam/curbstone 10 feet.

Story
Listen to the cassette tape, "Sir Oliver's Song" (first side).

Memory Verse
"I am the Lord your God...you shall have no other gods before Me."
Ex.20:2,3

WEEK 25   THURSDAY

Bible
Review Commandments I-III.
IV. "Remember the Sabbath day to keep it holy." (Ex.20:8-11) We are to
work six days and do our work then; the seventh day we are to rest.
God completed His work in creating the world in six days. He used
the seventh day to rest; He blessed it and made it holy.
Copy commandment IV on story page.

Reading
Read a poem.
Rhyming: Child names rhyming words for "vine," "vile," and "vest."
(Alone) Hand-eye coordination: Child uses scissors and glue to make
picture with construction paper.
Kinesthetic: Using two fingers, child traces letter shape V v (while saying
sound) on letter card, in the air, and on your back.

Music
Rise and Shine
A Tisket A Tasket

Arithmetic
More/less/equal
Have three cups and two straws. Are there the same amount of cups and
straws? No. There are more cups than straws. Repeat same concept
with different numbers of objects having some sets more, some less,
some equal.
On worksheet you have made (with 6-8 rows of two groups of shapes), put
a ring around the group that shows more in each row.

God's World
What all plants need: air, soil, water
Read:
j635 J67f   From Seed to Jack O Lantern (Hannah Lyons Johnson); large,
b&w photo of how pumpkins grow

Notes

j635 J67fs   <u>From Seed to Salad</u> (Hannah Lyons Johnson); large, b&w photos of seeds/ vegetables

Resources:
j581 S46   <u>Play with Plants</u> (Millicent E. Selsam); b&w drawings; experiments
j581 s46pla   <u>Play with Seeds</u> (Millicent E. Selsam); b&w drawings; experiments

Physical Education
Aerobics - continual (moving) activity to music. (Help your child pace him/ herself.)

Story
Listen to the second side of the cassette tape, "Sir Oliver's Song."

Memory Verse
"You shall not take the name of the Lord your God in vain, for the Lord will not hold him guiltless who takes his name in vain." Ex.20:7

WEEK 25   FRIDAY

Visit a greenhouse.

Preparation for next week:

General:
_____Read over lesson plans
_____List materials needed
_____Collect materials needed
_____Story pages, etc. to notebook

Library:
_____Return books used this week
_____Check out books for week after next

Field Trips:
_____Reconfirm next Friday's trip
_____Thank you note for last trip
_____Set up trip for week after next

WEEK 26   MONDAY

Bible
V. "Honor your father and mother, that your days may belong upon the land which the Lord your God is giving you." (Ex.20:12)

This is the only commandment with a promise. How can you honor your parents? (Never talk badly to them or about them to others; treat them special; talk with respect to them; obey them the first time they ask)
Copy commandment V on the story page.

Reading
Read a poem.
Introduce W w letter shape and sound. Child repeats sound and traces letter with fingers.
(Alone) Classifying: Have child sort W and w cards from others; then match with the W's and w's on the file folder.
Sequence and complete sentences: Have the child dictate story about visit to greenhouse.

Art
Make thank-you card and picture of the greenhouse; mail to greenhouse people.

Arithmetic
More/less
On flannelboard, have child tell which group had more? Less? On worksheet, have child put ring around group of objects that shows more in each row (6-8 rows of two groups of shapes).

Character Building
Respect: Talk about how child/other person can show respect to God, parents, life, marriage commitment. Talk about what happens when we don't show respect to them. (problems begin) What happens?
On Character Building story page, write: I do my best to show my respect to God, my parents, and human life.

Physical Education
Throw and catch a ball.

Story
A Child's Garden of Verses - "The Swing" and others

Memory Verse
"Remember the Sabbath day, to keep it holy. Six days you shall labor and do all your work, but the seventh day is the Sabbath of the Lord your God..." Ex.20:8-10a

WEEK 26   TUESDAY

Bible
VI. "You shall not murder." (Ex.20:13) We need to respect life. Life is sacred; God created every person. Everyone is special to God.
Copy commandment VI on the story page. Review commandments I-VI.

Reading
Read a poem.

(Alone) Left-to-right eye movement: Child draws line from left to right on worksheets you made (people and animals on left side; their houses on the right; 5-6 on each of 2 pages).

(Alone) Visual discrimination: Child sorts beans and seeds into different segments of egg carton (50-100 beans, seeds of up to 12 varieties).

Music
Are You Sleeping? (Frere Jacque) Nursery rhyme songs

Arithmetic
More/less/equal

Explain that equal means to have the same amount as something else.

Show examples of more, less and equal on the flannelboard. Add extra shapes to make groups equal.

On worksheet of eight rows of two groups, have child draw additional shapes to make the "less" group so that it's equal.

God's World
Plants

Review plant structure. What do plants need? (air, water, soil)

Talk about different types of plants (bush, tree, wildflower, garden flower, house plant, vegetables, plant, fruit and nut trees).

Look through gardening catalog at all the different varieties of plants.

Physical Education
Beanbag toss.

Story
Home for a Bunny (Margaret Wise Brown)

Growing Things (Miss Frances); Golden Book

Any books by Peter Spier

Memory Verse
"Honor your father and your mother, that your days may be long in the land which the Lord your God is giving you." Ex.20:12

WEEK 26   WEDNESDAY

Bible
VII. "You shall not commit adultery." (Ex.20:14) Marriage is special to God. He established it. He does not want a man or a woman to love any other woman or man as they do their marriage partner. They are to be faithful to each other. (Sir Oliver's Song cassette tape song: "Always be true...to the one you're married to.")

Copy commandment VII on the story page.

Reading
Read a poem.

Auditory discrimination: Child listens to set of two words and tells you if the beginning sounds are same or different.

vine, fine	water, well
fairly, very	walking, variety
wear, vacuum	willing, wife
victory, valley	young, wall
valiant, vote	want, weather

(Alone) Maze: Child takes matchbox car for drive through the maze.
Listening: Child repeats sequence of words after you:

Sabbath, reverence, holy	plant, structure, needs
working, rest, Creation	blotting paper, glass, seed
six days, one day, blessed	private zone, yours, no
honoring, father, mother	no, go, tell, parents
parents, loyalty, obedience	respect, privacy, personal
life, respect, holy	murder, hurting, specialness
partnership, lifelong, be true	faithfulness, marriage, commitment
husband, wife, anniversary	

Art
Spatter paint picture using tagboard/cardboard stencils in the shape of flowers (daffodil, tulip, 4-5 petals, etc.).

Arithmetic
More/less/equal
Piles of crayons: Which has more? Or are they equal? On worksheet, have child circle group that has more.

Health/Manners
Saying "No" to Strangers/Anyone re: Your Private Zone - Part 1
Read The Private Zone (Frances S. Dayee); private parts of body.
Introduce concept of NO - GO - TELL:
1. Say no.
2. Get away.
3. Tell parents right away.

On "Personal Health and Safety" story page, write: I will not allow anyone to touch my private zone. I will not touch anyone else's private zone.
Resource: Safety Zone (Linda D. Meyer); vs. abduction.

Physical Education
Tiptoe for ten feet.

Story
The Golden Egg Book (Margaret Wise Brown); Golden Book
A Child's Garden of Verses - "Rain" and others

Memory Verse
"You shall not murder." Ex.12:13

WEEK 26   THURSDAY

Bible
VIII. "You shall not steal." (Ex.20:15) God wants us to be honest. He
    wants us to honor and respect others and their property. He wants us
    to be thankful for what we have - to be content.
On story page, copy Commandment VIII.

Reading
Read a poem.
Rhyming: Child names rhyming words for "was," "wild," "wide," "wag."
(Alone) Hand-eye coordination: Using crayon, child traces over lines and
    figures you've made on a worksheet: | - \ / O.
Kinesthetic: Using two fingers and repeating sound, child traces W w on the
    card, in the air, and on your back.

Music
Nursery rhyme songs

Arithmetic
More/less/equal
Using bread tags or beans, have child make two piles to show more and
    less; another two piles to show equal.
On worksheet, have child draw additional circles/other shapes to make
    equal number in the two groups for each of eight rows.

God's World
Review plant structure and needs
Plant seed (pea, bean) between the side of a glass and 2 layers of wet
    paper towels in the glass. Fill cup with gravel, if necessary to keep
    towel by glass. Over next week, watch what happens. Record.
Resource:
j635.6 S46e   Eat the Fruit, Plant the Seed; b&w photos; avocado,
             citrus, etc.

Physical Education
Movement of your choice.

Story
The First Tulips in Holland (Phyllis Krasilovsky); oversize; lovely pictures

Memory Verse
"You shall not commit adultery." Ex.12:14

WEEK 26   FRIDAY

Bible
Walk/scavenger hunt in spring woods and then make collage with some
    things child found.

Preparation for next week:

General:
_____Read over lesson plans
_____List materials needed
_____Collect materials needed
_____Story pages, etc. to notebook

Library:
_____Return books used this week
_____Check out books for week after next

Field Trips:
_____Reconfirm next Friday's trip
_____Thank you note for last trip
_____Set up trip for week after next

WEEK 27   MONDAY

Bible
IX. "You shall not bear false witness against your neighbor." (Ex.20:16)
Like we talked about Friday, God wants us to be honest. He tells us to tell
the truth in love and to build others up. If someone says something
bad about a person you know, it's important we don't agree. If we
don't have anything good to say about someone, we shouldn't say
anything at all.
On story page, copy commandment IX.

Reading
Read a poem.
Introduce the letter shape and sound of X x (ks). Child repeats sound
while tracing letter shape.
(Alone) Classifying: Child sorts X and x cards from those of other letters;
then matches to the X's and x's on the file folder.
Sequence and complete sentences: Child dictates story about walk/
scavenger hunt in the woods.

Art
Cut out farm animals, make faces on them, glue to poster of farmyard scene
(to finish Wednesday).

Arithmetic
Read Inch by Inch (Leo Lionni).
Introduction to measurement. Tell child that we measure to find out the
size of things. Depending on what we're measuring, we use different
tools:
    To find out how fast we drive in the car, we use a speedometer.
    We use a volume control to change the loudness of the radio/TV.
    To find out how hot something is, we use a thermometer.

When can you think of, that we've used a thermometer?

See if he has a fever.

Find out how warm/cool it is outdoors.

Test to see if meat is done when roasting.

Show child each kind of thermometer. Talk about differences. Use oral thermometer to take child's temperature. Read it.

Child matches 0-10 numeral cards with 0-10 dots in file folder.

Child arranges 0-10 numeral cards in sequential order, beginning with 0.

Character Building

Contentment: Read book <u>Don't Count Your Chicks</u> (Ingri and Edgar Parin d'Aulaire).

When we aren't content, we aren't showing thankfulness to God.

On Character Building story page, write: God wants me to be content.

Physcial Education

Kicking and throwing the ball.

Story

<u>Shepherd Boy and the Wolf</u> (Aesop) j888

<u>Lion and the Mouse</u> (Aesop)

Memory Verse

"You shall not steal." Ex.20:15

"...I have learned in whatever state I am, to be content..." Phil.4:11b

WEEK 27   TUESDAY

Bible

X. "You shall not covet...anything that is to your neighbor's." (Ex.20:17)

God wants us to be so thankful for what we have; to be content and to be a good steward of what we have. He doesn't want us to compare. If we do compare, we may be ungrateful and then get angry with God, and then rebel and resent neighbors and friends. We might judge instead of trusting God.

Write commandment X on the story page.

Reading

Read a poem.

(Alone) Left-to-right eye movement: Child connects dots from X at left side of worksheet across to the right sheet (you make this worksheet; 8-12 rows).

(Alone) Visual discrimination: Child matches pattern cards (2 each of it, at, am, is, do, up, if, Al, to, me).

Speech: Child "reads" books to you.

Music

Old MacDonald Had a Farm

B-I-N-G-O

Arithmetic

To measure time, we use different tools.

To tell:	We use:	And measure in:
1.how quick a race is	stopwatch	seconds or parts of seconds
2.what time it is now	watch/clock	minutes, hours
3.what day it is	calendar	days, weeks, months

Show how to use each tool.

To see how long something is, we measure in inches, feet, yards, and miles. (Show ruler) There are twelve inches in a foot. (count them with child) To measure, we put the end where the 0 would be at one end of what we want to measure. Then we look to see how far it goes. (Measure pencil) This pencil is a little over 5 inches long.

Have child measure several things with you, and then independently. Measure lines on worksheet and put a ring around number that shows the correct answer of how many inches it is. (On worksheet, make 6 lines with choices of different measurements in inches.)

God's World

Farming - Talk about living on a farm and have child name as many animals as he can think of. Name more after reading one of the books in case you missed any.

Resources:

j636.4S427b	The Book of the Pig (Jack Denton Scott); b&w photos; ref.
j636.5C533	The Chicken and the Egg (Oxford Scientific Films); color photos.
j636.7C689m	My Puppy is Born (Joanna Cole); b&w photo; easy text.
j636.7F529p	A Puppy is Born (Heiderose and Andreas Fischer-Nagel); color photo; fairly easy text.
j636.T484u	Understanding Farm Animals (Ruth Thompson); color drawings; ref.
j636W766B	Baby Farm Animals (Merrill Windsor); National Geographic.
j636.1C48	The Big Book of Horses (Edward L. Chase); good for large color drawings.
j636.1M648b	Birth of a Foal (Jane Miller); b&w photo; easy text.
j636.1M967B	Baby Horses (Wm. Munoz, photog.); color photos.
j636.1P85t	The True Book of Horses (Elsa Posell); drawings, easy text.
j636.2C689c	A Calf is Born (Joanna Cole); b&w photos.
j637W948L	Look at a Calf (Dare Wright); large b&w photo; fairly easy text.
j636.F853f	Farm Babies (Russell Freedman); b&w photo; fairly easy text.
j636D923a	The Animals of Buttercup Farm (Phoebe and Judy Dunn); large color photos; easy text.
j636I78B	Baby Animals on the Farm (Hans-Heinrich Isenbart); large color photos; easy.
j636J17f	Farm Animals (A New True Book) (Karen Jacobson); large color photos; easy.

Physical Education
"Animal" walks and/or running.

Story
<u>Farm Animals</u> (Hans Helweg); Golden Book

Memory Verse
"You shall not bear false witness against your neighbor." Ex. 20:16

WEEK 27   WEDNESDAY

Bible
Review all Ten Commandments from the story page. Have child give an example for each one.

Reading
Read a poem.

Auditory discrimination: Child repeats clapping patterns after you.

(Alone) Closure: Child fills in missing parts of clown faces you've drawn on paper (1-5 pieces missing on each of 8-10 clowns).

Listening: Child repeats sequences of words after you:

honesty, truth, contentment	honesty, respect, property
tempting, stealing, lying, sad	truth, build up, thankfulness
choices, commitment, respect	contentment, practice, obey
thankfulness, stewardship, pray	farming, country, animals
comparing, coveting, complaining	crops, produce, grazing
commandments, God, holiness	name, reverence, sabbath
parents, honor, obey	life, respect, sacredness
commitment, marriage, be true	

Art
Complete the barnyard scene from Monday (add more animals, people, fence, etc.)

Arithmetic
How many inches in one foot? (12) What if we wanted to measure something longer than one foot? We need to use a yardstick. It is 36 inches long (count them with child as you/she point to the numerals on the yardstick).

Have child measure things around the room.

Health/Manners
Saying "no" about your private zone

Review Wednesday, Week 26 lesson (No-Go-Tell; have child repeat several times: No-Go-Tell). What is your private zone?

Roleplaying situations - someone at friend's house, relative/family friend, stranger at store

If someone tries to get me to do something I don't feel right about, I will use my smart head. I will say "no," I will "go," I will "tell" my parents.

Physical Education
Balance on balance beam/curbstone for 10 feet.

Story
The Treasure (Uri Shulevitz); contentment
Heidi (Johanna Spyri); Golden Book

Memory Verse
"You shall not covet...anything that is your neighbor's." Ex.20:17

WEEK 27   THURSDAY

Bible
Review sequence of Adam's sinning, which led to death for all mankind; and then Jesus' birth to save us from death. Jesus wants us to be an overcomer (to overwhelm, overpower and to get the better of bad influences; to win over wrong choices)!
Read/tell the story of Luke 22:1-38 (The Last Supper). Review story with child.

Reading
Read a poem.
Rhyming: Child names words to rhyme with: "fox," "wear."
(Alone) Hand-eye coordination: Child colors coloring book page with crayons.
Kinesthetic: Using two fingers while repeating sound, child traces X x on the card, in the air, and on your back.

Music
Farmer in the Dell
Shoofly

Arithmetic
Draw a picture of the child. Using measuring tape, measure different parts of the child, noting the measurement on the drawing next to that part of the body. (Ex.: wrist, head, arm length, foot, leg, chest, neck, height)
Have child measure lines on another worksheet you make, using ruler.
Draw a ring around the correct answer.

God's World
Farming - Animals (cont'd.)
Types of crops; responsibilities and benefits
Talk about the responsibilities to animals - providing food and water, shelter, medical care.
Talk about the responsibilities for the plants - caring for them by weeding, watering, planting, harvesting, and possibly preserving.
Talk about the benefits of learning about many animals and plants:
fresh, good quality food
fresh, good quality meat and eggs
learning to obey

learning to work hard
learning to work as a team with family
usually much land to play on and explore
Cut out/draw pictures of farm animals. Make into a farm scene.

Physical Education
"Animal" walks and/or running.

Story
The Little Kitten (Judy Dunn)
The Little Carousel (Marcia Brown)

Memory Verse
"He who heeds the word wisely will find good, and whoever trusts in the
Lord, happy is he." Prov.16:20

WEEK 27   FRIDAY

Visit arboretum.

Preparation for next week:

General:
_____Read over lesson plans
_____List materials needed
_____Collect materials needed
_____Story pages, etc. to notebook

Library:
_____Return books used this week
_____Check out books for week after next

Field Trips:
_____Reconfirm next Friday's trip
_____Thank you note for last trip
_____Set up trip for week after next

WEEK 28   MONDAY

Bible
Review story briefly of Luke 22:1-38 (Friday's lesson).
Read/tell story of Luke 22:39-62 (Garden of Gethsemane; Jesus praying;
    arrest; Peter's denial). Ask child questions about story; answer any
    questions child has about story.

Reading
Read a poem.
Introduce letter shape and sounds for Y y (yuh, ih, I). Child traces letter
    shape while repeating the three sounds.

(Alone) Classifying: Child sorts Y and y letter cards from others; then matches them with the Y's and y's on the file folder.

Sequence and complete sentences: Child dictates story about trip to arboretum.

Art

Draw and then paint designs for butcher paper "eggs." Cut out and use to decorate room.

Arithmetic

Have child show you on yardstick the following measurements: 20", 14", 5", 32". Show child how to hold ruler with one hand while drawing line with the other. Using ruler, have child practice drawing straight lines on a worksheet.

Character Building

Faithfulness: Talk about concept of faithfulness: sticking by a person or a cause/belief during good times and bad times no matter what the cost, no matter what other people say or think (even if they make fun of us). We need to be faithful to God and our family and our beliefs. We need to do what we know is right.

On Character Building story page, write: I will be faithful to God and my family and what I know is right to do.

Physical Education

Throwing and catching ball.

Story

Babar Learns to Cook (Laurent de Brunhoff)

Memory Verse

"If any one is in Christ, he is a new creation; the old has passed away, behold, the new has come." IICor.5:17a

WEEK 28   TUESDAY

Bible

Review yesterday's lesson. (Luke 22:39-62) What did we talk about yesterday that happened to Jesus in the Garden of Gethsemane?

Read/tell story of events in Luke 22:63-23:25. (Jesus as prisoner; people mistreating Him; His reaction) Review by asking questions to child and answering any child has.

Read/tell story of Luke 23:26-46 (on the cross). Stress Jesus' words and the people's reactions. Read Luke 23:47-56. (to the tomb)

Reading

Read a poem.

Left-to-right eye movement: Child "reads" two - three rows of five colored picture cards each (left to right; naming the pictures; top row to bottom row).

(Alone) Visual discrimination: Dominos

Speech: Child "reads" familiar book to you.

Music

Only a Boy Named David

This Little Light of Mine

Arithmetic

Have child show you various lengths you name on the ruler/yardstick.

Make worksheet with various lengths of up to 12" written down. Have child draw lines these sizes, starting at x's you've drawn.

God's World

Farming - Talk about the changes in farming, equipment especially. Read another book from the resource list of Tuesday, Week 27.

Physical Education

"Animal" walks and/or running.

Story

The Little Wooden Farmer (Alice Dalgliesh)

Jesus Forgives Peter (Molly McElroy); Arch Book

Memory Verse

"Then Jesus said to them, `Come after Me and I will make you become fishers of men.'" Mark 1:17

WEEK 28   WEDNESDAY

Bible

He arose! Read/tell the story of Jesus appearing to women, on the way to Emmaus, and to disciples (Luke 24:1-53), and arising into heaven. Did the people all know it was Jesus right away? (No) How did they feel after they saw Him taken up into heaven? (They were filled with joy!)

Reading

Read a poem.

Auditory discrimination: Child listens to set of two words and tells you if the beginning sounds are the same or different:

xylophone, xylene	yes, yam
zipper, young	ill, yet
zoo, zigzag	yellow, yummy
zero, Yule	wear, yelling
you, yes	yolk, yield

Memory: Child looks at 4-7 objects on tray/table; child closes eyes; take one or more objects off; child names object(s) missing.

Listening: Child repeats sequences of words after you:

Adam, overcome, temptation	manners, polite, kind
sin, consequence, death	farming, chores, country
Jesus Christ, born, overcomer	horses, cows, pigs, sheep
Satan, defeated, overcome	chickens, goats, roosters
Garden, praying, denial	barn, tractor, care
prison, torture, sentenced	cross, Calvary, Friday
obedience, sins, sacrifice	tomb, wrapped, buried
guest, host, hostess	

Art

Make clothespin puppets of Peter and two guards (to be used Thursday, Week 29).

Arithmetic

Measure some of child's dolls/toys. Which is longer, _____ or ____?

Have child draw lines of certain lengths on worksheet. On another worksheet divided into quarters, have child measure two lines in each section. Then child draws ring around longer line.

Health/Manners

Being a Good Guest and a Good Host(ess)

Act out spoof of terrible guest and then of terrible host. Then have the child name as many qualities of good guest and host(ess) as possible.

A. Qualities of good guest:

1. Cheerful, polite ("Please, may I use this?" and "Thank you.")
2. Respect for others' property and privacy (gentle with friends' toys; don't get into their parents' things).
3. Obey if friends' parents ask you not to touch/do something.
4. Thankful, good helper. (help clean up toys, etc.)

B. Qualities of good host(ess):

1. Cheerful, polite ("Please, could you pick this us?" and "Thank you.")
2. Honor your parents.
3. Obey your family's rules.
4. Be good example to guest (unselfish with toys, etc.)
5. Ask what guest wants to play; if okay with your family rules, play what guest wants to do.
6. Thankful that the guest came.
7. Play with all guests - not just one.
8. Thankful to parents that your friends could come over.

Roleplay good guest and good host(ess).

On "Manners" story page, write: I am a good guest. I am a good host(ess).

Physical Education

Bouncing ball

Story

The Little Golden Book of Dogs (Nita Jonas); Golden Book
Wiggles Golden Book

Memory Verse

"Jesus Christ is the same yesterday, today, forever." Heb.13:8

WEEK 28   THURSDAY

Bible

How did Jesus have victory over...

Temptation? (Matt.4:1-11; Mark 1:12-13; Luke 4:1-13) When Satan tempted Jesus, Jesus quoted God's Word to Satan and refused to be tempted.

Death? (I Cor.15:54-57) Jesus died so that we may have eternal life. He took all the sins of the world onto himself, even though He had none. He was perfect. He obeyed His Father and was crucified. If He had stayed dead, it would have been sad. But the evil one could not destroy Jesus through death. God raised Jesus from the dead and He raised Him into heaven to live with Him and judge.

Reading

Read a poem.

Rhyming: Child names words to rhyme with "yes," "yell," "yard," "yuck."

(Alone) Hand-eye coordination: Child sews shoelace/yarn through sewing card.

Kinesthetic: Using two fingers and repeating three sounds, child traces Y y letter shape on the card, in the air, and on your back.

Music

Hickory, Dickory Dock
Hallelu, Hallelu

Arithmetic

Review measurement: Show me one inch on a ruler. How many inches are there in one foot? How many inches are there in one yard?

Have child measure objects in room and then lines/objects drawn on paper. Draw ring around correct answer choice (several choices given per line/object).

God's World

Telling time - Day and night

Talk about how people have told time in the past: sun, sundial (shadow from blade on face of round sundial outisde), clocks (machine to keep track of the time).

Talk about what clocks are and how we use them. Look at clock. Name the parts (numbers, two hands: minute hand and hour hand).

Physical Education

"Animal" walks and/or running.

Story

The Little Goat (Judy Dunn); Golden Book
Right Now (David Kherdian and Nonny Hogrogian)

Memory Verse

"And this is the victory that has overcome the world - our faith." I John 5:4b

WEEK 28   FRIDAY

Visit a farm.

Preparation for next week:

General:
_____Read over lesson plans
_____List materials needed
_____Collect materials needed
_____Story pages, etc. to notebook

Library:
_____Return books used this week
_____Check out books for week after next

Field Trips:
_____Reconfirm next Friday's trip
_____Thank you note for last trip
_____Set up trip for week after next

WEEK 29   MONDAY

Bible

What does it mean to be "in Christ"? It means to have accepted Jesus, the Son of God, as the Lord of your life; that you give your life to Him and do all you can to follow Him. When you do this, the Holy Spirit of God fills you with His promises, new life, and victory over Satan. God gives us:

1. power to overcome, to WIN over temptation to do the wrong things.
2. promises to always be with us, to never leave us, to give us what we need when we need it.
3. new life; victory over old, bad habits and old ways of life.
4. victory over Satan. Victory is winning in a contest or struggle. Victory over Satan means winning in the contest of Satan trying to trick you, to tempt you into making wrong choices. All you have to do is to believe that and accept the win!

Reading

Read a poem.
Introduce letter shape and sound for Z z; child traces letter shape while repeating sound.
(Alone) Classifying: Child sorts out the Z and z letter cards from the others; then matches them to the Z's and z's on the file folder.
Sequence and complete sentences: Child dictates story about seeing farm animals.

Art

Make clothespin figures: two angels, two women, Jesus.

Teacher makes paper mache "tomb" from blown-up balloon covered with paper mache. Dry. Pop balloon. Cut out circle for the tomb opening (idea courtesy of Michelle Corcoran).

Arithmetic

Measurement of liquids and solids

Show child the following tools: 1/8 teaspoon; 1/4 teaspoon; 1/2 teaspoon; 1 teaspoon; 1 Tablespoon; 1/4 cup; 1/3 cup; 1/2 cup; 1 cup.

To measure small amounts of liquids or solids, we use measuring spoons and measuring cups. Have child repeat after you what each item is (using a complete sentence). Looking at the tools, which do you think holds the most? The least?

Independently, with newspaper on and under work area, have child carefully measure different amounts of oatmeal/cornmeal from one large bowl to another.

Character Building

Alertness: Alertness means being quickly aware of opportunities and of dangers. Talk about examples in our lives and how alert animals are. Talk about the awareness that there will be temptation to do wrong — that there are dangers. That we need to act quickly when we sense temptation — that we need to remember what the consequences are of disobedience, even if it's just a little bit of disobedience.

On Character Building story page, write: Alertness means being quickly aware of opportunities and dangers.

Physical Education

Kicking a ball

Story

Carousel (Donald Crews)

Any of the Margaret Wise Brown books

Memory Verse

"Jesus said to him, `I am the way, the truth, and the life. No one comes to the Father except through me.'" John 14:6

WEEK 29   TUESDAY

Bible

Using the clothespin puppets made previously, act out the crucifixion of Christ, the resurrection and the ascension of Christ:

Last Supper	Jesus in tomb
Garden of Gethsemane	Jesus arising
Jesus as prisoner	Jesus appearing to three groups of people
Jesus on cross	Jesus ascending into heaven

Reading

Read a poem.

Left to right eye movement: Child "reads" 2-3 rows (5 cards per row) of colored shape cards (right to left; top to bottom).

(Alone) Visual discrimination: Child matches halves of 20 pictures (faces, etc.).

Speech: Child "reads" book to you.

Music
Down in my Heart

Arithmetic
Review information from yesterday about different tools to measure liquids and solids. See how many names child can remember from equipment.

Have child work independently, with plastic/towel underneath, "measuring" water from one bowl into another.

Have child measure out specific amounts of cornmeal for you as directed and put in the other bowl.

God's World
Telling Time - Talk about the different kinds of clocks: watches, clocks of different sizes.

Talk about the different kinds of faces on clocks: digital, Roman numerals, regular numbers, lines where the numbers go.

Talk about units of time: hours, minutes, seconds.

Physical Education
Running broad jump

Story
A Tale for Easter (Tasha Tudor)
Rabbits (Toyoaki Ozaki)

Memory Verse
"...God is faithful, who will not allow you to be tempted beyond what you are able, but with the temptation will also make the way of escape, that you may be able to bear it." I Cor.10:13b

WEEK 29   WEDNESDAY

Bible
For the next two weeks we are going to learn about who God is.
Read A Book About God (Florence Mary Fitch); j230F54
God is:
1. all knowing - He knows everything about what's best for us. He knows everything we say and do and think. He knows what people in every part of the world think and do and say...all at once.
2. all powerful - God has all the power there is. He made the world — every part of it. He can cause anything to happen He wants to. Nothing can stop Him. There is nothing more powerful than God. He made the Red Sea part so His people could go through. He covered the entire earth with rain in Noah's time, flooding the earth.

God is more powerful than we'll ever know.

3. all present - God is everywhere all at once. He is always with us. He is also always with those people on the other parts of the earth. He never leaves us or forgets about us. He is always near us.

Although we cannot totally understand how God can do all this and be this, we need to just accept it on faith, and be so thankful! (As my prayer partner says, there's another "all" quality to God —He has it all together!)

Reading

Read a poem.

Auditory discrimination: Child repeats clapping patterns you make.

(Alone) Closure: Child fills in missing parts of 10-16 faces you've drawn on the chalkboard.

Listening: Child repeats sequences of words after you:

arising, surprise, angel	emptiness, rock, guards
appearing, triumph, victory	joyous, celebration, hurray!
victory, winning, contest	"in Christ," power, promises
new life, victory, winning	crucifixion, time, Easter
watches, clocks, sundial	sun, daylight, nighttime
aerobics, hopping, walking	rotation, twenty-four hours
running, jumping, kicking	emergency, calmness, quickly
phone number, address, name	

Art

Make Easter cards with rubber stamps, stickers, paint, crayons.

Arithmetic

Weight

We measure how heavy things are by scales. Using the bathroom scale, weigh child and several objects (Ex.: several books, a ball, several cans of food). Just because something is bigger, it doesn't necessarily mean that it's heavier, or that if something is smaller it will be lighter.

Health/Manners

Making emergency phone calls

Review home address (street number, town, state) and phone number.

Act out pretend emergency situation where you make phone call but talk real fast and hang up without giving complete, clear information.

Review what you learned last week from touring emergency communication center/police dispatcher office.

Practice picking up each phone in house (especially if some are touch tone and others rotary dial), dialing "911" (or emergency number in your area) and having child tell person in a clear, calm voice:

1. Where - address
2. Who - his/her name
3. What - emergency
4. When
5. Phone number

Listen to what the operator tells you to do (examples: first aid information, turn porch light on, stay on phone, etc.)

Roleplay several situations (fire at neighbors' house; parent fell down stairs).

Also tell about "O" (Operator).

On "Personal Health and Safety" story page, write: I will call '911', and tell 'Where,' address; 'Who,' my name; 'What', what happened; 'When', when it happened; and phone number.

Physical Education
Hop on one foot at a time; walk on the balance beam/curbstone.

Story
<u>Kiri and the First Easter</u> (Carol Greene); Arch Book

Memory Verse
"He who is in you is greater than he who is in the world." I John 4:4b

WEEK 29   THURSDAY

Bible
God the Father

There are three parts of God: God the Father, God the Son (Jesus), and God the Holy Spirit. We call this the Trinity (the unity of 3 parts into one God). God is all three parts at one time. Today, we're going to begin talking about God the Father. As a Father, God loves us, provides for us, leads us, and protects us.

    a. God loves us, more than we will ever know. Proverbs 103:11 says: "For as high as the heavens are above the earth, so great is his love for those who fear him."

    b. God provides for us, whatever we need. God fills that need, whether it's something to eat, or a shelter, or wisdom to know what to do. Because He never leaves us or forgets about us, He always knows what our needs are.

    c. God leads us. He has given us a chain of authority (people in authority over you) to lead us and guide us. He also leads us through the Word of God (the Bible).

Read (and begin to memorize) Psalm 100.

Reading
Read a poem.

Rhyming: Child names rhyming words for "zoo," "zero," "zoom."

(Alone) Hand-eye coordination: Child does puzzle(s).

Kinesthetic: While repeating sound and using two fingers, child traces Z z on letter card, in the air, and on your back.

Music
Christ the Lord is Risen Today

Arithmetic
To measure distance, we measure in miles. A map is a model to show distance and direction.

Notes

Let's review the four directions on a compass: North (N), South (S), East (E), and West (W). What does N stand for? S? E? W?

What is the opposite of North? South? East? West?

If N was this way, which way would S be? If E was this way, which way would W be? East is to the right of N. Show positions like 3-6-9-12 on the clock. On file folder, have child sort N, E, S, W cards and then match to empty squares near points on each of 6-8 compasses in which one direction is shown.

God's World

Telling time - Begin the telling time process. Use old clock and have child tell what number the hour hand is pointing to. Change hand for several examples. Help child see which number it's pointing to.

Physical Education

Movement of your choice.

Story

Time (Gillian Youldon)
The Three Little Pigs

Memory Verse

"...Christ lives in me." Gal.2:20b

WEEK 29   FRIDAY

Visit lily farm or other nursery/flower grower.

Preparation for next week:

General:
_____Read over lesson plans
_____List materials needed
_____Collect materials needed
_____Story pages, etc. to notebook

Library:
_____Return books used this week
_____Check out books for week after next

Field Trips:
_____Reconfirm next Friday's trip
_____Thank you note for last trip
_____Set up trip for week after next

WEEK 30   MONDAY

Bible

What did we talk about last Thursday that God the Father does? (He loves us, provides for us, and leads us.) Also:

d. God protects us. He sends angels down to watch over us. He doesn't let anything hurt us. He also gives us tools to use to protect ourselves: "the full armor of God."

Read Eph.6:10-18. Talk about each part of the armor. From construction paper, make each part (Ex.: belt-shaped piece with TRUTH written on it). Tape/pin each part over the child's regular clothes. Take a picture of the child in this "armor." When developed, put the picture in the notebook with a caption: "(Child's name)'s armor of protection from God."

Reading

Read from Edgar Lear's Nonsense Alphabet: A, B & C.

(Note: This is the beginning of six weeks of review of the letters of the alphabet. To record the information of each of the sounds, an "Alphabet Book" will be made. Each letter will have its own page, a full-size sheet of construction paper. On each page, print the capital and small letters at the top of the page. Then a picture will be found/ drawn to represent each of the letter sounds. At the end of all the alphabet, three holes will be punched in the pages and the book will be inserted into the child's notebook, or string/yarn will be used to tie the book together and it can fit in a pocket of the notebook. Again, as with all the books, gummed hole reinforcements are recommended.)

"A a" page - find pictures to represent each of the three sounds of "a." Glue to the page in the order of the sounds: aah, ay, ah.

Sequence and complete sentences: Child dictates story about last week's visit to lily farm.

(Alone) Sequence: Child arranges alphabet cards (a-e) in alphabetical order.

Art

Rubbings of leaves, bark, cones, etc. with paper and sides of crayons (with paper off).

Arithmetic

On map/atlas, have child find compass notation.

(Construction note: Make map poster of a "town" with several streets, houses, a N-E-S-W notation, a scale of distance, a church, a library, several stores, and a park. Show child that each inch on the map is like 10 ft. in the "real" town. Measure off 10 feet in the room and show the distance.

Using map you made, have child show you north and then how to get from one place to another on the map. (Use verbal directions. Start at the house, go north 2 blocks, then turn west, etc.)

Character Building

Praising God: Read Psalm 100 and talk about how we can praise God each day. On Character Building Story Page, write: I praise God for all my blessings.

Physical Education

Throwing and catching ball

Story

The Friendly Book (Margaret Wise Brown); Golden Book

Memory Verse

"...God...knows all things." I John 3:20

WEEK 30   TUESDAY

Bible

God the Son

The Trinity consists of the three parts of God. What are they? (God the Father, Son and the Holy Spirit) We have already talked about God the Father. Now, we're going to start learning about God the Son. God the Son, Jesus Christ, came to the earth as a human being, born as a baby. He grew up and obeyed His Father all of His days. His purpose was to defeat Satan. He overcame death for all of us who believe in Him by taking on all the sins of the world, suffering and dying for us, and then he WON the victory over Satan by arising from the dead, appearing three times, and being lifted into heaven. God the Son is our Savior (the one who saves us from danger and destruction).

If there's time, have the child recount story of crucifixion and resurrection. Tell child that now Jesus judges everyone.

Reading

Read Edgar Lear's Nonsense Alphabet: D, E & F.

"B b" page in alphabet book; write B b at top of page. Glue one picture to represent the "b" sound.

(Alone) Classification: Child sorts picture cards into the following categories: furniture, clothing, people and animals.

(Alone) Visual discrimination: Child matches A to Z letter cards with A's to Z's on file folder.

Music

Praise God From Whom All Blessings Flow

My God is So Great

Holy, Holy, Holy

Arithmetic

Dictate directions to child as he follows on map. See if he follows directions and knows his orientations. See if he ends up where you have directed him.

God's World
Economics - Barter-exchanging goods or services without money
Introduction to coins (they will be discussed in more detail in the arithmetic
lessons in several weeks). Explain that different coins are worth
different amouns of money. Have child look at coins and tell what he
notices. Show words "In God we trust" on each and go over what
pictures are on each. Show child which one is a penny.

Physical Education
Running broad jump

Story
Pelle's New Suit (Elsa Beskow)
Small Rain - Verses from the Bible (chosen by Jessie Orton Jones) j220J77

Memory Verse
"...power belongs to God." Ps.62:11c

WEEK 30   WEDNESDAY

Bible
God the Son, Jesus Christ, being perfect, showed us how we should live
and act. In His life, He acted the right way every time and showed us
how we should treat others. He was obedient to God. He was
obedient to His parents. He was filled with goodness, kindness,
gentleness, self-control, love, joy, peace, patience, and faithfulness. He
gave us a new commandment to follow, in addition to the Ten
Commandments: "...love one another, as I have loved you..." (John
13:34) Although He was a king while He was on earth, He chose to
serve. He said that to have a servant's heart is very important.

Resources:
j232F54   The Child Jesus (Florence Mary Fitch)
j232T24b   A Boy Once Lived In Nazareth (Florence M. Taylor)

Reading
Read Edgar Lear's Nonsense Alphabet: G, H & I.
"C c" page in alphabet book: write C c on top of page. Glue two pictures
to represent the "c" sound.
(Alone) Hand-eye coordination: Child traces the following figures, shapes: |
- \ / O +
(Alone) Visual discrimination: Dominos

Art
Have child draw a picture of what he thinks God looks like.

Arithmetic
Money
Tell child that in the U.S.A., some of our money is in coins and some is in
currency (paper dollar bills). For the next two weeks, we are going to

be learning about the coins our country uses for money.

Show child penny. This is a penny. It is worth one cent. Ask child what the coin is again. (It is a penny) How much money is it worth? (It is worth one cent) How many pennies would it take to buy something that costs 5 cents? (5) Have child sort pictures of penny from pictures of other coins. Then match the penny pictures with 1 cents on the file folder.

Health/Manners

Basic first aid (Part 1)

Introduction: What is First Aid? It is immediate care to someone who's sick or has been hurt. Why should we learn first aid?

1. Help others
2. Help ourselves.
3. Be prepared in case of disaster.

What are the priorities?

1. Prompt rescue if needed (from fire, water, smoke). Don't move in other circumstances unless absolutely necessary.
2. Breathing (open airway).
3. Bleeding (control severe bleeding).
4. First aid for poisoning/ingestion of harmful chemicals. Other important things to remember: Help victim be calm, stay still, and be warm. Remain calm! Call for help.

j614.8G666w   <u>What To Do When There's No One But You</u> (Harriet Margolis Gore); thinking through emergency situations

Physical Education

Hop on one foot at a time; climb on inclined board.

Story

<u>Caps for Sale</u> (Esphyr Slobodkina)

<u>Catherine Marshall's Story Bible</u> (illus. by children); j220M367c; look at pictures; begin today and finish tomorrow.

Memory Verse

"The eyes of the Lord are in every place, keeping watch on the evil and the good." Prov.15:3

WEEK 30   THURSDAY

Bible

God the Holy Spirit

God the Holy Spirit is the third part of the Trinity. When we accept Christ as Lord, He gives us the Holy Spirit (John 20:22). It comforts us and guides us, like a still small voice inside us telling us what is right and wrong. It helps us make right decisions. We are to be thankful for the Holy Spirit of God within us, and to speak reverently of it (to speak with devotion and honor), just as we do with the other names for God.

(Devotion means first place in your life; the center of attention in your life.) Matthew 12:32b warns us what will happen if we do not speak of the Holy Spirit with respect: "…whoever speaks against the Holy Spirit, it will not be forgiven him, either in this age or in the age to come." We can't see God the Holy Spirit inside of us, but we can sense His leading us and comforting us.

Reading

Read Edgar Lear's Nonsense Alphabet - J, K & L.

\"D d" page in alphabet book: write D d at top of page. Glue picture to represent the "d" sound.

(Alone) Visual discrimination: Child matches letter cards (a-z) with a's to z's on file folder.

(Alone) Classification: Child sorts picture cards into the following categories (four good groups - at least 4 pictures for each of the four groups):
Bread/cereal group
Fruit/vegetable group
Dairy group
Meat/fish/eggs/protein group

Music

God Is So Good
Fairest Lord Jesus
Oh, How I Love Jesus

Arithmetic

Introduce nickel. Tell child (as you show him a nickel): This is a nickel. It is worth five cents. It would take five pennies to equal as much money as one nickel. (Look at the front and back with the child.) What is this called? (nickel) How much is it worth? (five cents)

Have child sort pictures of nickel from pictures of other coins. Then match the nickel with five cents on file folder, and five cents with nickel pictures.

God's World

Economics - Review that there are different coins for different amounts of money. Tell child that for larger amounts of money, instead of having larger coins or keeping huge amounts of pennies in our pockets (heavy!), that currency (paper money) was thought of. Show child $1, $5, $10. Show numbers on them to identify which value each is.

Talk about choices with money:
1. Tithing (10% or more given back to God)
2. Savings (short-term; long-term; horse, college, etc.)
3. Purchases (gifts, for ourselves)
4. Helping others

Resource:
j332E43M   Money (Benjamin Elkin)

Physical Education

Movement of your choice.

Story
My Little Golden Book About God (Jane Werner Watson); Golden Book
Catherine Marshall's Story Bible; finish looking at pictures

Memory Verse
"If God is for us, who can be against us?" Rom.8:31b
"But Jesus looked at them and said to them, 'With men this is impossible,
but with God all things are possible.'" Matt.19:26

WEEK 30   FRIDAY

Take or mail Easter cards to others.

Preparation for next week:

General:
_____Read over lesson plans
_____List materials needed
_____Collect materials needed
_____Story pages, etc. to notebook

Library:
_____Return books used this week
_____Check out books for week after next

Field Trips:
_____Reconfirm next Friday's trip
_____Thank you note for last trip
_____Set up trip for week after next

WEEK 31   MONDAY

Bible
Give examples of how the Holy Spirit has spoken in your life and give your
child examples of how He speaks to him. Review with child the fruits
of The Holy Spirit (love, joy, peace, patience, kindness, goodness,
faithfulness, gentleness, and self-control - Gal.5:22-23). (See how many
the child can remember, using the colored shape cards made during
weeks 21-22 to spark his memory.)

Reading
Read Edgar Lear's Nonsense Alphabet: M, N & O.
"E e" page in alphabet book: write E e on top of page. Glue pictures to
represent the two sounds of "e."
Sequence and complete sentences: Child dictates story about taking Easter
cards to others.
(Alone) Sequence: Child arranges letter cards (a-j) in alphabetical order.

Art

Draw and color "spring" things for mobile (finish Wednesday).

Arithmetic

Introduce dime. Tell child (as you show him a dime): This is a dime. It is worth ten cents. It would take ten pennies or two nickels to equal as much money as one dime. (Look at the front and back with the child.) What is this called? (dime) How much is it worth? (ten cents) Review penny and nickel, too.

Have child sort pictures of coins and match with his cents amount.

Character Building

Glorifying God in my life: Reflecting God's goodness in my life. Show how flashlight shines its light through a piece of plastic/paper. God's a light inside us. To glorify Him means letting His light shine through us to others.

Talk about how we can glorify God: in our speech; in how we dress; in how we act; in how we treat others.

On Character Building story page, write: To glorify God is to reflect God's goodness in my life.

Physical Education

Kicking the ball

Story

The Mother's Day Mice (Eve Bunting)

Just Look...A Book About Painting (Robert Cumming); art appreciation

Memory Verse

"For I am the Lord who heals you." Ex.15:26e

"And do not be conformed to this world, but be transformed by the renewing of your mind, that you may prove what is that good and acceptable and perfect will of God." Rom.12:2

WEEK 31   TUESDAY

Bible

Review of the Trinity

What does Trinity mean? (oneness of three separate and distinct parts of one God)

Name the 3 parts of God. (God the Father, Son, Holy Spirit)

What does God the Father do? (He loves us, provides for us, protects us, and leads us.)

What does God the Son do? (He was the example of how we should live. He's our Savior. He judges all people.)

What does God the Holy Spirit do? (He comforts and guides us.) Write a summary about the qualities and roles of God in the child's notebook.

Reading

Read Edgar Lear's Nonsense Alphabet: P, Q & R.

(Alone) Visual discrimination: Child matches A to Z letter cards with A's to Z's on file folder.

(Alone) Classification: Child matches numerals on cards with stamped objects of equal value on other cards (1-10).

"F f" page in alphabet book: write F f at top of page. Glue picture to represent the "f" sound.

Music

Walking with Jesus
Isn't He Wonderful?

Arithmetic

Review pennies, nickels, and dimes. Have child discriminate between by value and appearance.

Have child match coins with value on folder.

Have child match values with coins on folder.

God's World

Economics - Talk about why we put our money in banks.
1. Safety
2. Interest earned (bank pays us to use our money)
What are checks?

Physical Education

Broad jump; running

Story

Two Bear Cubs (Ann Jonas)
Frog and Toad Are Friends (Arnold Lobel)

Memory Verse

"Likewise the Spirit also helps us in our weaknesses." Rom.8:26a

WEEK 31 WEDNESDAY

Bible

Introduce: Communication with God

What is communication? (an exchange of information) God talks to us in several ways. Can you think of how? (Bible, Holy Spirit, Dad and Mom [chain of authority], pastor and Sunday school teachers) Today, we're going to talk about how God talks to us through the Bible and the Holy Spirit.

1. The Bible: The word "Bible" means "books." It's a group of 66 books written by many authors, many, many years ago by revelation (communication) from God. The Bible answers all our needs and calls on us to listen and obey. It helps us "build your life on what God has said" (p.8, N.I.V. Pictoral Bible). In the Bible, God tells us what He is like and how He wants us to live. It tells about Jesus.

2. God's Holy Spirit (the active presence of God in human life): God talks to us in our hearts as to how much He loves us and what we should do.

He speaks to each of us individually.

Reading

Read <u>Edgar Lear's Nonsense Alphabet</u>: S, T & U

"G g" page in alphabet book: write G g on top of page. Glue pictures representing the two "g" sounds onto the page.

(Alone) Closure: Child fills in the missing parts of the lines and figures: | - \ / O.

Listening: Child repeats sequences of words after you:

Trinity, three, unified	Father God, Son Jesus Christ, Holy Spirit
Father, cares for	protects, provides
legs, breastplate, feet	help, calm, call
shield, helmet, sword	911, information, listen
Savior, crucifixion, victory	economics, barter, money
Holy Spirit, comforter, guide	currency, coins, checks
all-knowing, all-powerful, all-present	
Jesus, example, loving, obedient	

Art

Cut out and glue with string Monday's shapes and pictures for mobile. Hang and enjoy.

Arithmetic

Introduce quarter. Tell child (as you show him a quarter): This is a quarter. It is worth twenty-five cents. It would take 25 pennies to equal as much as this one quarter. It is called a "quarter" because it is worth a quarter of a one dollar bill. (Look at the front and back with the child.) What is this called? (quarter) How much is it worth? (25 cents) Review other coins with child, too.

Have child match coins with amounts on file folders.

Health/Manners

Basic first aid (Part 2): Equipment

Review Week 31, Wednesday lesson.

Talk about equipment: bandages (strip of material used to hold a wound dressing or splint in place; it helps immobilize, support and protect a body part), bandaids, gauze square and bandage compress, gauze pad; adhesive tape (tape gauze pad on); Neosporin (antibacterial cream, helps prevent infection); tweezers, rubbing alcohol; soap and clear water; fels naptha soap.

Tell and show child where this is in your home and car. Whenever at restaurant/store show first aid kit, if seen.

Talk about Red Cross, an organization that helps people learn more about first aid and helping people who need help.

Physical Education

Bouncing ball

Story

<u>Oxcart Man</u> (Donald Hall)

<u>Raggedy Ann and Andy Book</u> (Jan Sukus); Golden Book

Bible Readings for Boys and Girls (illus. Lynd Ward); j220B582bi; choose several for today; will use tomorrow, too.

Memory Verse
"...God is love." I John 4:8b

WEEK 31   THURSDAY

Bible
God also speaks through two other main groups of people.

3. Our authority figures (Dad and Mom): God has given them charge over their children to teach, train, love, and care for. He reveals things (by the Bible, His Holy Spirit and other Christians) to them, to teach you. God speaks to you through your parents.

4. God also talks to you through your pastor and Sunday school teachers. In their study of God's Word, these people can share specific information about the Bible with you.

Reading
Read Edgar Lear's Nonsense Alphabet: V, W & X.

"H h" page in alphabet book: write H h at top of page. Glue picture to represent the "h" sound.

(Alone) Visual discrimination: Child matches letter cards (a-z) with the a's to z's on file folder.

(Alone) Classifying: Child sorts picture cards (at least 10 each) into four classifications: animals, people, food and clothing.

Music
Jesus (praise Him...love Him...serve Him...thank Him)

Arithmetic
Have child sort different coin cards into piles. Name each pile and tell how many (dimes, etc.) are in the pile. Match with cents value on file folder. Match cents cards to coin pictures on file folder.

God's World
Economics - Talk about how money is made or talk about how we save up for our goals (short-term and long-term: college/training and retirement) financial planning.

Physical Education
Movement of your choice

Story
Ask Mr. Bear (Marjorie Flack)
Bible Readings for Boys and Girls; choose several more pages

Memory Verse
"Even a child is known by his deeds, by whether what he does is pure and right." Prov.20:11

WEEK 31   FRIDAY

Tour bank.

Preparation for next week:

General:
_____Read over lesson plans
_____List materials needed
_____Collect materials needed
_____Story pages, etc. to notebook

Library:
_____Return books used this week
_____Check out books for week after next

Field Trips:
_____Reconfirm next Friday's trip
_____Thank you note for last trip
_____Set up trip for week after next

WEEK 32   MONDAY

Bible
Review: How does God talk to us? (through Bible, Holy Spirit, Dad and
    Mom, pastor and Sunday school teachers) How should we respond?
    (listen and obey) What does it mean to listen? (to hear with thoughtful
    attention; to hear what's being said and think about it) What does it
    mean to obey? (to follow the commands or guidance of someone) So
    what should we do when God speaks to us? (Hear, think about what's
    being said, and obey.)

Reading
Read Edgar Lear's Nonsense Alphabet: Y, Z
"I i" page in the alphabet book: write I i at top of page. Glue pictures to
    page representing the two sounds of "i."
Sequence and complete sentences: Child dictates story about trip to the
    bank.
(Alone) Sequence: Child arranges letter cards (a-o) in alphabetical order.

Art
Have child draw a crayon picture of himself.

Arithmetic
Ask child to show you five pennies and then one nickel. Ask child how
    many cents the five pennies are worth. How many is the nickel worth?
    They are both worth five cents. They are an equal amount. Also, do
    the same process for ten pennies with one dime.

Character Building

Being good listeners to God, through His channels.

Talk about qualities of a good listener:

1. Thinking about what's being said.
2. Paying attention to the one who's talking.
3. Choosing not to think about other things at the same time.

How can this apply to our relationship with God and listening to Him:

1. in the Bible? (taking time to learn)
2. with His Holy Spirit?
3. from Mom and Dad?
4. from Sunday School and Church? (not being distracted)

On Character Building story page, write: To be a good listener, I need to pay attention to who's talking and to think about what's being said (and nothing else).

Physical Education

Throwing and catching ball

Story

Bible Stories of Boys and Girls (Jane Werner, illus.) First Golden Book
Sending Messages (John Stewig) j001.5S852s
The Biggest Bear (Lynd Ward)

Memory Verse

"All scripture is given by inspiration of God..." II Tim.3:16a

WEEK 32   TUESDAY

Bible

How can we talk with God? We can talk with God through prayer. What is prayer? (approaching God in word or thought) Prayer is important because it is powerful. God listens to us. Jesus is the "go-between" for us and God. He is our priest. He promises if we ask anything of God and ask it in His name (Jesus), believing we will receive it, we will. That's why we end our prayers, "in Jesus' name. Amen." Jesus and the Holy Spirit of God pray on our behalf to God when we pray.

When are we to pray? (all the time: morning, noon and night; we are to pray constantly)

On new story page, entitled "Communication with God," write:

God talks to me through the Bible. It teaches us who God is and how He wants us to live.

God talks to me through His Holy Spirit living inside me.

God talks to me through my parents.

God talks to me through my pastor and Sunday school teachers.

When God talks to me, I need to listen (hear and think about it) and obey.

I can talk with God. Talking with God is called prayer.

Prayer is important. It is powerful. God listens to us.

If I ask anything of God in Jesus' name with faith, He will answer my prayer.

God wants me to pray all the time.

Reading
Read a poem.

"J j" page in the alphabet book: write J j on top of page. Glue picture to page representing the "j" sound.

(Alone) Classifying: Child sorts picture cards into categories of the four food groups.

(Alone) Visual discrimination: Child matches A to Z cards with the A's to Z's on file folder.

Music
The B-I-B-L-E

God is So Good

Arithmetic

Review 5 pennies = 5 cents = 1 nickel; 10 pennies = 10 cents = 1 dime. Show child that two nickels = one dime, so ten 1 cents = two 5 cents = one 10 cents.

Show child that to make 7 cents, you start with one 5 cent and then add two pennies. Or you can have 7 pennies. They would both be equal.

God's World
Having your own business - Talk about breaking a job down into parts. Do one thing at a time and plan ahead.

Talk about basics of supply and demand. Give an example of making a certain kind of toy, etc.

Resource:

j658.9A489g   Good Cents - Every Kid's Guide to Making Money
                  (by The Amazing Life Games Co.) (See p.123-128)

Physical Education
Broad jumping; running

Story
Big Joe's Trailer Truck (Joe Mathieu); Golden Book

From Sheep to Scarf (Ali Mitgutsch); j677.31M683f

Memory Verse
"Your word is a lamp to my feet and a light to my path." Ps.119:105

WEEK 32   WEDNESDAY

Bible
How should I pray? God wants me to pray with the right motivation, to give thanks to Him, to glorify God (praise Him), to build people up (not to break myself or others down). God wants me to ask in faith, believing that the thing I ask for WILL happen. God wants me to pray by myself and with other Christians. God doesn't want me to pray a fancy prayer to try to impress others. God wants me to ask for God's will to be done.

Reading

Read a poem.

"K k" page in the alphabet book: write K k on top of page. Glue picture on page, representing the "k" sound.

(Alone) Closure: Child fills in the missing parts of the shapes which you've written on a worksheet: | - \ / O.

(Alone) Visual discrimination: Dominos

Art

Make Mother's Day gift.

Arithmetic

Review pieces of money with child.

Using pictures mounted on index cards with cents value, have child match up coins to make different values (ex.: for card that says three cents, child would get three pennies and put it next to the card).

Health/Manners

Basic first aid (Part 3) - Open Wounds

Have child identify first aid kit ingredients. (large bandage, gauze pad, adhesive tape, tweezers, rubbing alcohol, antibacterial cream, soap and water)

First thing in helping others in non-emergency situation is cleaning our hands.

Tell child there are four kinds of wounds:

1. Abrasions (scrapes)

   Little bleeding; need to clean so no infection

2. Incisions (cuts)

   Bleeding

3. Lacerations (jagged cut/tear)

   Bleeding

4. Punctures (hole from something sharp)

   Not much bleeding

First aid:

1. Stop bleeding immediately

   a. direct pressure (use pad/dressing)

   b. once clot forms, don't remove/disturb

   c. elevate above level of heart

2. Protect wound from germs

   a. wash in and around victim's wound to remove bacteria and foreign matter (dirt, gravel, etc.)

   b. rinse thoroughly

   c. blot wound dry with gauze pad/clean cloth

   d. put Neosporin (or other antibacterial ointment) on

   e. put clean bandage on

3. Get medical attention if necessary

   a. Watch for infection (swelling, redness, "hot" feeling, throbbing, tenderness, etc.)

Practice with each type of wound

Physical Education
Tiptoe a distance of 10 feet; skipping

Story
The Little Puppy (July Dunn); Golden Book
The Story of Lumber (Louise Lee Floethe); j674F62s

Memory Verse
"Ask, and it will be given to you; seek, and you will find; knock, and it will
be opened to you." Matt.7:7

WEEK 32   THURSDAY

Bible
What does God want me to pray for? He wants me to pray for others to get
to know Jesus, and to help them. I can also pray for growth with God
and with the rest of my life. Jesus gives us an example of a prayer to
pray. It is called "The Lord's Prayer" (Matt.6:9-13; Luke 11:2-4). Read/
repeat this to your child.

Reading
Read a poem.
"L l" page in the alphabet book: write L l at top of page. Glue picture
representing the "l" sound onto page.
(Alone) Visual discrimination: Child matches cards (a - z) with the a's to z's
on file folder.
(Alone) Classifying: Child matches numeral cards with objects of a certain
number, 1-10.

Music
Praise Him, Praise Him (p.35Wee)
Review songs from Tuesday.

Arithmetic
Review, that to make odd amounts, we start with the coin nearest to the
amount we want and then add up with other coins. (Ex.:3 cents, 6
cents, 8 cents, 11 cents) Have child get correct coins to match with
picture card amounts.

God's World
Having your own business - Talk about advertising and the ways you could
advertise and market a product.
Play store with empty boxes, containers, and play money.

Physical Education
Movement of your choice.

Story
Prayer for a Child (Rachel Field)
Lumberjack (William Kurelek); j674K96L; look at color paintings

Memory Verse

"For your Father knows the things you have need of before you ask him."
Matt.6:8b

"I have called upon You, for You will hear me, O God..." Ps.17:6a,b

WEEK 32   FRIDAY

Visit an organization that helps others.

Preparation for next week:

General:
_____Read over lesson plans
_____List materials needed
_____Collect materials needed
_____Story pages, etc. to notebook

Library:
_____Return books used this week
_____Check out books for week after next

Field Trips:
_____Reconfirm next Friday's trip
_____Thank you note for last trip
_____Set up trip for week after next

WEEK 33   MONDAY

Bible

Why is knowing God's Word (what the Bible says) important? Then we know what God wants and what we should pray for. (Rom.10:17, I John 5:14,15) If we ask with the wrong motivation, God won't hear our prayers. Why is faith important? If we don't ask in faith, we won't get results and our prayers won't be answered. (Matt.17:20: Mark 6:5,6; Rom.14:23b) Jesus can't do mighty miracles where there's unbelief. We need to always be thankful. Why is perseverence important (to continue repeating)? It shows God we have great faith. (Matt.15:22-28; Luke 11:5-10; Luke 18:1-8) God will listen to us.

Reading

Read a poem.
"M m" page in the Alphabet book: write M m at top of page. Glue picture representing the "m" sound onto page.
Sequence: Child arranges letter cards (a-t) into alphabetical order.

Art

Make Mother's Day cards for Mom and Grandmas. (Use rubber stamps, crayons, paints, etc.)

Arithmetic

Play "Garage Sale": Have child "pay" for various marked items with coins separated into sections of muffin pan. Change roles. Decide what you can get for the (x) cents you have.

Character Building

The power of prayer: Read examples of answered prayer in the Bible (ex.: James 5:16-18) and talk about the power of prayer in your life.

On Character Building story page, write: Prayer is powerful.

Physical Education

Kicking ball

Story

<u>David</u> (Maud and Miska Petersham); j220.92D14P

<u>Aesop's Fables</u>; j888A25cat. Choose one or two for today; use this week

Memory

"Pray without ceasing." I Thess.5:17

WEEK 33 TUESDAY

Bible

What are some of God's promises we can use in prayer?

1. God acts on our behalf. (Is.64:4)
2. "...before they call I will answer; and while they are still speaking, I will hear." (Is.65:24)
3. "Call to Me and I will answer you..." (Jer.33:3a)
4. "For with God nothing will be impossible." (Luke 1:37)
5. "And my God will supply all your need according to His riches in glory by Christ Jesus." (Phil.4:19)
6. "If you ask anything in my name, I will do it." (John 14:14)

On story page on communication with God, write:

God wants me to pray for His will to be done.

It is important that I know what the Bible says so I know what God wants and what to pray for.

God wants me to pray with faith.

God wants me to be persistent in prayer.

God gives me lots of promises to use in my prayers. He loves me a lot!

Reading

Read a poem.

"N n" page in the alphabet book: write N n at top of page. Glue picture representing the "n" sound onto page.

(Alone) Visual discrimination: Child matches A - Z cards onto A's to Z's on file folder.

(Alone) Closure: Child fills in the missing parts of the following figures and shapes: | - \ / O.

Music
Whisper a Prayer
Some of child's favorite songs

Arithmetic
Review of coins: name and value (in cents)
Have child match money amount (ex.:7 cents) with pictures of coins of
    equal value and money picture (coins) with pictures of items of various
    "price."
Have child sort coins into correct slots using muffin pan.

God's World
Writing - changes in written communication
Talk about how written communication has changed over the years and/or
    read:

j676G441p	<u>Paper, Paper Everywhere</u> (Gail Gibbons); color illus.
Resource:	
j655E64f	<u>The First Book of Printing</u> (Sam Beryl Epstein); ref.; history

Physical Education
Broad jump; running

Story
<u>Ruth</u> (Maud and Miska Petersham) j220.92R97P
<u>Aesop's Fables</u> - choose several

Memory Verse
"...pray for one another..." James 5:16b
"...casting all your care upon Him, for He cares about you." I Pet.5:7

WEEK 33   WEDNESDAY

Bible
Introduce: "Love each other." Besides the Ten Commandments which we
    are to obey, Jesus gave us a final commandment: "Love each other."
    How? And what is love? Read I Corinthians 13:4-8a. List about love:

Love means being patient with another person.
Love means being kind to another person.
Love means not envying another person.
Love means not boasting to another person.
Love means not being proud toward another person.
Love means not being rude toward another person.
Love means not thinking only of yourself.
Love means not getting angry easily.
Love means not keeping a record of wrongs.
Love means telling the truth.

Love means protecting another person.
Love means trusting another person.
Love means hoping for another person.
Love means persevering.
Love never fails.

Reading
Read a poem.
"O o" page in the alphabet book: write O o at top of page. Glue pictures
   to page representing the three sounds of "o."
Listening: Child repeats sequences after you:

communication, God, me	listen, Bible, Holy Spirit
parents, church, hear	respond, listen, obey
talking, me, always	prayer, listening, God
Jesus' name, with faith, now	Mother's Day, appreciation, Mom
business, job, parts	advertising, supply, cash
writing, bark, paper	storekeeper, working, managing
Red Cross, helping, disasters	bloodbank, training, first aid

Art
Draw and color picture of Mom.

Arithmetic
Shapes and numbers in nature
Read Listen to a Shape (Marcia Brown) and use it as a resource this week.
Look/talk about with child the different shapes in nature (leaves, flowers,
   grass, icicles, honeycombs, etc.)

Health/Manners
Basic first aid (Part 4) - Bites and Stings
A. Animal Bites:
   Wash area with soap and water; flush area with water.
   Apply bandage; see doctor.
B. Insect Bites/Stings (can cause death if allergic reaction, ususally local
      pain and irritation):
   1. Minor bites and stings: remove stinger, cold applications; soothing
      lotions (calamine)
   2. Ticks (can transmit disease germs): cover tick with heavy oil (mineral
      oil, salad oil, machine oil). Allow it to remain for half an hour. If
      tick doesn't get off at once, remove all with tweezers. Thoroughly
      but gently wash area with soap and water.
C. Poisonous Snake Bites:
   Reduce circulation of blood through bite area; delay absorption of
      venom. Get to hospital quickly. While doing that keep victim still
      and calm; have victim lie down; immobilize the bitten extremity and
      keep it at or below heart level; 2-4" above bite apply 1" wide band
      snugly, but so finger can be slipped underneath.

Physical Education
Bouncing ball

Story
The Tower of Babel (William Wiesner); j221.1W65t
Aesop's Fables - choose several more; j888A25cat

Memory Verse
"Your word I have hidden in my heart, that I might not sin against You."
Psalm 119:11

WEEK 33   THURSDAY

Bible
Friendship - A friend is someone we like/love. God tells us we should not
be friends to some people. ("Make no friendship with an angry man,
And with a furious man do not go." Prov.22:24) ("Do not be deceived:
'Evil company corrupts good habits.'" I Cor.15:33) God does not want
us to be tempted to learn bad habits. He wants us to choose our
friends. Once we have chosen friends that would please God, we need
to remember what Proverbs 17:17a says: "A friend loves at all times."
There are certain ways we can learn to be a good friend. For the next
nine school days we are going to talk about those qualities. Remember
the Golden Rule: Do to others what you would want them to do to you.

Reading
Read a poem.
"P p" page in the alphabet book: write P p at top of page. Glue picture to
page representing the "p" sound.
(Alone) Visual discrimination: Child matches cards (a - z) with a's to z's on
file folder.
Child draws the following shapes next to the models you've drawn on a
worksheet: | - \ / O.

Music
His Banner Over Me is Love (p.34Wee)
Some of the child's favorite songs

Arithmetic
Look at Marcia Brown's book again, Listen to a Shape. Talk about numbers
of things in God's world (number of petals, number of legs on an
animal and insect, parts in compound leaf, etc.).

God's World
Planning and marking out a flag garden/herb garden
Make an herb garden (circular shape divided into sixths) or make a "flag"
garden with red, white and blue petunias.

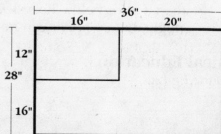

Resources:
    j716B16   The Indoor and Outdoor Grow-it Book (S. Sinclair
                     Baker); lots of ideas, line drawings
    j716C77f   Fun-Time Window Garden (Emogene Cooke)

Physical Education
Movement of your choice

Story
Noah and the Rainbow (Bible); j222.1B58n
A Day in The Life of a Librarian (David Paige); j020P142D

Memory Verse
"And all things, whatever you ask in prayer, believing, you will receive."
Matt. 21:22

WEEK 33   FRIDAY

Make lunch for Mom.

Preparation for next week:

General:
_____Read over lesson plans
_____List materials needed
_____Collect materials needed
_____Story pages, etc. to notebook

Library:
_____Return books used this week
_____Check out books for week after next

Field Trips:
_____Reconfirm next Friday's trip
_____Thank you note for last trip
_____Set up trip for week after next

WEEK 34   MONDAY

Bible
Qualities of a good friend
1. Love - read "E" page in Big Thoughts for Little People (God loves
   everyone) and pages I and II from Giant Steps for Little People (Love
   your father...and Jesus said to love...). Answer questions for each page.
2. Goodness - read from Giant Steps for Little People: p.VI (If you do
   what's right...); p.X (Sometimes you'll be laughed at...); p.XI (If you say
   that you love God...); p.XII (Always try to do what's right...). Answer
   questions on each page.

Reading

Read a poem.

"Qu qu" page in the alphabet book: write Qu qu on top of page. Glue picture to page representing the "qu" sound.

Sequence and complete sentences: Child dictates story about taking Mom out to a restaurant to lunch.

(Alone) Sequence: Child arranges cards (a - z) in alphabetical order.

Art

Make clay paperweight for Father's Day gift.

Arithmetic

Begin review of concepts learned this year:

Spatial concepts (top/middle/bottom; above/below; over/under; before/ after/between)

See Weeks 1-3 for specific activities.

Character Building

Flexibility: To be flexible means to be willing to change my plans in order to:

1. Accept the best course of action.
2. React to unexpected conditions.
3. Best help the people I serve.

Give child example(s) of each condition. Talk about each of these conditions of flexibility in the child's life.

On Character Building story page, write: I need to be flexible to make the best choice.

Physical Education

Throwing and catching ball

Story

Story of your choice

Memory Verse

"Therefore, whatever you want men to do to you, do also to them..." Matt.7:12a

WEEK 34   TUESDAY

Bible

Qualities of a good friend (cont'd.)

3. Joyfulness - read rhymes from these pages and answer questions from: Big Thoughts for Little People, "C" -crying, "J" -joyful, "N" -nice, "P" - polite; Giant Steps for Little People, XIX (Once I knew a little girl.).

Reading

Read a poem.

"R r" page in the alphabet book: write R r at top of the page. Glue picture

representing the "r" sound to the page.
(Alone) Visual discrimination: Child matches A to Z cards to the A's to Z's on file folder.
(Alone) Classification: Child sorts picture cards into the four food group categories.

Music
This is My Commandment

Arithmetic
Review of shapes and colors. See Weeks 4,5,7,9 for specific activities.

God's World
Planning a garden - Read parts of the following book to decide:
1. Size of the garden
2. What types of plants you want to plant (flowers, vegetables, both)
3. Amount of work involved (planting, weeding, watering, harvesting)
Resource:
j635O28I   In My Garden - A Child's Gardening Book
(Helen and Kelly Oechsli)

Physical Education
Broad jump; running

Story
Molly's Woodland Garden (Anne and Harlow Rockwell)
I Know a Lady (Charlotte Zolotow); friends with older lady

Memory Verse
"Do not be deceived: `Evil company corrupts good habits.'" I Cor.15:33
"Make no friendship with an angry man...lest you learn his ways..."
Prov.22:24-25a

WEEK 34   WEDNESDAY

Bible
Qualities of a good friend (cont'd.)
4. No anger or arguing - read rhymes and answer questions from: Giant Steps for Little People: IX (don't get into arguments) and XXV (anger can be dangerous); Big Thoughts for Little People: "Q" (quarreling).

Reading
Read a poem.
"S s" page in the alphabet book: write S s at top of the page and glue pictures to represent the two sounds of "s" onto the page.
(Alone) Visual discrimination: Dominos
Child draws the following letters/shapes onto a worksheet: T H V O +.

Art
Sponge art - use sponge in tempra paint to color in/make vegetable shapes.
When dry, cut and tape into "basket" of yellow/brown construction paper.

223

Arithmetic
Review of counting: child counts on own to 30 while pointing to numbers.

Health/Manners
Basic first aid (Part 5) - Blisters, Contact Poisons
1. Blisters: Don't break, if all pressure can be relieved. Otherwise, wash entire area with soap and water, make small puncture hole at base of blister with needle sterilized in rubbing alcohol. Apply sterile dressing; protect area. If blister already broken, treat as an open wound.
2. Contact poisons:
   a. Chemical burns: (poisons, harsh chemicals)
      Remove contaminated clothing and immediately drench and flush with large quantities of water. Wash with soap and water for five minutes. Don't leave victim alone.
   b. Poisonous plants:
      Remove clothing. Wash thoroughly with soap, water, and rubbing alcohol; apply calamine lotion, if reaction mild. If severe reaction or known previous sensitivity, seek medical advice.

Physical Education
Hopping, galloping

Story
Eric Plants a Garden (Jean Hudlow); planning & all steps
Janey (Charlotte Zolotow)

Memory Verse
"A friend loves at all times..." Prov.17:17a

WEEK 34   THURSDAY

Bible
Qualities of a good friend (cont'd.)
5. Kindness - read rhymes and answer questions from: Giant Steps for Little People: V (gentleness is always good) and Big Thoughts for Little People: "K" (kindness)

6. Doing for others, being helpful - read rhymes and answer questions from: Giant Steps for Little People: XVI (How should you treat others?) and Big Thoughts for Little People: "D" (doing what needs to be done) and "H" (helping).

Reading
Read a poem.
"T t" page in the alphabet book: write T t at top of the page and glue picture to represent the "t" sound onto the page.
(Alone) Visual discrimination: Child matches letter cards (a-z) to the a's to z's on the file folder.

(Alone) Classification: Child makes ten piles, one for each number. Into each he puts any card that shows the numeral or the number of objects that corresponds to the number (four each of numbers 1-10).

Music
Praise the Lord Together

Arithmetic
Review seriation/order (first/second/third; smallest to largest; youngest to oldest; lightest to darkest; lightest to heaviest). See Weeks 6, 11 and 12 for specific activities.

God's World
Planning a garden - Read parts of In My Garden - A Child's Gardening Book which was recommended for this past Tuesday to talk about:
Size of plants (tall, bushy, etc.)
Companion plants
Resource:
j595.7H71go   Good Bugs and Bad Bugs in Your Garden - Back-Yard Ecology (Dorothy Childs Hogner)

Physical Education
Movement of your choice

Story
"Kimbie" Visits the Zoo (Jack E. Young)
The Adventures of Goat (Lucille Hammond); Golden Book

Memory Verse
"Therefore, as we have opportunity, let us do good to all, especially to those who are of the household of faith."

WEEK 34   FRIDAY

Visit the zoo.

Preparation for next week:

General:
_____Read over lesson plans
_____List materials needed
_____Collect materials needed
_____Story pages, etc. to notebook

Library:
_____Return books used this week
_____Check out books for week after next

Field Trips:
_____Reconfirm next Friday's trip
_____Thank you note for last trip
_____Set up trip for week after next

WEEK 35   MONDAY

Bible
Qualities of a good friend (cont'd.)

7. Sharing - read rhymes and answer questions from: Big Thoughts for Little People: "U" (unselfish) and "V" (visitors - hospitality) and Giant Steps for Little People: XIII (God wants you to share with others).

Reading
Read a poem.

Read poems: "Gardening Is Heaps of Fun," "In the Garden," and "Gardening" -p.42V.

"U u" page in the alphabet book: write U u on top of the page and glue three pictures to represent the three sounds of "u" onto page.

Sequence and complete sentences: Child dictates story about trip to the zoo.

(Alone) Sequence: Child arranges cards (a-z) into alphabetical order.

Art
Make "zooscape" (to be completed Wednesday). Color and cut zoo animals. Glue to butcher paper/construction paper zoo.

Arithmetic
Review numbers 0-10 and match numerals with pictures of objects of a corresponding number. See Weeks 13-23 for specific activities.

Character Building
Kindness: Roleplay with child examples of when a person was kind and then examples of being unkind - by what he said and what he did.

On Character Building story page, write: I can show kindness to others in how I talk and act.

Physical Education
Kicking the ball

Story
Let's Make Paper Dolls (Vivian Huff); j736.98H889L

Flicka Ricka Dicka and the New Friend (Lindman)

Memory Verse
"Let all that you do be done with love." I Cor.16:14

WEEK 35   TUESDAY

Bible
Qualities of a good friend (cont'd.)

8. Forgiveness - read rhymes and answer questions from: Big Thoughts for Little People: "F" (forgive) and Giant Steps for Little People: VII (acting kind toward others).

Reading

Read a poem.

"V v" page in the alphabet book: write V v at top of the page and glue picture representing the "v" sound to page.

(Alone) Visual discrimination: Child matches A to Z cards with the a's to z's on the file folder (capital to small matching).

Hand-eye coordination: Child draws: T H V O + onto worksheet, practicing several times.

Music

Favorites from the year

Arithmetic

Review concepts of many/few and more/less/equal. See Weeks 25-26 for specific activities.

God's World

Plan your garden/your child's garden. Plant it at a later time at your convenience.

Physical Education

Broad jump; running

Story

The Carrot Seed (Ruth Kruss)
A Friend is Someone Who Likes You (Joan Walsh Anglund)

Memory Verse

"Be at peace among yourselves." I Thes.5:13b
"Be of the same mind toward one another." Rom.12:16a

WEEK 35   WEDNESDAY

Bible

Qualities of a good friend (cont'd.)

9. Thankfulness - read rhymes and answer questions from: Big Thoughts for Little People: "S" (singing) and "T" (thankful), and Giant Steps for Little People: XXX (thank the Lord for all you have).

Reading

Read a poem.

"W w" page in the alphabet book: write W w on top of page and glue picture representing the "w" sound to page.

(Alone) Classifying: Child sorts picture cards into following categories: furniture, animals, clothing, people.

Listening: Child repeats sequences after you:

love, neighbors, God	friendship, upbuilding, care
goodness, flexibility, love	gardening, plan, size, work
hoe, shovel, rake, hose	companion plants, weeding, watering

joyfulness, peace, kind, help   zoo, zookeeper, animals
lion, tiger, elephant, giraffe   polar bear, panda bear, grizzly bear
monkey, coyote, wolf, duck   share, forgive, thank, blessing
tools, caution, safety   Father's Day, respect, Dad, love
giggle, laugh, chuckle

Art
Complete the "zooscape" begun Monday. Use pipe cleaners/strips of construction paper for "bars" on the cages.

Arithmetic
Review measurement: inches, feet, yards; degrees; teaspoon, tablespoon, cup.
See Weeks 27-29 for specific activities.

Health/Manners
Basic first aid (Part 6)
Review material presented from Week 30-34

Physical Education
Bouncing ball

Story
Thy Friend, Obadiah (Brinton Turkle)

Memory Verse
"And be kind to one another, tenderhearted, forgiving one another, just as God in Christ also forgave you." Eph.4:32

WEEK 35   THURSDAY

Bible
How can we be a good friend? (be loving, be good, be joyful, not argue or get angry, be kind, be helpful, share, forgive, be thankful)
What are blessings? (any good thing we have)
Where do our blessings come from? ("Every good and perfect gift is from above, coming down from the Father of the heavenly lights..." James 1:17a,b)

Reading
Read a poem.
"X x" page in the alphabet book: write X x at top of page and glue picture representing the "x" sound onto page.
(Alone) Classifying/Visual discrimination: Child matches the cards (a-z) with the A's to Z's on the file folder.
(Alone) Hand-eye coordination: Child draws the following letters on a worksheet: T H V O + (several times each).

Music
Love, Love
Favorites from the year

Arithmetic

Review money: name and identify coins; match with their monetary value.
See Weeks 32-33 for specific activities.

God's World

Tools - Talk about safety with tools:
1. Sharp point down when holding/carrying.
2. Put tool back in its right place when done with it.
3. Use with caution - and only when Mom/Dad are with you.
Talk about the following three tools; show them and let them touch them.
Talk about their use: Hammer, Pliers, Measuring Tape.

Physical Education

Movement of your choice

Story

Johnny Crow's Party (L. Leslie Brooke)
Richard Scarry's Please and Thank You Book ("Good Friends and
Neighbors")

Memory Verse

"Therefore, comfort each other and edify one another..." I Thes.5:11a

WEEK 35   FRIDAY

Visit a fish hatchery.

Preparation for next week:

General:
_____Read over lesson plans
_____List materials needed
_____Collect materials needed
_____Story pages, etc. to notebook

Library:
_____Return books used this week
_____Check out books for week after next

Field Trips:
_____Reconfirm next Friday's trip
_____Thank you note for last trip
_____Set up trip for week after next

WEEK 36   MONDAY

Bible

Review of concepts covered in Weeks 1-9.

Reading

Read a poem.

"Y y" page in the alphabet book: write Y y at top of the page and glue three pictures to page, representing the three sounds of "y."

Sequence and complete sentences: Child dictates story of visit to the fish hatchery.

(Alone) Sequence: Child arranges cards (a-z) in alphabetical order.

Art

Make Father's Day cards for Dad and Grandpas using rubber stamps, crayons, paints, etc.

Arithmetic

Review the days of the week and the months of the year. Have child repeat each of the series.

Character Building

Initiative - Talk about examples of initiative:

If we saw a baby ready to stick a pin into an electrical outlet, what could you do? (Take initiative and respond quickly to help her stay safe)

If you saw Mom carrying a heavy bag of groceries and had a trunkful more, what could you do? (Even though she had not asked you to help, offer or begin to help)

On Character Building story page, write: Initiative means stepping out to help or explore something in a positive/good way.

Physical Education

Throw and catch ball

Story

<u>Around and Around</u> (Betty Miles)
<u>Mousekin Finds a Friend</u> (Edna A. Miller)

Memory Verse

"...speak evil of no one, to be peaceable, gentle, showing all humility to all men." Titus 3:2

WEEK 36   TUESDAY

Bible

Review of concepts covered in Weeks 10-18.

Reading

Read a poem.

"Z z" page in the alphabet book: write Z z at top of the page and glue picture representing the "z" sound to page.

(Alone) Classification/Visual discrimination: Child sorts through all the alphabet cards A to Z and a to z and puts them in alphabetical order (one stack for A's and a's; another stack for B's and b's, etc.).

Music
Climb, Climb Up Sunshine Mountain

Physical Education
Review of concepts.

God's World
Tools - Talk about the following tools; show them to the child and let him touch them. Talk about their use: Screwdriver, Wrench, Sandpaper, Level

Resources:

j670C68e	Early American Crafts: Tools, Shops and Products (C. B. Colby); full-page b&wh photos; good pictures of old-time tools
j680S592s	Carpentry is Easy When You Know How (Arco Pub. Co.); large color step-by-step direction for easy carpentry projects

Physical Education
Broad jump; running

Story
Frog and Toad All Year (Arnold Lobel)
The Toolbox (Anne and Harlow Rockwell)

Memory Verse
"Forgive, and you will be forgiven." Luke 6:37c

WEEK 36   WEDNESDAY

Bible
Review of concepts covered Weeks 19-27.

Reading
Read a poem.
Read through the alphabet book, saying the letter sound as you point to that page (child says sounds, too).
(Alone) Hand-eye coordination: Child draws T H V O + on worksheet, practicing several times.

Art
Draw and color a picture of you and Dad doing a favorite thing together.

Arithmetic
Review of concepts.

Health/Manners
Introductions (to help others be able to talk with each other)
Show respect by saying older person/woman/girl's name first.

(Adult) "Mrs. Price, I'd like to have you meet my friend, Amy. Amy, this is Mrs. Price."

(Friends) "Susan, I'd like you to meet Tommy Jones. Tommy, this is Susan Kenny."

(Adult) "Mr. Smith, I'd like you to meet my sister, Kelly. Kelly, this is Mr. Smith."

(Adult) "Grandpa, I'd like you to meet my friend, Adam. Adam, this is Mr. Peterson, my grandfather."

Practice introductions, shaking hands, and greeting by the other party. "Hello/Hi. It's nice to meet you, their name."

Physical Education
Running

Story
My Journals and Sketchbooks: Robinson Crusoe (Anie Politzer) oversize; look at sketches

Memory Verse
"Praise the Lord! Oh, give thanks to the Lord, for He is good! For His mercy endures forever." Ps.106:1

WEEK 36   THURSDAY

Bible
Review of concepts covered in Weeks 28-35.

Reading
Read a poem.

Read through the alphabet book, having the child say the letter sounds as you point to that page.

Sequence and complete sentences: Child dictates story about what he/she wants to do in the summer.

Sequence and complete sentences: Child dictates story about what he/she plans to do for Dad in taking him to lunch tomorrow.

Music
Praise God from Whom All Blessings Flow

Arithmetic
Review of concepts

God's World
Tools - Talk about using tools to build a building with, how to take care of the tools, sharpen them, etc.; need to practice with use.

Read:

j690S677p   Pete's House (Harriet Langsam Sobol); b&wh photos; step-by-step from plans to finished house.

Then talk about using the "tools" you've learned this year in school to build your life with.

Resources:
    j690.52M114u   Unbuilding (David Macaulay); good for b&wh full-page drawings of process
    j937M117c   City - A Story of Roman Planning and Construction (David Macaulay)
    j913.32M117p   Pyramid (David Macaulay)
    j725.4M117m   Mill (David Macaulay)
    j726.6M117c   Cathedral: The Story of Its Construction (David Macaulay)
    j728Y94T   The Tipi: A Center of Native American Life (David & Charlotte Yue)

Physical Education
Movement of your choice

Story
Story of your choice

Memory Verse
"...speaking the truth in love..." Eph.4:15a

WEEK 36   FRIDAY

Make lunch for Dad.

CONGRATULATIONS! You have completed a year of learning! Thank God for His blessings to you and your family. May God bless you as you represent Him through His Son Jesus Christ.

Coordinating School Times For A Preschooler and a Kindergartener

Following is a schedule (two hours in length) that provides for joint and individual activities between a preschooler and a kindergartener (or older student).

TIME	PRESCHOOLER	KINDERGARTENER
9:00-9:05	———————— Prayer, Pledge of Allegiance and Calendar Time————————	
9:05-9:20	Bible Class	
9:20-9:25	Listen to drill	Phonogram drill
9:25-9:35	Independent reading activity	Phonogram test/Reading activity
9:35-9:45	Check work, teach skill, concept	Play
9:45-10:00	Play	Writing words in Notebook
10:00-10:15	Art/Music Class	
10:15-10:30	Arithmetic (Work with one while other doing indep. activ.; switch)	
10:30-10:40	Character Building Class/Health Class/God's World Class	
10:40-10:50	Physical Education Class	
10:50-11:00	Story	

Enjoy every moment of your year together!

Notes About The Kindergarten Arithmetic Program

On the following pages, you will find an outline and specific daily activities for your kindergartener. There are several points that I would like to make that hopefully will become part of your "routine" on a daily basis.

First is that of the **calendar time** at the beginning of school, after the prayer and pledge. During that time, we name the days of the week, the months of the year, and then count on the calendar from 1-30/31. Then the current day's space is colored, after which we repeat the specific date of the day. After that, for the kindergartener (preschoolers can listen in, too!), I recommend **counting on a number line** (you can make one easily by cutting several pieces of construction paper in three parts the long way, marking each into ten parts with a number and taping them to the bulletin board/wall, connected. We have ours in rainbow segments: 0-10 is red, 11-20 is orange, etc.).

We count up to 50 (to start with, then eventually getting to 100). After the child is very familiar with the numbers, you can start counting by 10;s, then by 2's, and 5's. Keep repeating this (you'll be thinking of it in your sleep!) as **repetition is important in establishing concepts**.

Also, after the addition and subtraction facts are learned, daily practice even a little at a time is important. Even bathtimes can provide quick drills. Enjoy every minute with your kindergartener!

Kindergarten Arithmetic

Basic Concepts

I.   Basic concepts (Review)
   A. Top/middle/bottom
   B. Above/below and over/under
   C. Colors: identification and visual discrimination

II.   Shapes
   A. Review circle, square and triangle: identification and discrimination
   B. Introduce oval, rectangle and diamond: identification and visual
      discrimination

III. Fractional parts of a whole
   A. Review: 1/2, 1/3, 1/4, 1/6.
   B. Introduce: 1/8, 3/8, 2/3, 3/4.

IV.   Seriation
   A. Review 1st, 2nd, 3rd; lightest to heaviest, lightest to darkest, youngest to
      oldest, series of pictures in story, smallest to largest.

V.   Numerals and corresponding number of objects
   A. Review 1-10.
   B. Introduce 11-30.
   C. Introduce 31-100 with numeral and place on number line only.

VI.   Counting
   A. Review to 30
   B. Introduce to 100
   C. Introduce counting by 2's, 5's and 10's.

VII. Measurement
   A. Expand on preschool application of using ruler and yardstick; measuring
      spoons and cups.

VIII. Maps
   A. Review four basic directions.
   B. Use those to follow instructions to find spot/object.

IX.   Money
   A. Review of penny, nickel, dime and quarter.
   B. Introduce half-dollar, $1.00, $5.00, $10.00, and $20.00
   C. Use money to "pay" for "purchases" at "store."

X. Addition
   A. Introduction to concept, signs and terms.
   B. Facts with sums up to 10.

XI. Subtraction
    A. Introduction to concept, signs and terms.
    B. Facts with largest number 10 or less.

Kindergarten Arithmetic Program

Lesson Plans

Week 1

Monday
No school (Labor Day).

Tuesday
Review colors. Have child name all eight basic colors plus white. Show
    child Primary colors (red, yellow and blue). All the other colors are
    made from them.
Have child sort stack of cards by colors (pictures of objects in each of the
    colors as well as cards of the colors themselves; at least four for each of
    the colors plus white).

Wednesday
Review concept of top/middle/bottom. Using the flannelboard, the table as
    a middle line, and relationships with themselves (top of your hand),
    have child demonstrate proficiency with the concepts.
Divide a coloring book page into thirds by folding. Have child color the
    top part one color, the middle another, and the bottom part a third
    color.

Thursday
Review concepts of above/below, over/under using discussion of animals
    and birds, where they travel in relationship to the ground. Have child
    follow instructions using the flannelboard to demonstrate understanding
    of concepts.
Review days of the week; child repeats.
Child sorts numeral cards (0-10) and matches to numerals in file folder.

Week 2

Monday
Review shapes: circle, triangle and square. Have child trace shape of card
    with fingers while saying shape name. Explain that triangle shapes can
    vary somewhat: that each side does not need to be the same length;
    show examples.
Child sorts wallpaper shapes on cards into piles of circles, triangles and
    squares.
Using a crayon, child traces over your drawings on a worksheet for the
    three shapes. Make sure he starts at the x and traces the correct
    direction. Have three of each shape for child to trace.

Tuesday

Show child a rectangle. Explain that it can be a "tall" one or a short, wide rectangle. It always has four lines connected to make four sides. The sides can be of any length. Have child trace shape while saying shape name.

Using crayon, have child trace rectangles you've drawn on a worksheet.

Wednesday

Introduce oval shape. Explain that a circle is perfectly round and an oval is longer on one side or another. It can be "standing up" or "lying down"; it's still an oval. Trace card with fingers.

Using crayon, have child trace ovals you've drawn on a worksheet.

Thursday

Introduce diamond shape. Have child trace while repeating name.

Using crayon, have child trace diamond shapes you've drawn on a worksheet.

If desired, these shapes, and pictures cut from cardboard stencils could be made into a "book."

Week 3

Monday

Have child name each of the shapes learned: circle, square, triangle, oval, rectangle and diamond, as he points to each.

Child sorts wallpaper shapes on cards (with all six shapes) into piles by shape; then matches each card with the corresponding pattern in a file folder matching game by shapes.

Tuesday

Review shape names. Introduce colored wooden shapes (Ex.: Design Discoveries by Discovery Toys). Have child sort them by color and then by shape.

Child traces shapes on worksheet then makes his own shapes, drawing his next to the models you've drawn.

Wednesday

Child draws shapes on worksheet after tracing yours.

Child uses wooden shapes to make patterns of his own and following instructions of manufacturer.

Thursday

Child again practices drawing each of the shapes, this time on the chalkboard.

Child uses wooden shapes to make patterns and designs.

Week 4

Monday

Review a fraction being a part of a whole. Using a piece of bologna, cut it to show halves and quarters. Have child show you: 1/4, 2/4 (what does that equal?), 3/4 (is 3/4 more than 1/4? 1/2?). Review the symbols for each of the fractions: 1/2 means one part of two, etc.

On worksheet, have child color in the part specified on shapes divided into the proper segments. (color 1/3)

Have child match parts to the whole (parts onto shapes in a file folder). Use circles divided into 1/2's and 1/4's and squares divided likewise, and also such divided into triangle segments.

Tuesday

Review thirds and sixths.

Have child match parts to the whole using file folder.

On a worksheet, have child color specific parts (1/3, 2/6, etc.)

Wednesday

Using shape parts from file folder matching, have child find a 1/2 part and a 1/3 part. Which is larger?

Introduce eighths. Start with circle; cut in 1/2; then to 1/4's and then to 1/8's. Show symbol of 1/8; one part in eight.

On worksheet, have child color specific part of a whole from written symbol.

Thursday

Show child circles and squares with divisions marked. Have child tell you how many divisions.

Have him sort cards with fractional symbols on them into piles of like amounts; then match to circular/square representation with fractional part colored in with colored pencil/crayon.

Week 5

Monday

Seriation: 1st, 2nd, 3rd. Have cards or dolls or toys lined up. Have child describe the 1st, 2nd, 3rd.

On worksheet, have child color the first shape blue, the second red, the third yellow.

Have child do three movements and then ask: What did you do first? second? third?

Tuesday

Say three words in a sequence to the child. Which word did I say first? Etc.

Line up four shapes: three alike, one different. Which is different: the first, second or third?

On worksheet with three houses or other objects, have child number them (left to right)/trace numbers you draw. Then color.

Wednesday

Lightest to heaviest: Have child feel 4 to 5 objects and have him arrange them in order of lightest to heaviest.

Have child arrange sets of color gradations (4 each per color) in order.

Have child arrange a set of stacking cups in order from smallest to largest, after you've mixed them up.

Thursday

Youngest to oldest: child arranges photos/pictures in order.

Looking at story book with child, focus on series of several pictures. What happened first?

Weeks 6 - 12

For the next seven weeks, child will be reviewing and learning about the numerals 0-30, and the concepts they represent by matching with a group of corresponding number of objects. Each day's format will be basically the same except for the number studied. Therefore instead of repeating, I will explain the daily format once for you to refer to each time.

Teacher and child count up the number line until you get to the number being studied. Teacher shows number card for the number and shows child how to write it (where to start, which direction to go, etc.). Then child, while saying the name of the numeral, uses two fingers and traces the numeral in the air, on the table, and then with pencil over faintly outlined numeral you have made on a worksheet. Then child practices writing the numeral himself. Child puts pencil down. Teacher holds up number card with numeral on it; child holds up corresponding number of fingers. After several numerals have been studied, you mix up the cards. Then child counts out set of 25 counters (for 1-10 use only) into groups of whatever number is being studied.

Then child does a number of independent activities relating to the particular number in study:

a. Child stamps/uses stickers the corresponding number of times to represent studied number. Then he writes the numeral on the page.

b. Child colors in number line for correct amount of value on the same page. Each number will have one page like this for a "My Counting To 30" book.

c. Child clips correct number of clothespins to outside edge of paper plate labeled with numeral on inside.

d. Child matches numeral cards with dots/groups of objects in file folder matching game.

This is the format for Weeks 6-12.

Week 6

<u>Monday</u>	0, 1, 2
<u>Tuesday</u>	3, 4
<u>Wednesday</u>	5
<u>Thursday</u>	6

Week 7

<u>Monday</u>	7
<u>Tuesday</u>	8
<u>Wednesday</u>	9
<u>Thursday</u>	10

Week 8

<u>Monday</u>	11
<u>Tuesday</u>	12
<u>Wednesday</u>	13
<u>Thursday</u>	14

Week 9

<u>Monday</u>	15
<u>Tuesday</u>	16
<u>Wednesday</u>	17
<u>Thursday</u>	18

Week 10

<u>Monday</u>	19
<u>Tuesday</u>	20

<u>Wednesday</u>   21

<u>Thursday</u>   22

Week 11

<u>Monday</u>   23

<u>Tuesday</u>   24

<u>Wednesday</u>   25

<u>Thursday</u>   26

Week 12

<u>Monday</u>   27

<u>Tuesday</u>   28

<u>Wednesday</u>   29

<u>Thursday</u>   Thanksgiving!

Weeks 13-15

For each series of numbers, on a daily basis, child and teacher will point to numbers as they count up the number line, noting especially the numbers in the series being studied.

Child writes numbers in the series, getting help from you or the number line, if needed. Then after practicing, child writes numbers at correct spot on a large number line being created totally by the child.

Independently:

  a. Child matches like number cards (Ex.:39 with another 39); four sets of each number in the series studied.

  b. Child fills in the blanks for missing numbers on a worksheet you make for each series.

Week 13

Monday   Complete #30 in book.

Tuesday   30's

Wednesday   40's

Thursday   Review 30-50

Week 14

Monday   50's

Tuesday   60's

Wednesday   70's

Thursday   Review 50-80

Week 15

Monday   80's

Tuesday   90's

Wednesday   Review 80-100

Thursday   Review and talk about place value: 1's, 10's, 100's, 1000's. Our decimal system is based on groups of 10.

Weeks 16 - 22

For the next seven weeks, the child will be learning the concept of addition and the specific number facts with sums up to and including ten. The following format is to be repeated each week with the specific addition facts mentioned.

Monday
Review concept of adding (making a larger group by adding two groups together), the signs: "+" and "=" and the term "sum." Review the fact that it doesn't matter if the problem is written across or down, the answer will be the same.
Show child concept of each fact by using fingers or counters to "act out" problems on the paper/chalkboard.
Have child write down each of the facts being studied.

Tuesday
Have child answer fact by flashcards.
Have child match "problem" card with "sum" on the file folder matching game.

Wednesday
Flashcards
Have child do worksheet of addition problems; he writes in the sum for each of the problems of the week and any "toughies" from previous weeks.

Thursday
Have child answer facts given by you verbally; no flashcards.
Have child do worksheet with problems as review and/or have child match "problem" card with "sum" on folder.

Week 16 0+ and 1+ facts

Week 17 2+ facts

Week 18 3+ facts

Week 19 4+ facts

Week 20 5+ facts

Week 21 6+ facts

Week 22 7+, 8+, 9+ facts

Weeks 23 - 29

Use same format as outlined before, except with subtraction. (Subtraction is taking something away from a group of things to get a smaller amount; term: "difference")

Week 23 0-, 1-, 2- facts

Week 24 3-, 4- facts

Week 25 5-, 6- facts

Week 26 7- facts

Week 27 8- facts

Week 28 9- facts

Week 29 10- facts

Week 30

Review of addition and subtraction. Mix up addition and subtraction problems on worksheets and on flashcards and folders. Tailor this to the "challenging" areas, if any, of your child. Make sure you include problems written across and down on your file folder games, flashcards and worksheets.

Week 31

Monday
    Review name, sight identification, and value (x cents) for penny and nickel.
    Have child sort group of coins into pennies and nickels.
    On worksheet, have groups of pennies. Have child count and write the answer (4 cents, etc.).

Tuesday
    Review name, sight identification and value of dimes.
    Have child sort coins into three groups. Count the number of each group.
    Have child match coins with cents values written on file folder.

Wednesday
    Ask child for each coin. What is it called? How much is it worth? Write its monetary value.
    On worksheet with x cents written, have child put proper coins to total that value (up to 20 cents).

Thursday
    Have child match x cents value cards to file folder with coins taped in (as individual coins and groups of coins).
    Play store with child. Have him "buy" things and count out money.

Week 32

Monday
    Introduce quarter (name, sight identification, value is 25 cents).
    Have child match x cents value cards to file folder with groups of coins (up to 25 cents value per group).

Tuesday
    Show child half-dollar, $1.00 bill, $5.00 bill, $10.00 bill, and $20.00 bill. On each, have child point to the numeral that shows the value.

Wednesday
    Introduce equal value. Work with child to find as many combinations of coins to equal 25 cents as you can.
    Match x cents value cards with coins in file folder (groups of coins up to 50 cents in value).

Thursday
    Review of each piece of money (name, sight identification, value).
    Find combinations of coins to make 50 cents value.
    Matching coins to x cents markers on items "for sale" (up to 50 cents in value).

Week 33

<u>Monday</u>
Review of ruler: How many inches? Show me 6" on ruler, etc. Show child how to hold ruler so you can draw a straight line of a certain length.
On worksheet, have several specific distances listed (4", etc.). Have child draw line of corresponding length.

<u>Tuesday</u>
Explain that 12 inches equals one foot. Have three rulers and a yardstick. Show, by counting, that 1 yard = 3 feet, and that they both are 36" long.
Have child use yardstick to measure items in the room.
Have child put 1/4" diameter stickers on to specific lengths on yardstick to correspond with lengths listed on worksheet.

<u>Wednesday</u>
Using catalog pictures of items in your home, give child a worksheet with several pictures of items to measure. Have child measure the height and record the measurement next to the picture. To check, go back to each item with the child and have him show you how he measured.

<u>Thursday</u>
Using map or maze made for Preschool Readiness activity, have child follow written directions you list (also indicating verbally the starting point). (Example: go 5" , go 2" |, go 4"   , go 1" | and have him put a sticker on the ending point. Check it over with him.

Week 34

<u>Monday</u>
Review solid and liquid measurement, using the following equipment: 1/4 t, 1/2 t, 1 t, 1 T, 1/4 cup, 1/3 cup, 1/2 cup, 1 cup. Name each and show child how much it holds.
Have child practice measuring (by himself) with cornmeal from one bowl to another (with newspaper underneath!).

<u>Tuesday</u>
Have child practice measuring liquid (water or colored water).

<u>Wednesday</u>
Review directions - north, south, east and west - with child. Show him how each of the abbreviations (N, E, S, W) look. Using map or maze again, have child follow "Treasure Hunt" with clues such as: go 4" W, 2" N, etc. Have him mark his "spot" with a small sticker.

<u>Thursday</u>
Have child follow clues on another "Treasure Hunt."

Week 35

<u>Monday</u>
    Review shapes and seriation and colors. (Weeks 1-3, 5)
    Have child match number cards 1-100 (2 of each).

<u>Tuesday</u>
    Review fractions. (Week 4)
    Have child arrange number cards (1-50) into numerical order.

<u>Wednesday</u>
    Review place value. (Week 15)
    Have child match number cards 1-100 (2 of each).

<u>Thursday</u>
    Review of money. (Weeks 31-32)
    Have child arrange number cards (1-50) into numerical order.

Week 36

<u>Monday</u>
    Review measurements and maps. (Weeks 33-34)
    Have child match number cards 1-100 (2 of each).

<u>Tuesday</u>
    Review of counting by 2's, 5's and 10's.
    Have child arrange number cards (1-50) into numerical order.

<u>Wednesday</u>
    Review all addition facts learned. (Weeks 16-22)
    Have child match number cards 1-100 (2 of each).

<u>Thursday</u>
    Review all subtraction facts learned. (Weeks 23-29)
    Have child arrange number cards (1-100) into numerical order.

KINDERGARTEN READING
Basic Concepts

Using the <u>Phonics for Reading and Spelling</u> approach to teach all the language arts skills, the child learns:

    I. Sounds of all 70 phonograms for the English language.
   II. Correct method of printing all letters, capital and small.
  III. Increased vocabulary skills.
  IV. Increased grammar proficiency.
   V. 460 spelling words.
  VI. Phonetic decoding skills to analyze new word.
 VII. Ability to read books independently.
VIII. Ability to write paragraphs, proofread them, and rewrite.

What Is "Phonics for Reading and Spelling" Approach To Teaching Reading?

The <u>Phonics for Reading and Spelling</u> is a multisensory approach to teaching all language arts skills: writing (composition), printing, vocabulary, reading, listening, spelling, grammar, following directions, and other skills. This is done by having the child say a sound, see the letters used, hear the teacher say the sound, and write the letters that make the sound. It is a method based on phonics. The 70 phonograms for the English language are taught as well as grammar and spelling rules. The basics are reinforced and reviewed to ensure that the child gets off to a very strong start. It is one that has proven to be highly successful in teaching children and adults to read. Although the book upon which this curriculum is based seems at some times disorganized and confusing, by reading it and then following the structure of the lesson plans, it should be no problem to follow at all.

The preschool reading program is based on learning the first 26 phonograms (to correspond with the letters of the alphabet). This program reviews the sounds as well as teaching of the writing of letters. It is a program that stresses excellence and rewards the learner with the confidence of a job well done.

In addition to the text, <u>Phonics for Reading and Spelling</u>, and this Guide, there are McCall-Crabbs booklets that test your child's reading comprehension - available from Christian Life Workshop. I highly recommend using the 70 Phonogram cards by Wanda Sanseri (available through Christian Life Workshops); on the back of each card, it tells you exactly what to say.

The gift of reading is one of the most precious, and, unfortunately, one of the most overlooked/neglected gifts we can give our children. So many of the skills they will use for the rest of their lives will be dependent on their ability to read. It is oftentimes tied with children's (and adults') self-esteem. For these reasons and the belief that it takes ten times longer to correct a problem than to teach it right in the first place, I felt strongly that this reading system is the very best you can offer your child. Even if you go at a slower pace than the Guide recommends, use the system and know it will work for you and your child.

Kindergarten Reading Program

Lesson Plans

Week 1

Monday

Talk with child about basics of how he/she can be the best learner this year by obeying the rules and following the suggestions of the teacher:

1. There is always one talker and one listener in a conversation. You cannot talk and listen at the same time. When the teacher is talking, you need to listen. When you talk, I will listen.

2. When you are listening, fold your hands so you will be able to concentrate better. Lay pencil down and keep hands folded.

3. To learn well, you must help your body sit in a way that it will not get tired so easily. Sit with your bottom way back in the chair and stack the spinal "blocks" nice and straight.

4. You will be using one hand to write with and the other to hold the paper. Show them the correct way to slant their paper, depending on hand preference, and to hold their pencils.

5. You have a smart head. I expect you to use it and to think well. You will be able to remember the rules and the sounds because you are smart and we will practice until you know them all perfectly.

6. To be a good learner, we need to think about what you're doing in school - not about something else.

Tuesday

Explain what a phonogram is: "one or more letters that makes one voice sound."

Using the information on p.54-55 in the text, teach your child how to write the first two "clock" letters: **a** and **c**. You may refer to the top line as the "roof," the middle (dotted) line as the ceiling, and the bottom line as the "floor." Some letters even go into the "basement"!

Wednesday

Review how to hold the pencil, how to hold the paper, how to sit, and where (on the clock) we start to make "clock" letters.

Teach child how to make the following letters: **d**, **f**, **g** and review the letter sounds for each. Have child practice by making several of each letter. Also, review several a's and c's and the sounds they make.

Thursday

Teach child how to write **o**, **s**, **qu** and their sounds. Review all clock letters (sounds and letter shapes).

Week 2

Monday
>Daily review: Say and write phonograms; dictate phonograms to the child without showing the card; child reads back the phonograms, one at a time, to the teacher; teacher writes them on the chalkboard; child proofreads paper.
>Introduce letter shapes (writing) and sounds for: **b**, **e**, **h**.

Tuesday
>Review previously learned phonograms (a, c, d, f, g, o, s, qu, b, e, h) by method shown in Week 2, Monday.
>Introduce letter shapes (writing) and sounds for: **i**, **j**, **k**, **l**.

Wednesday
>Review previously learned phonograms (a, c, d, f, g, o, s, qu, b, e, h, i, j, k, l, m) by method shown in Week 2, Monday.
>Introduce letter shapes (writing) and sounds for: **m**, **n**.

Thursday
>Review previously learned phonograms by method shown in Week 2, Monday. Introduce letter shapes (writing) and sounds for: **p**, **r**, **t**.

Week 3

Monday
>Review previously learned phonograms by method shown in Week 2, Monday.
>Introduce letter shapes (writing) and sounds for: **u**, **v**, **w**.
>Dictate alphabet, using only sounds; you write letter on board after child repeats the letter sounds.

Tuesday
>Review previously learned phonograms by method shown in Week 2, Monday. Introduce letter shapes (writing) and sounds for: **x**, **y**, **z**.
>Dictate and write on chart the information on page 1 (first half) of the notebook, page 81 of the text (Consonants and Vowels). When I named the vowels to our children, I named the letters (in a normal voice): a,e,i,o,u (and then in a whisper) "and sometimes `y'." Somehow, by adding a little fun to it, the material is remembered more easily.

Wednesday
>Review first 26 phonograms by method shown in Week 2, Monday.
>Review vowels.

Thursday
>Review previously learned phonograms by method shown in week 2, Monday.
>Introduce phonograms (writing and sounds): **er**, **sh**.

Week 4

Monday
    Review previously learned phonograms by method shown in Week 2, Monday.
    Introduce phonograms (writing and sounds): **oo, ee**.

Tuesday
    Review previously learned phonograms by method shown in Week 2, Monday.
    Introduce phonograms (writing and sounds): **th, ou**.

Wednesday
    Review previously learned phonograms by method shown in Week 2, Monday.
    Introduce phonograms (writing and sounds): **ir** (we remembered this by making up a line we usually said after the phonogram: "I are the first child." Even though it's poor grammar, it's good memory!), **ck**.

Thursday
    Review previously learned phonograms by method shown in Week 2, Monday.
    Introduce phonograms (writing and sounds): **ng, ed**.

Week 5

Monday
    Review previously learned phonograms by method shown in Week 2, Monday.
    Introduce phonograms (writing and sounds): **ur, ay**. (We remembered "ur" by adding "You are a nurse, Grandma." The children's grandma was a nurse. You could change the name.)

Tuesday
    Review previously learned phonograms by method shown in Week 2, Monday.
    Write phonograms from page 7 of the notebook (p.100-101 in text) on chart as child repeats the phonogram sounds after teacher.
    Introduce phonograms (writing and sounds): **wor, ow**.

Wednesday
    Review previously learned phonograms by method shown in Week 2, Monday.
    Introduce phonograms (writing and sounds): **ai, wh**.

Thursday
    Review previously learned phonograms by method shown in Week 2, Monday.
    Introduce phonograms (writing and sounds): **oy, oi**.

Week 6

Monday
    Review previously learned phonograms by method shown in Week 2,
       Monday.
    Introduce phonograms (writing and sounds): **ear**, **aw**.

Tuesday
    Review previously learned phonograms by method shown in Week 2,
       Monday.
    Introduce phonograms (writing and sounds): **au**, **ch**.

Wednesday
    Review previously learned phonograms by method shown in Week 2,
       Monday.
    Introduce phonograms (writing and sounds): **ew**, **oa**.

Thursday
    Review previously learned phonograms by method shown in Week 2,
       Monday.
    Introduce phonograms (writing and sounds): **ui**, **ea**.

Week 7

Monday
    Review previously learned phonograms by method shown in Week 2,
       Monday.
    Introduce phonograms (writing and sounds): **ai**, **or**.

Tuesday
    Review previously learned phonograms by method shown in Week 2,
       Monday.
    Begin writing words from Ayres list (p.119 of text) on Spelling List page in
       notebook: **me**, **do**, **and**, **go**, **at** (using any markings and notes shown in
       text) by the following method:
    To write words in the notebook:
      1. Say word and ask child what the first sound of the word is.
      2. Child responds with sound.
      3. Tell child to write that sound on his paper. He puts his pencil down
         when he's done.
      4. Ask what the next sound is; child responds; you tell child to write the
         phonogram that makes that sound next to the first one.
      5. Repeat until all phonograms written to complete the word.
      6. Child dictates back, one phonogram at a time, while the teacher
         writes it on the chalkboard. (Teacher guides child through process:
         "Which sound did you hear next?")
      7. Child checks his paper with the chalkboard to make certain his
         word looks the same. If not, he corrects.

8. Teach grammar rules as you encounter them in the spelling list.
9. Use any markings and notes from the text.
10. Review: saying word, spelling with phonograms, and saying the word the way it's pronounced: ("We say_____").

<u>Wednesday</u>

Review previously learned phonograms by method shown in Week 2, Monday.

Review yesterday's spelling list; practice any missed words.

Write the following spelling words by method shown in Week 7, Tuesday: **on**, **a**, **it**, **is**, **she**.

<u>Thursday</u>

Review previously learned phonograms by method shown in Week 2, Monday.

Review yesterday's spelling list; practice any missed words.

Write the following spelling words by method shown in Week 7, Tuesday: **can**, **see**, **run**, **the**, **in**.

Week 8

<u>Monday</u>

Review previously learned phonograms by method shown in Week 2, Monday.

Review yesterday's spelling list; practice any missed words.

Write the following spelling words by method shown in Week 7, Tuesday: **so**, **no**, **now**, **man**, **ten**.

<u>Tuesday</u>

Review previously learned phonograms by method shown in Week 2, Monday.

Review yesterday's spelling list; practice any missed words.

Write the following spelling words by method shown in Week 7, Tuesday: **bed**, **top**, **he**, **you**, **will**.

<u>Wednesday</u>

Review previously learned phonograms by method shown in Week 2, Monday.

Review yesterday's spelling list; practice any missed words.

Write the following spelling words by method shown in Week 7, Tuesday: **we**, **an**, **my**, **up**, **last**.

<u>Thursday</u>

Review previously learned phonograms by method shown in Week 2, Monday.

Review yesterday's spelling list; practice any missed words.

Write the following spelling words by method shown in Week 7, Tuesday: **not**, **us**, **am**, **good**, **little**.

Week 9

<u>Monday</u>
Review previously learned phonograms by method shown in Week 2, Monday.
Review yesterday's spelling list; practice any missed words.
Teach subject and object pronouns: **I/me**, **he/him**, **she/her**, **you/you**, **we/us**, **they/them**. List these on chart. Write sentences on the chart using each of them once. Have child give an example for one.

<u>Tuesday</u>
Review previously learned phonograms by method shown in Week 2, Monday.
Write second half of page 1 of the notebook (page 81 of text): "silent final e's" on chart.
Write the following spelling words by method shown in Week 7, Tuesday: **ago**, **old**, **bad**, **red**, **of**.

<u>Wednesday</u>
Review previously learned phonograms by method shown in Week 2, Monday.
Review yesterday's spelling list; practice any missed words.
Write the following spelling words by method shown in Week 7, Tuesday: **be**, **but**, **this**, **all**, **your**, **you**.

<u>Thursday</u>
Review first 54 phonograms by method shown in Week 2, Monday.
Review yesterday's spelling list; practice any missed words.
Write the following spelling words by method shown in Week 5, Tuesday: **out**, **time**, **may**, **into**, **him**.

Week 10

<u>Monday</u>
Review phonograms missed recently.
Review yesterday's spelling list; practice any missed words.
Write these spelling words: **today**, **look**, **did**, **like**, **six**.

<u>Tuesday</u>
Review phonograms missed recently.
Review yesterday's spelling list; practice any missed words.
Write these spelling words: **boy**, **book**, **by**, **have**, **are**.

<u>Wednesday</u>
Review phonograms missed recently.
Review yesterday's spelling list; practice any missed words.
Write the following spelling words: **had**, **over**, **must**, **make**, **school**.

<u>Thursday</u>
Review phonograms missed recently.
Review yesterday's spelling list; practice any missed words.
Write these spelling words: **street**, **say**, **come**, **hand**, **ring**.

Week 11

Monday
Review phonograms missed recently.
Review yesterday's spelling list; practice any missed words.
Write these spelling words: **live**, **live**, **kill**, **late**, **let**.

Tuesday
Review phonograms missed recently.
Review yesterday's spelling list; practice any missed words.
Write these spelling words: **big**, **mother**, **three**, **land**, **cold**.

Wednesday
Review phonograms missed recently.
Review yesterday's spelling list; practice any missed words.
Write these spelling words: **hot**, **hat**, **child**, **ice**, **play**.

Thursday
Review phonograms missed recently.
Review yesterday's spelling list; practice any missed words.
Write these spelling words: sea, see. (End of Section A-G.) Review words
   at random from Section A-G.

Week 12

Monday
Review phonograms missed recently.
Review last Thursday's spelling list; practice any missed words.
Write these spelling words: **day**, **eat**, **sit**, **lot**, **box**.
Give Test #1 from the Spelling Scale (first 10 words). Correct; record results
   without showing to child.

Tuesday
Review phonograms missed recently.
Review yesterday's spelling list; practice any missed words.
Write these spelling words: **belong**, **door**, **floor**, **yes**, **low**.

Wednesday
Review phonograms missed recently.
Review yesterday's spelling list; practice any missed words.
Write these spelling words: **soft**, **stand**, **yard**, **bring**, **tell**.

Thursday
Thanksgiving!

Week 13

Monday
    Review phonograms.
    Review yesterday's spelling list; practice any missed words.
    Write these spelling words: **five**, **ball**, **law**, **ask**, **just**.

Tuesday
    Review phonograms missed yesterday.
    Review yesterday's spelling list; practice any missed words.
    Write these spelling words: **gust**, **way**, **get**, **home**, **much**.

Wednesday
    Review phonograms of which the child is uncertain.
    Review yesterday's spelling list; practice any missed words.
    Write these spelling words: **call**, **long**, **love**, **then**, **house**.

Thursday
    Review phonograms of which the child is uncertain.
    Review yesterday's spelling list; practice any missed words.
    Write these spelling words: **year**, **to**, **I**, **as**, **send**.

Week 14

Monday
    Review phonograms.
    Review yesterday's spelling list; practice any missed words.
    Write these spelling words: **one**, **lone**, **alone**, **has**, **some**.

Tuesday
    Review phonograms missed yesterday.
    Review yesterday's spelling list; practice any missed words.
    Write these spelling words: **how**, **her**, **them**, **other**, **baby**.

Wednesday
    Review phonograms of which the child is uncertain.
    Review yesterday's spelling list; practice any missed words.
    Write these spelling words: **well**, **about**, **men**, **man**, **for**.

Thursday
    Review phonograms of which the child is uncertain.
    Review yesterday's spelling list; practice any missed words.
    Write these spelling words: **ran**, **run**, **was**, **that**, **his**.

Week 15

Monday
    Review phonograms.
    Review yesterday's spelling list; practice any missed words.
    Write these spelling words: **led**, **lay**, **apple**, **dog**, **bread**.

<u>Tuesday</u>
Review phonograms missed yesterday.
Review yesterday's spelling list; practice any missed words.
Write these spelling words: **eats**, **food**. (Ends Section H.) Review words at random from Section H.

<u>Wednesday</u>
Review phonograms of which the child is uncertain.
Introduce the following phonograms: **ey**, **eigh**.

<u>Thursday</u>
Review phonograms of which the child is uncertain.
Introduce the following phonograms: **ei**, **igh**.

Week 16

<u>Monday</u>
Review phonograms.
Introduce the following phonograms: **ie**, **kn**.

<u>Tuesday</u>
Review phonograms missed yesterday.
Introduce the following phonograms: **gn**, **wr**.

<u>Wednesday</u>
Review phonograms of which the child is uncertain.
Introduce the following phonograms: **ph**, **dge**.

<u>Thursday</u>
Review phonograms of which the child is uncertain.
Introduce the following phonograms: **oe**, **gh**. Have your child take Test #2 of the Spelling Scale (15 words).

Week 17

<u>Monday</u>
Review phonograms.
Introduce the following phonograms: **ti**, **ci**.

<u>Tuesday</u>
Review phonograms missed yesterday.
Introduce the following phonograms: **si**, **ough**.
This is the end of all 70 phonograms! Hooray! When your child has mastered them, you may have a celebration for him/her. You might consider a reward of a toolbox or sewing kit, symbolic of learning the tools to the English language.

Wednesday
Review phonograms of which the child is uncertain.
Write these spelling words: **nine**, **face**, **miss**, **ride**, **rides**.

Thursday
Review phonograms of which the child is uncertain.
Write these spelling words: **tree**, **sick**, **god**, **north**, **while**.

Week 18

Monday
Review all 70 phonograms.
Review yesterday's spelling list; practice any missed words.
Write these spelling words: **spent**, **foot**, **feet**, **blow**, **blows**.

Tuesday
Review phonograms missed yesterday; practice any missed words.
Review yesterday's spelling list; practice any missed words.
Write these spelling words: **block**, **spring**, **plant**, **river**, **cut**.

Wednesday
Review phonograms of which the child is uncertain.
Review yesterday's spelling list; practice any missed words.
Write these spelling words: **song**, **sing**, **sang**, **sung**, **winter**.

Thursday
Review phonograms of which the child is uncertain.
Review yesterday's spelling list; practice any missed words.
Write these spelling words: **stone**, **free**, **lake**, **lace**, **page**.

Week 19

Monday
Review all 70 phonograms.
Review yesterday's spelling list; practice any missed words.
Write these spelling words: **nice**, **end**, **fall**, **went**, **back**.
Have child dictate a paragraph to you. You write it down, then your child
    copies it.

Tuesday
Review phonograms missed yesterday.
Review yesterday's spelling list; practice any missed words.
Write these spelling words: **away**, **paper**, **put**, **each**, **soon**.

Wednesday
Review phonograms of which the child is uncertain.
Write these spelling words: **came**, **Sunday**, **show**, **Monday**, **moon**.

Thursday

Review phonograms of which the child is uncertain.
Review yesterday's spelling list; practice any missed words.
Write these spelling words: **yet**, **find**, **give**, **new**, **letter**.
Begin reading easy book from the bibliography of the library. There is a listing in The Writing Road to Reading. There's also a listing of over 340 children's books - with title, author, size of print, and questions about the books - in First Grade: Learning At Home. Have your child use a bookmark under the line of type (s)he's reading and have him/her put her finger under the word (s)he's on, to help with tracking.

Week 20

Monday

Review all 70 phonograms.
Review yesterday's spelling list; practice any missed words.
Write these spelling words: **take**, **Mr.=Mister**, **abbreviation**, **period**.
Have child dictate a paragraph to you and then copy your writing.

Tuesday

Review phonograms missed yesterday; practice any missed words.
Review yesterday's spelling list; practice any missed words.
Write these spelling words: **after**, **thing**, **what**, **than**, **its**, **his**, **her**.

Wednesday

Review phonograms of which the child is uncertain.
Review yesterday's spelling list; practice any missed words.
Write these spelling words: **it's=it is**, **contraction**, **apostrophe**.

Thursday

Review phonograms of which the child is uncertain.
Review yesterday's spelling list; practice any missed words.
Write these spelling words: **very**, **or**, **thank**, **dear**, **west**.
Test #3 (20 words) of the Spelling Scale; record results.

Week 21

Monday

Review all 70 phonograms.
Review yesterday's spelling list; practice any missed words.
Write these spelling words: **sold**, **told**, **best**, **form**, **far**.
Write paragraph independently.

Tuesday

Review phonograms missed yesterday.
Review yesterday's spelling list; practice any missed words.
Write these spelling words: **gave**, **alike**, **add**, **brave**, **corn**.
Proofread paragraph written yesterday; rewrite.

Wednesday
Review phonograms of which the child is uncertain.
Review yesterday's spelling list; practice any missed words.
Write these spelling words: **dance**, **dinner**, **doll**, **egg**, **looks**.
Complete one lesson in McCall-Crabbs booklet.

Thursday
Review phonograms of which the child is uncertain.
Review yesterday's spelling list; practice any missed words.
Write these spelling words: **rich**, **zoo**, **zip**, **zero**. (End of Section I.)
Review Section I words at random.

Week 22

Monday
Review all 70 phonograms.
Review yesterday's spelling list; practice any missed words.
Write these spelling words: **seven**, **forget**, **happy**, **noon**, **think**.
Write paragraph independently.

Tuesday
Review phonograms missed yesterday.
Review yesterday's spelling list; practice any missed words.
Write these spelling words: **sister**, **cast**, **card**, **south**, **deep**.

Wednesday
Review phonograms of which the child is uncertain.
Review eight words of which the child is uncertain from previous spelling lists.
Write these spelling words: **inside**, **blue**, **post**, **town**, **stay**.
Complete one lesson in McCall-Crabbs comprehension booklet.

Thursday
Review phonograms of which the child is uncertain.
Review another eight words of which the child is uncertain from previous spelling lists.
Write these spelling words: **grand**, **outside**, **dark**, **band**, **game**.
Read from an easy book.

Week 23

Monday
Review all 70 phonograms.
Review another eight words from previous spelling lists.
Write these spelling words: **boat**, **rest**, **east**, **son**, **sun**.
Write paragraph independently.

Notes

Tuesday
Review of phonograms missed yesterday.
Review another eight words from previous spelling lists.
Write these spelling words: **help**, **hard**, **race**, **cover**, **fire**.
Proofread paragraph written yesterday; rewrite.

Wednesday
Review of phonograms of which child is uncertain.
Review another eight words from previous spelling lists.
Write these spelling words: **wire**, **tire**, **age**, **gold**, **read**.
Complete one lesson in the McCall-Crabbs comprehension booklet.

Thursday
Review of phonograms of which child is uncertain.
Review another eight words from previous spelling lists.
Write these spelling words: **read**, **red**, **fine**, **cannot**, **may**.

Week 24

Monday
Review all 70 phonograms.
Review yesterday's spelling list; practice any missed words.
Write these spelling words: **may**, **line**, **left**, **ship**, **train**.
Write paragraph independently.

Tuesday
Review phonograms missed yesterday.
Review yesterday's spelling list; practice any missed words.
Write these spelling words: **saw**, **pay**, **large**, **near**, **down**.
Proofread paragraph written yesterday; rewrite.

Wednesday
Review phonograms of which the child is uncertain.
Review yesterday's spelling list; practice any missed words.
Write these spelling words: **why**, **bill**, **want**, **girl**, **part**.
Complete one lesson in McCall-Crabbs comprehension booklet.

Thursday
Review phonograms of which the child is uncertain.
Review yesterday's spelling list; practice any missed words.
Write: "Her first nurse works early" (p.2 of notebook; see pages 84-85 of text). Talk about the 5 ways to write the "er" sound. Add spelling words to chart columns as they are encountered.
Test #4 (25 words) of the Spelling Scale; record results.
Read from an easy book.

Week 25

<u>Monday</u>
Review all 70 phonograms.
Review yesterday's spelling list; practice any missed words.
Write these spelling words: **still**, **place**, **report**, **never**, **found**.
Write paragraph independently.

<u>Tuesday</u>
Review phonograms missed yesterday.
Review yesterday's spelling list; practice any missed words.
Write these spelling words: **side**, **kind**, **life**, **here**, **car**.
Proofread paragraph written yesterday; rewrite.

<u>Wednesday</u>
Review phonograms of which the child is uncertain.
Review yesterday's spelling list; practice any missed words.
Write these spelling words: **word**, **every**, **under**, **most**, **made**.
Complete one lesson in McCall-Crabbs comprehension booklet.

<u>Thursday</u>
Review phonograms of which the child is uncertain.
Review yesterday's spelling list; practice any missed words.
Write these spelling words: **said**, **say**, **work**, **our**, **more**.
Read from an easy book.

Week 26

<u>Monday</u>
Review all 70 phonograms.
Review yesterday's spelling list; practice any missed words.
Write these spelling words: **when**, **from**, **form**, **wind**, **wind**.
Write paragraph independently.

<u>Tuesday</u>
Review phonograms missed yesterday.
Review yesterday's spelling list; practice any missed words.
Write these spelling words: **print**, **air**, **fill**, **along**, **lost**.
Proofread paragraph written yesterday; rewrite.

<u>Wednesday</u>
Review phonograms of which the child is uncertain.
Review yesterday's spelling list; practice any missed words.
Write these spelling words: **name**, **room**, **hope**, **same**, **glad**.
Complete one lesson in McCall-Crabbs comprehension booklet.

<u>Thursday</u>
Review phonograms of which the child is uncertain.
Review yesterday's spelling list; practice any missed words.

Write these spelling words: **with**, **mine**, **chair**, **forgot**, **girls**.
Read from an easy book.

Week 27

Monday
Review all 70 phonograms.
Review yesterday's spelling list; practice any missed words.
Write these spelling words: **hang**, **meat**, **mouse**, **sits**, **store**, **supper**. (End of Section J.) Review Section J words at random.
Write paragraph independently.

Tuesday
Review phonograms missed yesterday.
Review yesterday's spelling list; practice any missed words.
Write these spelling words: **became**, **brother**, **rain**, **keep**, **start**.
Proofread paragraph written yesterday; rewrite.

Wednesday
Review phonograms of which the child is uncertain.
Review yesterday's spelling list; practice any missed words.
Write these spelling words: **mail**, **male**, **female**, **eye**.
Complete one lesson in McCall-Crabbs comprehension booklet.

Thursday
Review phonograms of which the child is uncertain.
Review yesterday's spelling list; practice any missed words.
Write these spelling words: **I**, **glass**, **party**, **upon**, **two**.
Read from an easy book.

Week 28

Monday
Review all 70 phonograms.
Review yesterday's spelling list; practice any missed words.
Write these spelling words: **twin**, **twice**, **twenty**, **between**, **they**.
Write paragraph independently.

Tuesday
Review phonograms missed yesterday.
Review yesterday's spelling list; practice any missed words.
Write these spelling words: **would**, **any**, **many**, **could**, **should**.
Proofread paragraph written yesterday; rewrite.

Wednesday
Review phonograms of which the child is uncertain.
Review yesterday's spelling list; practice any missed words.
Write these spelling words: **city**, **only**, **where**, **week**, **weak**.
Complete one lesson in McCall-Crabbs comprehension booklet.

Thursday
Review phonograms of which the child is uncertain.
Review yesterday's spelling list; practice any missed words.
Write these spelling words: **first**, **sent**, **cent**, **mile**, **seem**.
Test #5 (30 words) of the Spelling Scale; record results.
Read from a book.

Week 29

Monday
Review all 70 phonograms.
Review 8 words from previous spelling lists.
Write these spelling words: **see**, **even**, **without**, **afternoon**, **Friday**.
Write paragraph independently.

Tuesday
Review phonograms missed yesterday.
Review yesterday's spelling list; practice any missed words.
Write these spelling words: **hour**, **our**, **wife**, **state**, **July**.
Proofread paragraph written yesterday; rewrite.

Wednesday
Review phonograms of which the child is uncertain.
Review yesterday's spelling list; practice any missed words.
Write these spelling words: **head**, **story**, **open**, **short**, **lady**.
Complete one lesson in McCall-Crabbs comprehension booklet.

Thursday
Review phonograms of which the child is uncertain.
Review yesterday's spelling list; practice any missed words.
Write these spelling words: **reach**, **better**, water, **round**, **cost**.
Read from a book.

Week 30

Monday
Review all 70 phonograms.
Review yesterday's spelling list; practice any missed words.
Write these spelling words: **price**, **become**, **class**, **horse**, **care**.
Write paragraph independently.

Tuesday
Review phonograms missed yesterday.
Review yesterday's spelling list; practice any missed words.
Write these spelling words: **try**, **move**, **delay**, **pound**, **behind**.
Proofread paragraph written yesterday; rewrite.

Wednesday
Review phonograms of which the child is uncertain.
Review yesterday's spelling list; practice any missed words.
Write these spelling words: **around**, **burn**, **camp**, **bear**, **bare**.
Complete one lesson in McCall-Crabbs comprehension booklet.

Thursday
Review phonograms of which the child is uncertain.
Review yesterday's spelling list; practice any missed words.
Write these spelling words: **clear**, **clean**, **spell**, **poor**, **finish**.
Read from an easy book.

Week 31

Monday
Review all 70 phonograms.
Review yesterday's spelling list; practice any missed words.
Write these spelling words: **hurt**, **maybe**, **across**, **tonight**, **tenth**.
Write paragraph independently.

Tuesday
Review phonograms missed yesterday.
Review yesterday's spelling list; practice any missed words.
Write these spelling words: **sir**, **these**, **those**, **club**, **seen**.
Proofread paragraph written yesterday; rewrite.

Wednesday
Review phonograms of which the child is uncertain.
Review yesterday's spelling list; practice any missed words.
Write these spelling words: **see**, **felt**, **full**, **fail**, **set**.
Complete one lesson in McCall-Crabbs comprehension booklet.

Thursday
Review phonograms of which the child is uncertain.
Review yesterday's spelling list; practice any missed words.
Write these spelling words: **stamp**, **light**.
Begin teaching about word endings (first half of p.5 of the Notebook; see p.96-97 of text).
Read a book.

Week 32

Monday
Review all 70 phonograms.
Review yesterday's spelling list; practice any missed words.
Continue with word endings (second half of p.5 of the notebook).
Write paragraph independently.

Tuesday
    Review phonograms missed yesterday.
    Review yesterday's spelling list; practice any missed words.
    Finish with word endings (p.6 of notebook).
    Proofread paragraph written yesterday; rewrite.

Wednesday
    Review phonograms of which the child is uncertain.
    Review yesterday's spelling list; practice any missed words.
    Write these spelling words: **coming**, **come**, **night**, **pass**, **shut**.
    Complete one lesson in McCall-Crabbs comprehension booklet.

Thursday
    Review phonograms of which the child is uncertain.
    Review yesterday's spelling list; practice any missed words.
    Write these spelling words: **easy**, **ease**, **birds**, **bone**, **cloud**.
    Test #6 (35 words) of the Spelling Scale; record results.

Week 33

Monday
    Review all 70 phonograms.
    Review yesterday's spelling list; practice any missed words.
    Write these spelling words: **garden**, **goose**, **knife**, **mouth**, **oak**.
    Write paragraph independently.

Tuesday
    Review phonograms missed yesterday.
    Review yesterday's spelling list; practice any missed words.
    Write these spelling words: **peach**, **pole**, **queen**, **rope**, **season**.
    Proofread paragraph written yesterday; rewrite.

Wednesday
    Review phonograms of which the child is uncertain.
    Review yesterday's spelling list; practice any missed words.
    Write these spelling words: **space**, **stands**, **wagon**, **wheat**, **window**. (End
        of Section K.) Review Section K words at random.
    Complete one lesson in McCall-Crabbs comprehension booklet.

Thursday
    Review phonograms of which the child is uncertain.
    Review yesterday's spelling list; practice any missed words.
    Begin review of Ayres spelling list: Sections A-K: review (approximately 40
        words/day) words from lessons Week 7, Tuesday - Week 9, Tuesday.

Week 34

<u>Monday</u>
Review all 70 phonograms.
Review yesterday's spelling list; practice any missed words.
Review words from Week 9, Wednesday - Week 11, Tuesday.
Write paragraph independently.

<u>Tuesday</u>
Review phonograms missed yesterday.
Review Spelling List words, Week 11, Wednesday - Week 13, Tuesday.
Proofread paragraph written yesterday; rewrite.

<u>Wednesday</u>
Review phonograms of which the child is uncertain.
Review Spelling List words, Week 13, Wednesday - Week 15, Tuesday.

<u>Thursday</u>
Review phonograms of which the child is uncertain.
Review Spelling List words, Week 17, Wednesday - Week 19, Tuesday.
Read from a book.

Week 35

<u>Monday</u>
Review all 70 phonograms.
Review Spelling List words, Week 19, Wednesday - Week 21, Tuesday.
Write paragraph independently.

<u>Tuesday</u>
Review phonograms missed yesterday.
Review Spelling List words, Week 21, Wednesday - Week 23, Tuesday.
Proofread paragraph written yesterday; rewrite.

<u>Wednesday</u>
Review phonograms of which the child is uncertain.
Review Spelling List words, Week 23, Wednesday - Week 25, Wednesday.
Complete one lesson in McCall-Crabbs comprehension booklet.

<u>Thursday</u>
Review phonograms of which the child is uncertain.
Review Spelling List words, Week 25, Thursday - Week 27, Wednesday.
Read from a book.

Week 36

<u>Monday</u>
    Review all 70 phonograms.
    Review Spelling List words, Week 27, Thursday - Week 29, Wednesday.
    Write paragraph independently.

<u>Tuesday</u>
    Review phonograms missed yesterday.
    Review Spelling List words, Week 29, Thursday - Week 31, Wednesday.
    Proofread paragraph written yesterday; rewrite.

<u>Wednesday</u>
    Review phonograms of which the child is uncertain.
    Review Spelling List words, Week 31, Thursday - Week 33, Wednesday.
    Complete one lesson in McCall-Crabbs comprehension booklet.

<u>Thursday</u>
    Review phonograms of which the child is uncertain.
    Take Test #7 of the Spelling Scale (40 words). Record results.

Congratulations!

If you are interested in learning more about <u>First Grade: Learning At Home</u>,
    write for more information to:

Noble Publishing Associates
P.O. Box 2250
Gresham, OR 97030

Other Home-Schooling Titles
From Noble Publishing

The Original 21 Rules of This House

Sure, kids will be kids. But kids have to learn how to be well-behaved members of their own families. The biggest problem often lies with *parents* who swing from one mood to another so that the rules never stay the same. With *The Original 21 Rules of This House*, you will be able to stick to a reasonable standard, and say the same things day after day. The reproducible coloring book, individual rule posters and laminated (jelly-proof) master list work together to help everyone of all ages obey the house rules.

Item #1041–$10.95

Uncommon Courtesy For Kids

Young gentlemen and little ladies don't just spring out of nowhere. Children have to be trained. Now, using the same format that works so well with the *21 Rules*, we take on the challenge of teaching 56 rules of proper etiquette. You'll be amazed at how much your children learn as each poster goes onto the refrigerator. The laminated placemat lists all 56 rules, and the reproducible coloring book illustrations are funny, but effective.

Item #1042–$12.95

Rules for Young Friends

It's not easy to *have* a friend or, for that matter, to *be* a friend. Friends can do either harm or good to your character. But Christ died to save our friends, too. With a few basic rules, boundaries can be set that keep each friendship on the right track. With this third in the series of *Rule Kits*, we coach children on how to be a good influence on the neighborhood without becoming "companions of fools."

Item #1036–$12.95

Choreganizers ™

Where is the work ethic of years gone by? It's alive and well with *Choreganizers*. This system organizes household chores with cards hung neatly on individual *ChoreCharts*. *Mom Money* is issued for good attitudes toward work, and, once a week, *The Chore Store* opens with an inventory of wholesome treats to buy. *Choreganizers* works amazingly well with children ages 3 to 13.

Item #1725–$16.95

The Christian Home School

by Gregg Harris

Since 1988, this book has introduced thousands of families to Christian home education. Now, after two years out of print, it's back! In a friendly style that even your public school relatives can enjoy, Gregg presents the reasons for home schooling and shares the steps for getting started on a firm, Biblical foundation.

Item #1010–$12.95

Teaching Tips

3-Tape Set

by Valerie Bendt

Are you looking for some new and creative teaching ideas? *Teaching Tips* is a three-tape series that is all that and more. Valerie introduces the design and use of unit studies, teaches us how to turn unit studies into one-of-a-kind books with our children, and gives us tips on how to encourage life-long readers. Great stuff!

Item #1727–$19.95

Peter Rabbit, Winnie & Charlotte

Study Guides

by Ann Ward

Ann Ward draws her insight and experience from years as an elementary school teacher and home-school mother. These non-consumable study guides of the works of Beatrix Potter, *Charlotte's Web, Winnie-the-Pooh, and The House at Pooh Corner* will introduce your child to some of the finest classics in children's literature. Each lesson builds reading/listening, comprehension and vocabulary.

Peter Rabbit Item #1481–$9.95
Charlotte/Winnie # 1482–$9.95
Set of Two # K1483–$16.95

Listen, Color & Learn

by Shari Pittenger

Children have more energy than they know what to do with. That's part of the reason they can't sit still during family devotions. If only there were a way to direct all that energy so that it would actually help your children pay better attention. Now there is. These devotional coloring books for the Psalms are designed to make Bible study and prayer times with your children more rewarding.

Individual Volumes $5 Each

Available from your local bookstores or you can call 1-800-225-5259

Home Schooling Children With Special Needs

by Sharon C. Hensley, M.A.

Many children have special needs—from mild to severe. Home schooling works especially well for such children because it allows them to learn without the fear of social rejection. Sharon Hensley understands the challenges and offers great resources, ideas and hope. Highly recommended! Order it for a friend.

Item # 8500–$12.95

Home Schooling Children With Special Needs — Tape Set

Children who have special needs need special parents. This seven-tape set is designed to give you Biblical inspiration and practical information to deal with whatever challenges you face. The various speakers are home-school parents, dedicated pastors, and skilled professionals who create a balance between experience and training. If you have a child with special needs, let us help you become a special mom or dad.

Item #1472–$39.95

The IHELP Planner
Individualized Home Education for Life Preparation

by Rhonda Robinson

Initially created to assist children with special needs, this new lesson planner and goal-setting tool helps *any parent* create an individualized education program (IEP) for *any child*. The unique forms assist even the novice home schooler in establishing realistic goals that build on the strengths of each child. *IHELP* also helps you pursue your goals on a daily basis, in the midst of all your household activities. It's especially effective at documenting all those teachable moments that arrive without warning. You'll have clear records of your student's progress. *IHELP* really boosts the confidence of the teacher. Like *The Home School Organizer*, the *IHELP* Planner comes with easily reproducible forms.

Item #8510–$34.95

Searching For Treasure

by Marty Elwell

The Book of Proverbs was written and compiled by King Solomon primarily to help parents teach their children how to live wisely in this foolish world. With *Searching For Treasure* Marty Elwell, a pastor's wife, home-school mother, and author, makes the Proverbs easily understandable and applicable for children and adults. Illustrations by Steve Rose make the point stick by using New Testament principles and stories with Old Testament proverbs. The includes a Game Board and Game Cards.

Item # 1760 - $20.00 / Coloring Book #1765 - $5.00

The Right Choice: Home Schooling

by Chris Klicka

This book has become the standard bearer of the Christian home-schooling movement around the world. Easy to read, hard hitting, well documented, thorough, logical-- these are the terms that describe the strengths of *The Right Choice*. If you could read only one book on home schooling, this would be the one. Supplemental chapters by Gregg Harris and foreword by D. James Kennedy make this book complete.

Item #1493–$12.95

Government Nannies:
The Cradle to Grave Agenda of Goals 2000 & Outcome Based Education

by Cathy Duffy

With *Government Nannies*, Cathy Duffy (who is also the author of *The Christian Home Educator's Curriculum Manuals* on page 1), examines the devastating impact new federal education policy will have on children and families. The ramifications of *Goals 2000* and outcome-based education are felt everywhere– in public schools, private schools *and home schools*. All are explored, making this the most thorough and readable book on the subject. It truly is a "cradle-to-grave agenda" with government interference from womb to tomb. If you read only one book about the current educational situation, make it this one. The time is short. Act now, to make a difference. People who read this book soon after order additional copies to give away to their friends. It's that kind of book.

Item #1700–$12.95

The Home School Organizer

by Sono Harris

There are a lot of details to keep track of in home schooling. Lesson plans have to be roughed out, resources have to be listed, records have to be kept--not just for legal purposes. They help you become more effective as a teacher. *The Home School Organizer* provides all the reproducible materials and tab sections you need to get organized and stay organized. The *Organizer* won an award for its category from *Practical Home Schooling Magazine*.

Item #1033–$34.9

Encouragement Along the Way

by B. Howard

Be honest. There are those days when home schooling is not much fun at all. Pressure from all sides conspire to get you down. It so easy to forget why you decided to keep the kids home in the first place. Is it really worth it? Bobbie Howard answers heart to heart with this devotional thoughts book for home-school moms. It also makes a great gift book!

Item #1755–$12.9

Available from your local bookstores or you can call 1-800-225-5259

The Noble Planner™
Time Management System

by G. Harris

The Noble Planner derives its name from Isaiah 32:8, "*The noble man makes noble plans and by noble deeds he stands.*" Few things have greater impact in life than how we manage our time. *The Noble Planner* allows you to do so with a distinctively Christian approach based on loving God with all your heart, soul, mind and strength. You'll plan your week "in the after-glow of worship." The results are a clear life *purpose*, passionate *goals*, informed *plans* and forceful *actions*. Procrastination and disorganization are defeated for good. If you currently use a *Daytimer™*, a *Franklin Quest™*, or any other 2-page-per-day planner, you'll love the unique planners and calendars of *The Noble Planner*. If you don't use a planner yet, you don't know what you're missing! Test drive *The Noble Planner* for 30 days.

Your satisfaction is guaranteed, and you have no time to lose.

Noble Time-Management Seminar Tapes
Recorded on eight 90-minute cassette tapes. Life Changing! (Available Summer of 1995) **Item #95TP–$34.95**

Master Filler Only
Includes Goal Worksheets, Season of Life Master Plans, Project Plans, Calendars, Daily Planners, Area of Life Tabs and Directory and Samples of all other forms. Fits into any 8.5" x 5.5" 3-ring or 7-ring binder.
Item #95MF–$34.95

Filler With Leather-like Vinyl Binder
Quality 7-ring, 1.5" capacity, Sewn and Sealed Binder
Burgundy Binder **Item #90BU–$69.96**
Charcoal Black Binder **Item #90CH–$69.95**

Noble Planner Accessories
Archive 3-D Ring Binder **Item #95AR–$8.95**
7-hole Punch (4 sheets) **Item #95DP–$21.95**
7-hole NASV Bible **Item #94BI–$25.00**

> "Life-changing application…That is what The Noble Planner is all about. The Noble Planner helps you apply God's truth in your everyday life with vision, passion, insight, self-discipline, and amazing balance. I highly recommend it." **Dr. Bruce Wilkinson**, Walk Thru The Bible Ministries

---

Children: Blessing or Burden?
Exploding the Myth of the Small Family

by Max Heine

If you sometimes feel like children are a bother, you'll *love* this book. Max Heine, a reporter for a daily newspaper, offers the most balanced, easy-to-read, documented, Biblical presentation on the topic of "family planning" to date. And it's a joy to read. The author explains why in recent decades children have been viewed as a burden instead of a blessing, and what the effects of that mistake have been. While making a powerful case for having bigger families, he's careful to help us avoid condemning ourselves or others. For all those who are advocates of the family, and for anyone making important decisions about having children, this book is essential reading. *Children: Blessing or Burden?* will help you to see your family as God's masterpiece. May your tribe increase!

Item #1400–$9.95

The Yellow Pages Guide to Educational Field Trips

Edited by Gregg Harris, with April Purtell, Michael & Elizabeth Gaunt, & Ross Tunnell

We think this book is the ultimate resource for field trips! Here's why:
1) It turns every major professional listing and institutional listing that you find in your Yellow Pages into a field trip destination.
2) It provides background information and vocabulary words for each destination.
3) It gives you suggestions for questions to ask while on the field trip, and information on what the Bible has to say about the profession. If you're already using field trips to make learning exciting, this book will make them even better. If you haven't utilized field trips yet, this book provides the structure you need to start.

Item #1750–$19.95

The New Attitude
Audio Experience
by Josh Harris

This exciting new 2-tape set features two messages from the *New Attitude Teen Conference*. Each 60-minute cassette includes interviews and challenging, Biblically based messages filled with humor as well as gripping illustrations.

Tape One: This Is Your Life!
A look at how your value system affects the way you live. Here Josh shares his story of wanting OUT of home schooling. What should your focus be in high school? This is a message you won't want to miss.

Tape Two: It's All About Attitude
What does it take to be someone who makes an impact on the world? Using Biblical examples, Josh challenges teens to take a new attitude towards learning, work and their future.

This can change your life!

Item #1742–#13.95

Available from your local bookstores or you can call 1-800-225-5259

These Home Schooling Titles From Noble Publishing ca... ...rchased at your local Christian Bookstore, or you can order them directly from Noble Press by calling:

1-800-225-5259

Home Schooling Workshop Tape Sets

by Gregg Harris

The eight sessions recorded in each of these tape sets have helped launch and maintain the dedication of over 90,000 families in home schooling. We receive letters every week from those who made their decision in Gregg's Basic Workshop and others who found the resolve to continue in his Advanced Workshop. If you are new to home schooling, or if you are getting weary of it, don't wait for the workshop to come to your area. Order the tapes and listen. It's amazing what God can do through the simple truths presented here.

The Basic Home Schooling Workshop
on 8 Audio Cassette Tapes

by Gregg Harris

Get started on the best possible foundation by experiencing the workshop that has helped launch 90,000 families into home schooling. The Basic Workshop is geared toward the Christian family that is new to home schooling, with special emphasis on questions of interest to parents of elementary school children. Though it is designed to provide practical steps and strategies, it also offers the inspiration and motivation you'll need to keep going when discouraged.

8-tape set #1497–$39.95
Notes #1919–$9.95

The Advanced Home Schooling Workshop
on 8 Audio Cassette Tapes

by Gregg Harris

The home-schooling community is getting older. There are far more teenagers being taught at home today than ever before. But even before your children become teens, once you've home schooled for three or four years, a whole slew of new questions and concerns come to mind.

• Should we allow our young people to date?
• How do we handle youth groups?
• What will the "future" hold for our children?
• Should I retire when I finish home schooling?

These and many more questions are answered in the Advanced Workshop.

8-tape set #1215–$39.95
Notes #1321–$9.95

Sweet Land of Liberty

by C. Coffin

The thirteen original colonies were founded by men and women of great courage and great faith. In this sequel to *The Story of Liberty*, Charles Coffin takes us on an exciting tour of each colony and relates the history of how each one was used by God.

Coffin's training as a newspaper reporter for a Boston paper (he reported directly to Lincoln during the Civil War) makes this fast-paced and extremely interesting. Amazing details add life and meaning to each chapter. By the end of the book, you'll see how God indeed orchestrated the founding of the United States of America.

Item #1451–$12.95

Science in the Creation Week

by David Unfred

In seven days God made the heaven and earth. What a great outline for a science curriculum! As the creation account unfolds, Mr. Unfred gives us a clear and easy-to-understand presentation of the physics of light, the chemistry of the basic elements, an introduction to astronomy and the fundamentals of plant and animal biology. Designed for grades 2-6, you can teach several grades at the same time, simply by giving the assignment to students at their ability levels.

Item #1002–$19.9

The Classic Series

By Don and Linda Hurst

The Classics is a literature-based, multi-level curriculum design for (but not limited to) children in grades 3 through 6. It is designed to provide quality educational activities to meet the fering needs of children while freeing the teacher from the tedious tasks of researching, planning, and gathering lesson materials. This allows the teacher to utilize her time teaching.

Noble Publishing will be releasing eleven Unit Studies by Don and Linda Hurst in the fall of 1996. The Studies will include: *Little House on the Prairie, The Adventures of Tom Sawyer, Across Five Aprils, Old Yeller, Charlotte's Web*, and many more. For more information on *The Classic Series*, please call our office at (503) 667-3942.

Available from your local bookstores or you can call 1-800-225-5259